Inquiry and the *National Science Education Standards*

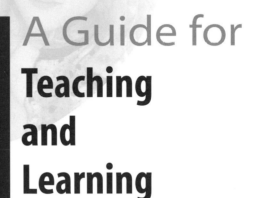

A Guide for Teaching and Learning

Committee on Development of an Addendum to the National Science Education Standards on Scientific Inquiry

Center for Science, Mathematics, and Engineering Education

National Research Council

National Academy Press
Washington, D.C.

NATIONAL ACADEMY PRESS • 2101 Constitution Avenue, NW • Washington, DC 20418

NOTICE: The project that is the subject of this report was approved by the Governing Board of the National Research Council, whose members are drawn from the councils of the National Academy of Sciences, the National Academy of Engineering, and the Institute of Medicine. The members of the committee responsible for the report were chosen for their special competences and with regard for appropriate balance.

The Center for Science, Mathematics, and Engineering Education (CSMEE) was established in 1995 to provide coordination of all the National Research Council's education activities and reform efforts for students at all levels, specifically those in kindergarten through twelfth grade, undergraduate institutions, school-to-work programs, and continuing education. The Center reports directly to the Governing Board of the National Research Council.

This study by the Center's Committee on Development of an Addendum to the *National Science Education Standards* on Scientific Inquiry was developed under grants from the National Science Foundation, National Aeronautics and Space Administration, and Governing Board Initiative of the National Academies. Any opinions, findings, or recommendations expressed in this report are those of the members of the committee and do not necessarily reflect the views of the funders.

Library of Congress Cataloging-in-Publication Data

Inquiry and the National Science Education Standards : a guide for teaching and learning / Center for Science, Mathematics, and Engineering Education, National Research Council.

p. cm.

Includes bibliographical references and index.

ISBN 0-309-06476-7 (pbk.)

1. Science—Study and teaching—Standards—United States. 2. Inquiry (Theory of knowledge) I. Center for Science, Mathematics, and Engineering Education.

LB1585.3 .I57 2000

507.1'073—dc21

00-008103

Additional copies of this report are available from the National Academy Press, 2101 Constitution Avenue, NW, Lock Box 285, Washington, DC 20055. Call (800) 624-6242 or (202) 3334-3313 (in the Washington metropolitan area).

This report is also available online at http://www.nap.edu.

Printed in the United States of America.

First Printing, April 2000
Second Printing, August 2000
Third Printing, November 2000

THE NATIONAL ACADEMIES

National Academy of Sciences
National Academy of Engineering
Institute of Medicine
National Research Council

The **National Academy of Sciences** is a private, nonprofit, self-perpetuating society of distinguished scholars engaged in scientific and engineering research, dedicated to the furtherance of science and technology and to their use for the general welfare. Upon the authority of the charter granted to it by the Congress in 1863, the Academy has a mandate that requires it to advise the federal government on scientific and technical matters. Dr. Bruce M. Alberts is president of the National Academy of Sciences.

The **National Academy of Engineering** was established in 1964, under the charter of the National Academy of Sciences, as a parallel organization of outstanding engineers. It is autonomous in its administration and in the selection of its members, sharing with the National Academy of Sciences the responsibility for advising the federal government. The National Academy of Engineering also sponsors engineering programs aimed at meeting national needs, encourages education and research, and recognizes the superior achievements of engineers. Dr. William A. Wulf is president of the National Academy of Engineering.

The **Institute of Medicine** was established in 1970 by the National Academy of Sciences to secure the services of eminent members of appropriate professions in the examination of policy matters pertaining to the health of the public. The Institute acts under the responsibility given to the National Academy of Sciences by its congressional charter to be an adviser to the federal government and, upon its own initiative, to identify issues of medical care, research, and education. Dr. Kenneth I. Shine is president of the Institute of Medicine.

The **National Research Council** was organized by the National Academy of Sciences in 1916 to associate the broad community of science and technology with the Academy's purposes of furthering knowledge and advising the federal government. Functioning in accordance with general policies determined by the Academy, the Council has become the principal operating agency of both the National Academy of Sciences and the National Academy of Engineering in providing services to the government, the public, and the scientific and engineering communities. The Council is administered jointly by both Academies and the Institute of Medicine. Dr. Bruce M. Alberts and Dr. William A. Wulf are chairman and vice chairman, respectively, of the National Research Council.

COMMITTEE ON DEVELOPMENT OF AN ADDENDUM TO THE *NATIONAL SCIENCE EDUCATION STANDARDS* ON SCIENTIFIC INQUIRY

Peter Dow (Chair), First Hand Learning, Inc.
Richard A. Duschl, School of Education, King's College London
Hubert M. Dyasi, City College (City University of New York)
Paul J. Kuerbis, The Colorado College
Lawrence Lowery, University of California at Berkeley
Lillian C. McDermott, University of Washington
Lynn Rankin, Exploratorium Institute of Inquiry
Mary Lou Zoback, Western Earthquake Hazards Program, U.S. Geological Survey

Staff, Center for Science, Mathematics, and Engineering Education

Rodger Bybee
Kristance Coates
Linda DePugh
Jay Hackett
Susan Loucks-Horsley
Steve Olson
Harold Pratt
Lisa Vandemark
Tina Winters

COMMITTEE ON SCIENCE EDUCATION K–12

Jane Butler Kahle (*Chair*), Miami University, Oxford, OH
J. Myron Atkin, Stanford University, Stanford, CA
Caryl Edward Buchwald, Carleton College, Northfield, MN
George Bugliarello, Polytechnic University, Brooklyn, NY
Beatriz Chu Clewell, The Urban Institute, Washington, DC
William E. Dugger, Technology for All Americans, Blacksburg, VA
Norman Hackerman, The Robert A. Welch Foundation, Houston, TX
Leroy Hood, University of Washington, Seattle, WA
William Linder-Scholer, SciMathMN, Roseville, MN
Maria Alicia Lopez Freeman, California Science Project, Monterey Park, CA
John A. Moore, University of California, Riverside, CA
Darlene Norfleet, Flynn Park Elementary School, University City, MO
Carolyn Ray, Urban Systemic Initiative, Cleveland, OH
Cary Sneider, Boston Museum of Science, Boston, MA
Rachel Wood, Delaware State Department of Public Instruction, Dover, DE
Robert Yinger, School of Education, Baylor University, Waco, TX

Reviewers

This report has been reviewed in draft form by individuals chosen for their diverse perspectives and technical expertise, in accordance with procedures approved by the National Research Council's Report Review Committee. The purpose of this independent review is to provide candid and critical comments that will assist the authors and the Center for Science, Mathematics, and Engineering Education in making the published report as sound as possible and to ensure that the report meets institutional standards for objectivity, evidence, and responsiveness to the study charge. The review comments and draft manuscript remain confidential to protect the integrity of the deliberative process. The committee wishes to thank the following individuals for their participation in the review of this report:

Lloyd Barrows, University of Missouri

Ken Bingman, Shawnee Mission West High School

Al Janulaw, California Science Teachers Association and Creekside Middle School

Dean Kamen, DEKA Research and Development Corporation

John Layman, University of Maryland (Retired)

Michael Martinez, University of California at Irvine

Joseph McInerney, Johns Hopkins University School of Medicine

Gail Paulin, Tucson Unified School District

Laurie Peterman, Anoka-Hennepin School District

Ursula Sexton, WestEd

Although the individuals listed above have provided many constructive comments and suggestions, responsibility for the final content of this report rests solely with the authoring committee and the National Research Council.

Contents

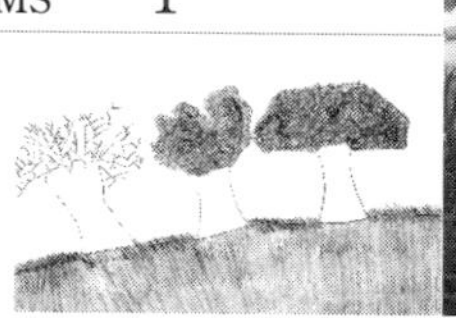

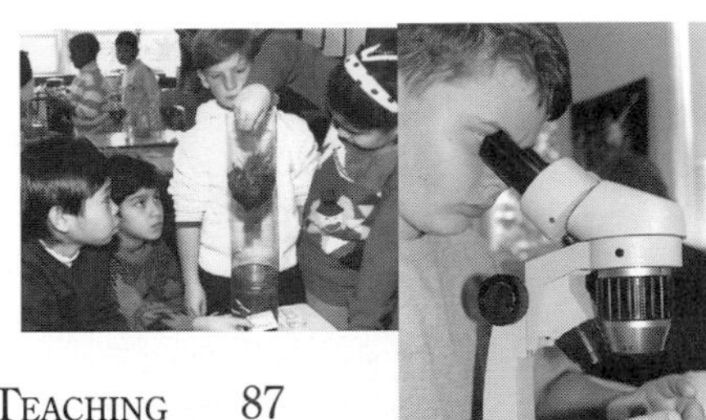

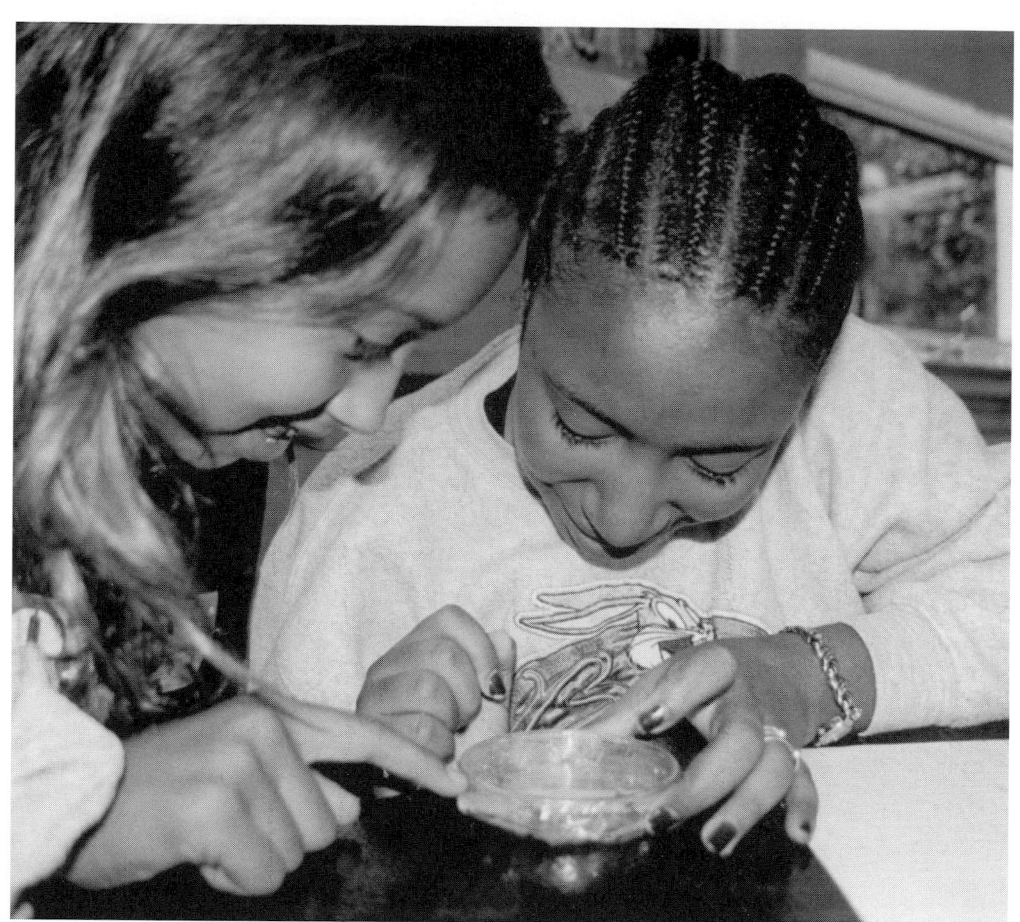

Foreword: A Scientist's Perspective on Inquiry

When I was growing up in the 1950s in the suburbs of Chicago, the educational experiences that meant the most to me were all associated with my struggling to meet a challenge that had captured my interest and initiative. I remember writing a long report on "The Farm Problem" in the seventh grade in which my task was to explain why our government was paying farmers for *not* growing a crop. In the eighth grade I had to explain to the rest of my class how a television set works. And in the ninth grade I remember poring over books on spectroscopy in the Chicago public library to prepare a report on its uses in chemistry.

All three of these tasks, and many others that interested me as a student, involved what we now call "inquiry." Teaching science through inquiry allows students to conceptualize a question and then seek possible explanations that respond to that question. For example, in my field of cell biology, cell membranes have to be selectively permeable — they have to let foodstuffs like sugars pass inward and wastes like carbon dioxide pass out, while holding the many big molecules that form the cell inside. What kind of material could have these properties and yet be able to expand as the cell grows?

It is certainly easy to remember another and more familiar type of science teaching from my childhood. In this approach — which remains depressingly common today — teachers provide their students with sets of science facts and with technical words to describe those facts. In the worst case, this type of science teaching assumes that education consists of filling a student's head with vocabulary words and associations, such as mitochondria being "the powerhouses of the cell," DNA being the "genetic material," and motion producing "kinetic energy." Science classes of this type treat education as if it were preparation for a quiz show or a game of trivial pursuit.

This view of science education has many problems. Most students are not interested in being quiz show participants. They fail to see how this type of knowledge will be useful to them in the future. They therefore lack motivation for this kind of "school learning."

Most important, this kind of teaching misses a tremendous opportunity to give all students the problem-solving, communication, and thinking skills that they will need to be effective workers and citizens in the 21st century.

Inquiry is in part a state of mind — that of inquisitiveness. Most young children are naturally curious. They care enough to ask "why" and "how" questions. But if adults dismiss their incessant questions as silly and uninteresting, students can lose this gift of curiosity. Visit any second-grade classroom and you will generally find a class bursting with energy and excitement, where children are eager to make new observations and try to figure things out. What a contrast with many eighth-grade classes, where the students so often seem bored and disengaged from learning and from school!

The *National Science Education Standards* released by the National Research Council in 1995 provide valuable insights into the ways that teachers might sustain the curiosity of students and help them develop the sets of abilities associated with scientific inquiry. The *Standards* emphasize that science education needs to give students three kinds of scientific skills and understandings. Students need to learn the principles and concepts of science, acquire the reasoning and procedural skills of scientists, and understand the nature of science as a particular form of human endeavor. Students therefore need to be able to devise and carry out investigations that test their ideas, and they need to understand why such investigations are uniquely powerful. Studies show that students are much more likely to understand and retain the concepts that they have learned this way.

For example, one skill that all students should acquire through their science education is the ability to conduct an investigation where they keep everything else constant while changing a single variable. This ability provides a powerful general strategy for solving many problems encountered in the workplace and in everyday life. The Lawrence Hall of Science in Berkeley, California, has developed a set of fifth-grade science lessons that give students extensive experience in manipulating systems with variables. These lessons begin with the class working in groups of four to construct different sized pendulums from string, tape, and washers. After each group counts the number of swings of their pendulum in 15-second intervals — yielding quite different results among groups — the groups conduct further trials that eventually trace the source of the variability to differences in the lengths of the strings. This leads to graphing as a means of displaying the data for future work with pendulums. Ideally, the teacher should use this particular sequence of lessons to teach students about the history of clocks, emphasizing the many changes in society that ensued once it became possible to divide the day and night into reliable time intervals.

Contrast this science lesson with a more traditional lesson about pendulums. In such a lesson, the teacher does most of the talking and demonstrating. Often, students display their knowledge about such variables as length of the pendulum, weight, and starting height by filling in a series of blanks on a worksheet.

The challenge for all of us who want to improve education is to create an educational system that exploits the natural curiosity of children, so that they maintain their motivation for learning not only during their school years but throughout life. We need to convince teachers and parents of the importance of children's "why" questions. I'm reminded of the profound effect that Richard Feynman's father had on his development as a scientist. One summer, in the Catskills Mountains of New York when Feynman was a boy, another boy asked him, "See that bird. What kind of bird is that?" Feynman answered "I haven't the slightest idea." The other boy replied, "Your father doesn't teach you anything!" But his father had taught Feynman about the bird — though in his own way. As Feynman recalls his father's words:

> "See that bird? It's a Spencer's warbler." (I knew he didn't know the real name.) ". . . You can know the name of that bird in all the languages of the world, but when you're finished, you'll know absolutely nothing whatever about the bird. You'll only know about humans in different places and what they call the bird. So let's look at the bird and see what it's doing — that's what counts."

The book you are about to read illuminates this approach to teaching science. It builds on the discussion of inquiry in the *National Science Education Standards* to demonstrate how those responsible for science education can provide young people with the opportunities they need to develop their scientific understanding and ability to inquire. The process must begin in kindergarten and continue, with age-appropriate challenges, at each grade level. Students must be challenged but also rewarded with the joy of solving a problem with which they have struggled. In this way, students recognize that they are capable of tackling harder and harder problems. As they acquire the tools and habits of inquiry, they see themselves learn. There can be nothing more gratifying, or more important, in science education.

Bruce Alberts
President, National Academy of Sciences

Preface

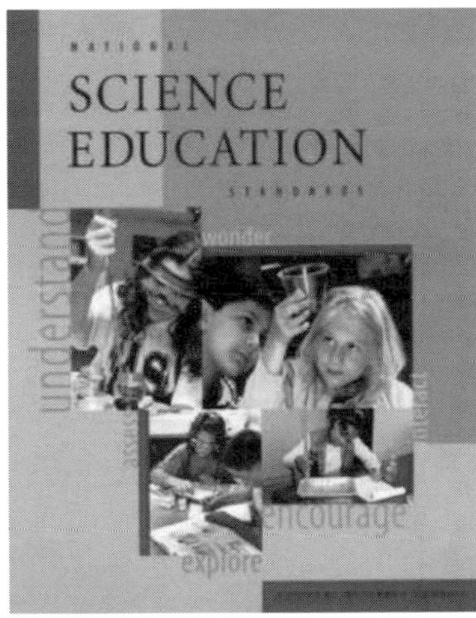

In December 1995 the National Research Council (NRC) released the *National Science Education Standards*, which, as stated in the "Call to Action" at the beginning of the *Standards*, spell out "a vision of science education that will make scientific literacy for all a reality in the 21st century." The release of the *Standards* was the culmination of an extensive process of consensus-building. In 1991 the President of the National Science Teachers Association, among others, asked the NRC to coordinate efforts to develop national standards for science education. Between 1991 and 1995, groups of teachers, scientists, administrators, teacher educators, and others organized by the NRC produced several drafts of the *Standards* and submitted those drafts to extensive review by others in these same roles. The result was a document that, since its release, has been a driving force behind improvements in U.S. science education.

A prominent feature of the *Standards* is a focus on inquiry. The term "inquiry" is used in two different ways in the *Standards*. First, it refers to the *abilities* students should develop to be able to design and conduct scientific investigations and to the *understandings* they should gain about the nature of scientific inquiry. Second, it refers to the teaching and learning strategies that enable scientific concepts to be mastered through investigations. In this way, the *Standards* draw connections between learning science, learning to do science, and learning about science.

As required by the charge to its authoring committee, *Inquiry and the*

National Science Education Standards has been designed to serve as a practical guide for teachers, professional developers, administrators, and others who wish to respond to the *Standards'* call for an increased emphasis on inquiry.

The committee charge further called for:

- a background discussion of inquiry;
- a summary of pertinent research and scholarly writings that argue convincingly for the value of inquiry in science education;
- Actions that teachers, administrators, parents, and others need to take; and
- A bibliography of resources for planning and implementation assistance.

In response to this charge, the guide is divided into eight chapters and three appendices:

■ Chapter 1, "Inquiry in Science and in Classrooms," sets the stage for describing the multiple roles of inquiry by comparing a geologist's scientific inquiry with that of a class of fifth-grade students and their enterprising teacher.

■ Chapter 2, "Inquiry in the *National Science Education Standards*," clarifies the vision of scientific inquiry framed in the *Standards.*

■ Chapter 3, "Images of Inquiry in K-12 Classrooms," examines science as inquiry by presenting and discussing a series of classroom vignettes at the elementary school, middle school, and high school levels.

■ Chapter 4, "Classroom Assessment and Inquiry," discusses the varied functions of and strategies for assessment in inquiry-oriented classrooms.

■ Chapter 5, "Preparing Teachers for Inquiry-Based Teaching," discusses the professional development of teachers from undergraduate preparation to continuous learning throughout their careers.

■ Chapter 6, "Making the Case for Inquiry," describes the results of research into inquiry-based teaching and learning.

■ Chapter 7, "Frequently Asked Questions About Inquiry," gives short answers to some of the questions frequently asked by classroom teachers, administrators, parents, and others.

■ Chapter 8, "Supporting Inquiry-Based Teaching and Learning," describes how leadership from principals and other administrators can further the use of inquiry in teaching and learning.

■ The appendices provide elaborations of the abilities and understandings of inquiry from the *Standards*; guidelines for selecting inquiry-oriented instructional materials; and a list of resources related to inquiry-based science education.

A number of the chapters in the report feature vignettes of teachers and students engaged in using and learning about inquiry. These vignettes are based on actual experiences witnessed by committee members and contributors to the report. Some details have been altered to emphasize particular points. The purpose of the vignettes is to illustrate the key ideas in the text, not to represent idealized classroom and professional development scenarios.

This guide has been produced under the direction of the Committee on Science Education K-12 (COSE K-12), a standing board within the Center for Science, Mathematics, and Engineering Education at the National Research Council. COSE K-12 formed the Committee on Development of an Addendum to the *National Science Education Standards* on Scientific Inquiry and charged the committee with producing a document that would help educators improve the quality of teaching, learning, and assessment through the use of inquiry. Funding for the project came from the National Science Foundation, the National Aeronautics and Space Administration, and the Governing Board Initiative of the National Academies.

The committee has written this guide to be used in a number of ways. Classroom teachers, science department chairs, science supervisors, and professional developers can use it directly to improve teaching and learning. School administrators and members of the public can use it to understand and promote inquiry-based teaching and learning. Professional developers and teacher educators can use it to improve the ways they work with teachers and better to model and design inquiry-oriented learning experiences for prospective and practicing teachers. University science faculty can use it to rethink the content and teaching strategies they use in courses attended by preservice teachers. Scientists can use it to guide their work with teachers. And the many other individuals and groups who believe that the process of inquiry should be part of every science classroom can use it to spark discussion and guide their efforts to effect change.

Readers who choose not to read this book from cover to cover should begin with Chapters 1 and 2, which provide a foundation for the remaining chapters. In Chapter 3 the vignettes represent different grade spans, depending on their grade level interest, so readers may want to be selective in which vignettes they read. Other chapter selections will depend on the particular role and need of the reader. For example, Chapter 5 speaks especially to teacher educators and professional developers and Chapter 8 to administrators and other leaders of science reform initiatives.

This guide is the first in a series of

planned addenda to the *Standards*. Addenda on science and technology and on classroom assessment are also being prepared. The Center also has produced several other documents that support standards-based reform in science education, including publications about selecting instructional materials, designing multi-year curriculum programs, and using the findings of the Third International Mathematics and Science Study to improve science curricula and teaching.

On behalf of the committee, I acknowledge with deep appreciation the contributions of Elizabeth Stage, Ron Anderson, Jim Minstrell, Denis Goodrum, Maryellen Harmon, Doris Ash, Lezlie DeWater, and David Hartney, who produced written material; Mike Atkin, Kathy DiRanna, Sally Crissman, Kathy Stiles, John Layman, JoAnne Vasquez, and Henry Heikkinen, who advised us on early drafts; and the many teachers and teacher developers whose inquiry-based teaching experiences illustrate the ideas in these pages. We especially thank Susan Loucks-Horsley and Jay Hackett, who served as project directors for different phases of this report; other dedicated Center staff who helped us conceptualize, improve, and produce this report, including Rodger Bybee, Harold Pratt, Lisa Vandemark, Kristance Coates, Linda DePugh, and Tina Winters; writer Steve Olson whose editing greatly improved the report; and dozens of teachers and administrators who participated in workshops where our ideas and frameworks were tried out, for their invaluable feedback.

Peter Dow, Committee Chair

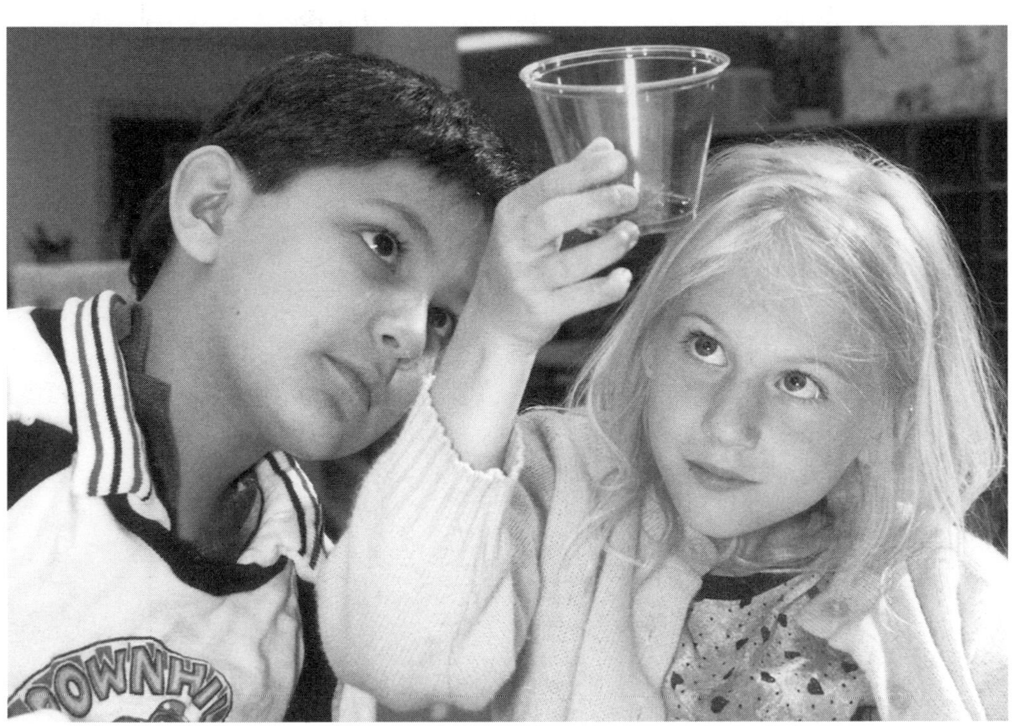

1 Inquiry in Science and in Classrooms

> Scientific inquiry refers to the diverse ways in which scientists study the natural world and propose explanations based on the evidence derived from their work. Inquiry also refers to the activities of students in which they develop knowledge and understanding of scientific ideas, as well as an understanding of how scientists study the natural world. *National Science Education Standards*, p. 23.

As pointed out in the *National Science Education Standards* (National Research Council, 1996), students who use inquiry to learn science engage in many of the same activities and thinking processes as scientists who are seeking to expand human knowledge of the natural world. Yet the activities and thinking processes used by scientists are not always familiar to the educator seeking to introduce inquiry into the classroom. By describing inquiry in both science and in classrooms, this volume explores the many facets of inquiry in science education. Through examples and discussion, it shows how students and teachers can use inquiry to learn how to do science, learn about the nature of science, and learn science content.

A good way to begin this investigation is to compare the methods and thinking process of a practicing scientist with the activities of an inquiry-based science lesson. The stories in this chapter set the stage for many of the themes to follow. The sidebars suggest some important aspects of the investigations of both scientists and students.

INQUIRY IN SCIENCE

A geologist who was mapping coastal deposits in the state of Washington was surprised to discover a forest of dead cedar trees near the shore. A significant portion were still standing, but they clearly had been dead for many years. He found similar

Makes observations

stands of dead trees at other places along the coast in both Oregon and Washington. He wondered, "What

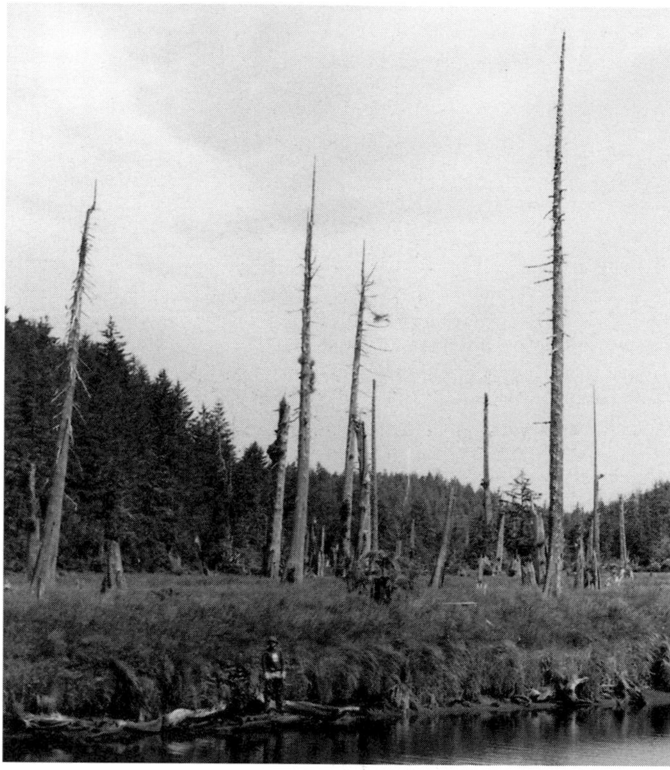

could have killed so many trees over so wide an area?"

Exhibits curiosity, defines questions, from knowledge background

Reflecting on his knowledge of earthquakes, crustal plate boundaries, and subsidence along coastlines, the geologist searched for possible explanations. "Did the trees die at the same time?" "Was their death related to nearby volcanic activity or some kind of biological blight?" "Given their coastal location, was there some relationship between the salt water and the destruction of the forests?"

He pursued his first question by dating the outer rings of the trees using carbon 14 radiometric methods. He found that they all had died about 300 years ago. As for the cause of the trees' death, his mapping indicated no evidence for widespread volcanic deposits in the areas of dead forests. Furthermore, the trees were not burned, nor did careful examination indicate any evidence of insect infestation.

Gathers evidence us technology mathemati

The geologist began thinking about the possible role of salt water in killing the trees. He recalled that a large section of the Alaskan coast dropped below sea level in 1964 when the tectonic plate that underlies much of the Pacific Ocean plunged beneath the North American tectonic plate that Alaska sits on as the result of a major "subduction zone earthquake." Many square miles of coastal forests in Alaska died when the coastline dropped and they were submerged in salt water following the earthquake. He knew that a similar subduction zone lies beneath the Washington and Oregon coast and gives rise to the volcanoes of the Cascade mountains. He wondered whether the trees in Washington and Oregon might have been drowned by sea water when a large section of the coast subsided during an earthquake 300 years ago.

Uses previous research

Propose a possible explanation

To check this explanation, he collected more data. He examined the sediments in the area. Well-preserved sections of sediment exposed in the banks of streams inland from the stands of dead trees showed a clean layer of sand below the soil — unlike any of the dark, clay-rich soil above and below the sand. "Where did the white sand come from?" he wondered.

The geologist knew that subduction zone earthquakes often produce tsunamis — tidal waves. He thought the sand layer could be sand washed ashore during a tsunami. If so, this would be further evidence of a major coastal earthquake. Fossils recovered from the sand layer indicated the sand came from the ocean rather than being washed down from inland, supporting the tsunami hypothesis.

He published several articles in peer-reviewed scientific journals hypothesizing that the dead trees and sand layer found along the coast were evidence that a major earthquake occurred about 300 years ago, just before European settlers arrived in the region (Atwater, 1987; Nelson et al., 1995).

Publishes explanation based on evidence

Several years later a Japanese seismologist, who was studying historic tide gauge records in Japan to document tsunamis from distant sources, identified a major earthquake somewhere along the Pacific rim on January 17, 1700, but the source of the earthquake was open to debate. Using historical records he was able to eliminate the possibility of a large earthquake from most known earthquake source regions around the Pacific. Aware of the geologist's work on dead forests in the Pacific northwest, the Japanese seismologist suggested that the source of the tsunami was a large subduction zone earthquake beneath present day Oregon and Washington (Satake et al., 1996).

Considers new evidence

Now the geologist had more evidence supporting his explanation that the sand layer was caused by a tsunami that accompanied an earthquake. Further examination of coastal sediments uncovered additional, but older, remains of dead trees and sand layers. He now thinks that earthquakes producing very large tsunamis, like the one he first identified, have repeatedly struck the Pacific Northwest coast in the past thousand years, just as these large earthquakes strike other subduction zones beneath Japan, the Philippines, Alaska, and much of Western South America. The coastal subsidence caused by the earthquake submerged the trees in salt water, which led to their death.

Adds to explanation

As sometimes occurs with scientific research, the geologist's findings influenced public policy. Public officials have revised the building codes for Washington and Oregon, based on the deeper understanding of earthquakes that grew out of this research. New buildings must be designed to resist earthquake forces 50 percent larger than under the old code.

Explanation informs public policy

This story illustrates several important features of scientific inquiry. A scientist noticed a phenomenon and had the curiosity to ask questions about it. No doubt many other people had also noticed the dead trees, but they either did not wonder about the cause of death or were not in a position to answer the question. Using his knowledge of geology and what he learned about trees and their habitats, the geologist made connections between the dead trees and other features of the environment, such as the coastal location. Those questions guided his investigation, which included the use of carbon 14 methods to date the dead trees and the gathering of available knowledge about the geology of the region. He developed an explanation for the death of the trees based on this preliminary evidence and gathered more evidence to test his explanation. He then published articles in which he discussed the relationship between the evidence he accumulated and the explanation he proposed. Later, a scientist in another part of the world read the publications and, because

LETTERS TO NATURE

Radiocarbon evidence for extensive plate-boundary rupture about 300 years ago at the Cascadia subduction zone

Alan R. Nelson, Brian F. Atwater, Peter T. Bobrowsky, Lee-Ann Bradley, John J. Clague, Gary A. Carver, Mark E. Darienzo, Wendy C. Grant, Harold W. Krueger, Rodger Sparks, Thomas W. Stafford Jr & Minze Stuiver

NATURE · VOL 378 · 23 NOVEMBER 1995 371

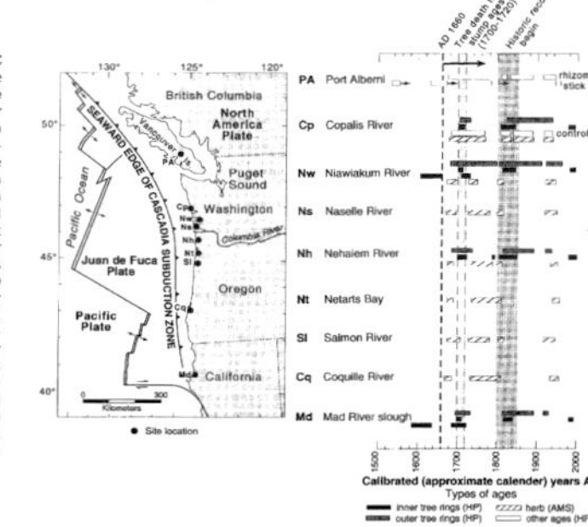

372 NATURE · VOL 378 · 23 NOVEMBER 1995

Geologist's report of his findings published in the journal *Nature*

scientists use universal descriptions and measurements, was able to compare his findings with those of the American scientist. The Japanese scientist obtained separate evidence — the occurrence of a tsunami on January 17, 1700 — that gave further support to the hypothesis that a subduction zone earthquake occurring on that date led to the death of a large number of trees along the Pacific Northwest coast.

THE NATURE OF HUMAN INQUIRY

The geologist's search for understanding of the natural world is a good illustration of the human characteristics that make inquiry such a powerful way of learning. Humans are innately curious, as anyone knows who has watched a newborn. From birth, children employ trial-and-error techniques to learn about the world around them. As children and as adults, when faced with an unknown situation, we try to determine what is happening and predict what will happen next. We reflect on the world around us by observing, gathering, assembling, and synthesizing information. We develop and use tools to measure and observe as well as to analyze information and create models. We check and re-check what we think will happen and compare results to what we already know. We change our ideas based on what we learn.

This complex set of thinking abilities, which helped early humans gather food and escape danger, constitutes the highly developed capacity we refer to as inquiry. In recent human history, some people have directed their curiosity toward issues other than subsistence and survival — for example, the movement of celestial objects, the causes of seasons, the behavior of moving objects, and the origins of organisms. Curiosity about such issues is unique to humans. People studied these phenomena, developing hypotheses and proposing explanations. The communication of hypotheses, ideas, and concepts among individuals shaped the strategies, rules, standards, and knowledge that we recognize today as scientific.

Inquiry into the natural world takes a wide variety of forms. It can range from a child's wondering how it is possible for ants to live underground to the search by groups of physicists for new atomic particles. Inquiry in classrooms also takes a wide variety of forms, as described later in this volume. But whatever its exact form, its role in education is becoming an increasing focus of attention. Today the world is being profoundly influenced by scientific discoveries. People need to make and evaluate decisions that require careful questioning, seeking of evidence, and critical reasoning. Learning environments that concentrate on conveying to students what scientists already know do not promote inquiry. Rather, an emphasis on inquiry asks that we think about what we know, why we know, and how we have come to know.

Inquiry is at the heart of the *National Science Education Standards.* The *Standards* seek to promote curriculum, instruction, and assessment models that enable teachers to build on children's natural, human inquisitiveness. In this way, teachers can help all their students understand science as a human endeavor, acquire the scientific knowledge and thinking skills important in everyday life and, if their students so choose, in pursuing a scientific career.

INQUIRY IN THE SCIENCE CLASSROOM

One of the best ways to understand school science as inquiry is through a visit to a classroom where scientific inquiry is practiced. The following vignette features a particular grade, but, as illustrated throughout this book, classroom inquiry can and does happen at all grade levels. Sidebars point out some ways inquiry is occurring.

Several of the children in Mrs. Graham's fifth grade class were excited when they returned to their room after recess one fall day. They pulled their teacher over to a window, pointed outside, and said, "We noticed something about the trees on the playground. What's wrong with them?" Mrs. Graham didn't know what they were concerned about, so she said, "Show me what you mean."

The students pointed to three trees growing side by side. One had lost all its leaves, the middle one had multicolored leaves — mostly yellow — and the third had lush, green leaves. The children said, "Why are those three trees different? They used to look the same, didn't they?" Mrs. Graham didn't know the answer.

Mrs. Graham knew

Exhibit uriosity, define uestions from current nowledge

that her class was scheduled to study plants later in the year, and this was an opportunity for them to investigate questions about plant growth that they had originated and thus were especially motivated to answer. Although she was uncertain about where her students' questions would lead, Mrs. Graham chose to take the risk of letting her students pursue investigations under her guidance. After all, they had had some experience last year in examining how seeds grow under different conditions. She hung up a large sheet of butcher paper where all the students could see it and said, "Let's make a list of ideas that might explain what's happening to those three trees outside." A forest of hands went up:

It has something to do with the sunlight.

It must be too much water.

Propose liminary lanations ypotheses

It must not be enough water.

The trees look different. They used to look the same.

It's the season, some trees lose their leaves earlier than others.

There is poison in the ground.

The trees have different ages.

Insects are eating the trees.

One tree is older than the others.

When the students were satisfied that they had enough ideas, Mrs. Graham encouraged them to think about which of their ideas were possible explanations that could be investigated and which were descriptions. She then invited each student to pick one explanation that he or she thought might be an answer. She grouped the students by choices: There was a "water group", a "seasons" group, an "insects" group, and so on. She asked each group to plan and conduct a simple investigation to see if they could find any evidence that answered their question. As they planned their investigations, Mrs. Graham visited each group of students

Plan and conduct simple investigation

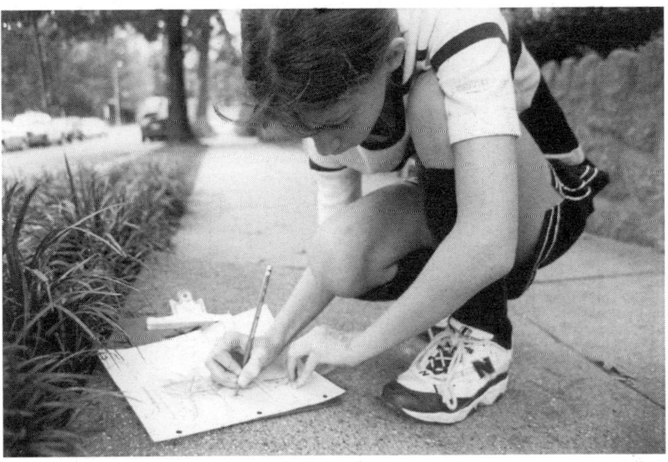

and carefully listened as they formulated their plans. She then asked each group to explain their ideas to their classmates, resulting in further refinement. Using this quick and public assessment of where they were, she was able to help them think about the processes they were using to address their question and consider whether other approaches might work better.

Gather evidence from observation

For the next three weeks, science periods were set aside for each group to carry out its investigation. The groups used a variety of sources to gather information about characteristics of trees, their life cycles, and their environments. For example, the "different ages" group answered their question fairly quickly. They contacted the PTA members who were involved in planting that part of the playground and found the original receipts for the purchase of the trees. A check with the nursery indicated that all three trees were identical and of approximately the same age when purchased. As some groups completed their investigations early, Mrs. Graham invited their members to join other groups still in progress.

Explain based on evidence

The water group decided to look at the ground around the trees every hour that they could. They took turns and jointly kept a journal of their individual observations. Since some students lived near the school, their observations continued after school hours and on weekends. They missed some hourly observations, but they had sufficient data to report to the class. "The tree without leaves is almost always standing in water, the middle tree is sometimes standing in water, and the green tree has damp ground but is never standing in water."

Consider other explanations

One of the students recalled that several months ago the leaves on one of his mother's geraniums had begun to turn yellow. She told him that the geranium was getting too much water. Mrs. Graham gave the group a pamphlet from a local nursery entitled "Growing Healthy Plants." The water group read the pamphlet and found that when plant roots are surrounded by water, they cannot take in air from the space around the roots and they essentially "drown." Based on their observations and the information they obtained from the pamphlet, the students concluded that the leafless tree was drowning, the middle tree was "kinda" drowning, and the third one was "just right."

The water group continued its work by investigating the source of the water. They found that the school custodian turned on a lawn sprinkler system three times a week. He left it running longer than necessary, and the excess water ran off the lawn and collected at the base of the trees. Since the ground was sloped, most of the water collected at one end of the tree-growing area. Together with the other groups, they reported their results to the rest of the class.

Communi[cate] explanati[ons]

As different groups gave their reports, the class learned that some observations and information — such as those from the group investigating whether the trees were different — did not explain the observations. The results of other investigations, such as the idea that the trees could have a disease, partly supported the observations. But the explanation that seemed most reasonable to the students, that fit all the observations and conformed with what they had

Dear Mr. Thompson,

Our class has noticed that the three trees outside our window look different from each other. One is totally bare, one's leaves are all different colors, and one has green leaves.

We contacted the nurserys that the PTA bought these trees from and they said the trees were the same kind and same age, so that is not the reason they are so different.

We found that the bare tree is always sitting in water. The tree with the different colored leaves is sometimes sitting in water. And the tree with the green leave is never actually sitting in water.

Our class has read that plants can actually drown in too much water, and we thought that this could be the reason that the trees look different.

We have noticed that you put on the sprinklers quite often, and water collects in the spot where the bare tree and the tree with colored leaves are. We were wondering if you could stop watering the plants so often.

From,
Mrs. Graham's 5th grade class

learned from other sources, was too much water. After their three weeks of work, the class was satisfied that together they had found a reasonable answer to their question. At Mrs. Graham's suggestion, they wrote a letter to the custodian telling him what they had found. The custodian came to class and thanked them. He said he would change his watering procedure and he did. Mrs. Graham then asked the students how they could find out if their explanation was correct. After some discussion they decided that they would have to wait until next year and see if all the trees got healthy again.

Test explanation

The following year, during the same month that they had observed the discrepancy, all three trees were fully clothed with green leaves. Mrs. Graham's former students were now even more convinced that what they had concluded was a valid explanation for their observations.

PARALLELS BETWEEN INQUIRY IN EDUCATION AND IN SCIENCE

One is struck by the parallels between Mrs. Graham's class and the inquiring geologist. The geologist began his investigation with a question about an unusual and intriguing observation of nature. So did Mrs. Graham's children. The scientist then undertook a closer examination of the environment — asked new and more focused questions — and proposed an explanation for what he observed, applying his knowledge of plate tectonics. The children applied their knowledge to formulate several explanations and new questions before undertaking further investigations. The scientist, knowing of investigations by other scientists, used their findings to confirm the validity of his original explanation. In Mrs. Graham's class, groups whose explanations were not confirmed lent strength to the "excess water" explanation. The geologist published his findings. The children "published" their findings in their reports to their classmates and later in a letter to the custodian. Although scientific research does not always influence public policy, the geologist's discoveries resulted in building code revisions in Washington and Oregon. The children's investigations led to revised lawn watering procedures at their school.

Inquiry in the classroom can take many forms. Investigations can be highly structured by the teacher so that students proceed toward known outcomes, such as discovering regularities in the movement of pendulums (as noted in the Foreword and in the classroom vignette on pages 146-147 of the *National Science Education Standards*). Or investigations can be free-ranging explorations of unexplained phenomena, like the tree leaf discrepancies in Mrs. Graham's schoolyard. The form that inquiry takes depends largely on the educational goals for students, and because these goals are diverse, highly structured and more open-ended inquiries both have their place in science classrooms.

The chapters that follow explore the dimensions of teaching and learning science as inquiry across a broad range of ages and scientific topics. The intention is to improve the quality of student learning by enabling them to acquire the abilities of inquiry, develop knowledge of scientific ideas, and understand the work of scientists.

2
Inquiry in the *National Science Education Standards*

When educators see or hear the word "inquiry," many think of a particular way of teaching and learning science. Although this is one important application for the word, inquiry in the Standards is far more fundamental. It encompasses not only an ability to engage in inquiry but an understanding of inquiry and of how inquiry results in scientific knowledge.

Because of the importance of inquiry, the content standards describing what all students need to know and be able to do include standards on science as inquiry. These inquiry standards specify the abilities students need in order to inquire and the knowledge that will help them understand inquiry as the way that knowledge is produced. In this way, the *Standards* seek to build student understanding of how we know what we know and what evidence supports what we know.

The abilities and understanding of inquiry are neither developed nor used in a vacuum. Inquiry is intimately connected to scientific questions — students must inquire using what they already know and the inquiry process must add to their knowledge. The geologist investigating the cause of the dead cedar forests along the Pacific Coast used his scientific knowledge and inquiry abilities to develop an explanation for the phenomenon. Mrs. Graham's fifth grade students used their observations and the information they gathered about plants to recognize the factors affecting the growth of trees in their schoolyard and to solve the "three-tree problem." For both scientist and students, inquiry and subject matter were integral to the activity. Their scientific knowledge deepened as they developed new understandings through observing and manipulating conditions in the natural world.

What is inquiry in education? The *Standards* note:

> Inquiry is a multifaceted activity that involves making observations;

> posing questions; examining books and other sources of information to see what is already known; planning investigations; reviewing what is already known in light of experimental evidence; using tools to gather, analyze, and interpret data; proposing answers, explanations, and predictions; and communicating the results. Inquiry requires identification of assumptions, use of critical and logical thinking, and consideration of alternative explanations. (p. 23)

Developing the ability to understand and engage in this kind of activity requires direct experience and continued practice with the processes of inquiry. Students do not come to understand inquiry simply by learning words such as "hypothesis" and "inference" or by memorizing procedures such as "the steps of the scientific method." They must experience inquiry directly to gain a deep understanding of its characteristics.

Yet experience in itself is not sufficient. Experience and understanding must go together. Teachers need to introduce students to the fundamental elements of inquiry. They must also assist students to reflect on the characteristics of the processes in which they are engaged.

This chapter addresses the several perspectives on inquiry included in the National Science Education Standards. It first provides some historical background to place the role of inquiry in context. It then gives the actual content standards on Science as Inquiry: what should students know and be able to do? A description of a set of elements or features essential to inquiry-oriented teaching and learning sets the stage for a discussion of instructional models that can help teachers structure activities to foster student inquiry. Finally, several myths that misrepresent inquiry in school science programs are described and debunked.

INQUIRY IN SCHOOL SCIENCE: HISTORICAL PERSPECTIVES

Inquiry has had a role in school science programs for less than a century (Bybee and DeBoer, 1993; DeBoer, 1991). Before 1900, most educators viewed science primarily as a body of knowledge that students were to learn through direct instruction. One criticism of this perspective came in 1909, when John Dewey, in an address to the American Association for the Advancement of Science, contended that science teaching gave too much emphasis to the accumulation of information and not enough to science as a way of thinking and an attitude of mind. Science is more than a body of knowledge to be learned, Dewey said; there is a process or method to learn as well (Dewey, 1910).

By the 1950s and 1960s, the rationale for inquiry as an approach to

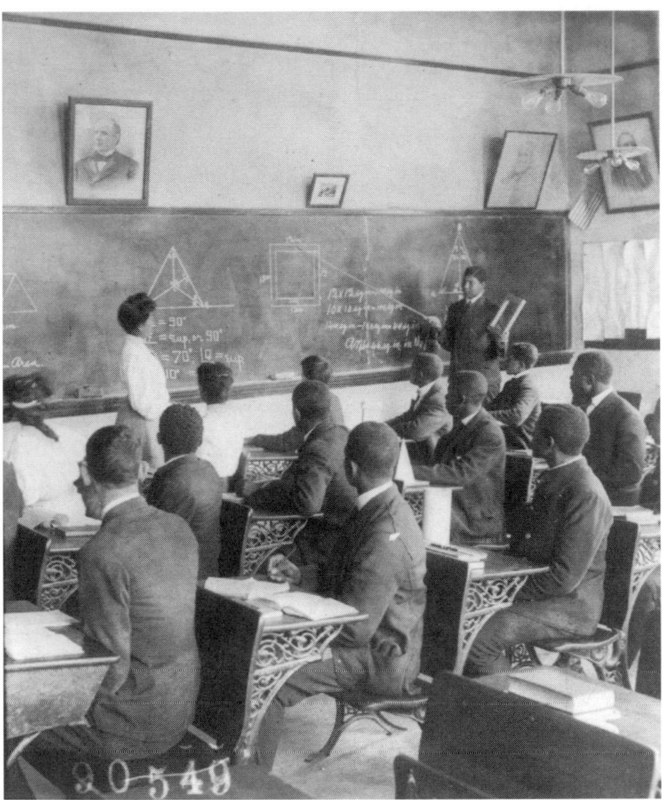

School classroom 1906

teaching science was becoming increasingly evident. If students were to learn the methods of science, then how better to learn than through active engagement in the process of inquiry itself? The educator Joseph Schwab (1960, 1966) was an influential voice in establishing this view of science education. Schwab argued that science should be viewed as conceptual structures that were revised as the result of new evidence. For example, the geologist described in the previous chapter followed this approach in developing an explanation for the widespread death of trees.

Science teaching and learning should reflect this perspective on science, Schwab said.

The implications of Schwab's ideas were, for their time, profound. His view suggested that teachers should present science as inquiry and that students should use inquiry to learn science subject matter. To achieve these changes, Schwab (1960) recommended that science teachers look first to the laboratory and use these experiences to lead rather than follow the classroom phase of science teaching. That is, students should work in the laboratory before being introduced to the formal explanation of scientific concepts and principles. Evidence should build to explanations and the refinement of explanations.

Schwab also suggested that science teachers consider three possible approaches in their laboratories. First, laboratory manuals or textbook materials could be used to pose questions and describe methods to investigate the questions, thus allowing students to discover relationships they do not already know. Second, instructional materials could be used to pose questions, but the methods

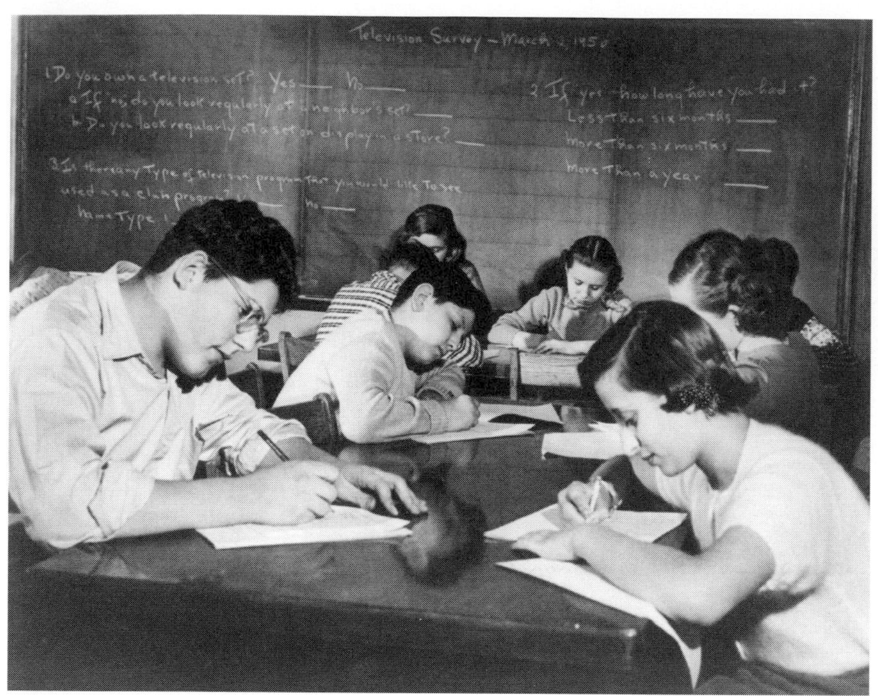

School classroom 1950

and conclusions reached by the scientists. Where possible, students read about alternative explanations, different and perhaps conflicting experiments, debates about assumptions underlying the research and the use of evidence, and other issues of scientific inquiry. Through this approach, students build an understanding of what constitutes scientific knowledge and how scientific knowledge is produced.

The work of Schwab, Dewey, and others, including Bruner and Piaget in the 1950s and 1960s, influenced the nature of curriculum materials developed in those decades and into the early 1970s. Russia's launch of the Sputnik satellite in 1957 further spurred the development of these materials, many of which were supported by the National Science Foundation and other federal agencies and private foundations. Underlying many of these instructional materials was the commitment to involve students in doing rather than being told or only reading about science. This reform placed as much, if not more, emphasis on learning the processes of science as on mastering the subject matter of science alone. Teaching models were

and answers could be left open for students to determine on their own. Third, in the most open approach, students could confront phenomena without textbook- or laboratory-based questions. Students could ask questions, gather evidence, and propose scientific explanations based on their own investigations.

Schwab proposed an additional approach, which he referred to as an "enquiry into enquiry." (Schwab chose to use this variation of the spelling of the word.) In this approach, teachers provide students with readings and reports about scientific research. They discuss the details of the research: the problems, data, role of technology, interpretations of data,

Space flight July 19, 1946

based on theories of learning that emphasized the central role of students' own ideas and concrete experiences in creating new and deepened understandings of scientific concepts.

Throughout the country, use, or at least awareness, of these new curriculum materials prompted educators to provide students with more laboratory and other "hands-on" experiences, more opportunities to pursue their own questions, and more focus on understanding larger scientific concepts rather than disconnected facts. Although the effective use of these new materials was not as widespread as anticipated (Weiss, 1978; Harms and Kahl, 1980; Harms and Yager, 1981), this new view of school science did prompt more study and careful thinking about major issues in science education. Furthermore, and of special significance to this volume, the changes of the 1950s, 1960s, and 1970s widely disseminated the idea of helping students to develop the skills of inquiry and an understanding of science as inquiry.

INQUIRY IN THE *NATIONAL SCIENCE EDUCATION STANDARDS*

The developers of the *National Science Education Standards* (National Research Council, 1996) had this historical perspective on which to base their work. Studies of teaching and learning in science classrooms had led to two observations. First, most teachers were still using traditional, didactic methods (Stake and Easley, 1978; Harms and Yager, 1981; Weiss, 1987). Examination of science classrooms revealed that many students were mastering disconnected facts in lieu of broader understandings, critical reasoning, and problem-solving skills. Some teachers, however, were using the new curriculum materials, such as those from the Biological Sciences Curriculum Study (BSCS), Science Curriculum Improvement Study (SCIS), Elementary Science Study (ESS), Intermediate Science Curriculum Study (ISCS), and Physical Sciences Study Committee (PSSC). Their students were spending large amounts of time in inquiry-based activities. They were making observations, manipulating materials, and conducting laboratory investigations. As a result, they were developing cognitive abilities, such as critical thinking and reasoning, as well as learning science content (Bredderman, 1982; Shymansky et al., 1983).

Those developing national standards were committed to including inquiry as both science content and as a way to learn science. Therefore, rather than simply extolling the virtues of "hands-on" or "laboratory-based" teaching as the way to teach "science content and process," the writers of the *Standards* treated inquiry as both a learning goal and as a teaching method. The concept of inquiry thus appears in several different places in the *Standards*.

INQUIRY IN THE CONTENT STANDARDS

The content standards for Science as Inquiry include both abilities and understandings of inquiry (Tables 2-1, 2-2 and 2-3). The general standards for inquiry (Table 2-1) are the same for all three grade spans (K-4, 5-8, 9-12). The more detailed fundamental abilities of inquiry and fundamental understandings about inquiry increase in complexity from kindergarten through grade 12, reflecting the cognitive development of students (Tables 2-2 and 2-3).

Table 2-1. Content Standard for Science as Inquiry

As a result of activities in grades K-12, all students should develop

- abilities necessary to do scientific inquiry.
- understandings about scientific inquiry.

Abilities Necessary to Do Scientific Inquiry

Table 2-2 presents the key abilities from the inquiry standards. These "cognitive abilities" go beyond what have been termed science "process" skills, such as observation, inference, and experimentation (Millar and Driver, 1987). Inquiry abilities require students to mesh these processes with scientific knowledge as they use scientific reasoning and critical thinking to develop their understanding of science.

The basis for moving away from the traditional process approach is to encourage students to participate in the evaluation of scientific knowledge. At each of the steps involved in inquiry, students and teachers ought to ask "what counts?" What data do we keep? What data do we discard? What patterns exist in the data? Are these patterns appropriate for this inquiry? What explanations account for the patterns? Is one explanation better than another?

In justifying their decisions, stu-

Table 2-2. Content Standard for Science as Inquiry: Fundamental Abilities Necessary to Do Scientific Inquiry

Grades K-4

- Scientific investigations involve asking and answering a question and comparing the answer with what scientists already know about the world.
- Scientists use different kinds of investigations depending on the questions they are trying to answer.
- Simple instruments, such as magnifiers, thermometers, and rulers, provide more information than scientists obtain using only their senses.
- Scientists develop explanations using observations (evidence) and what they already know about the world (scientific knowledge).
- Scientists make the results of their investigations public; they describe the investigations in ways that enable others to repeat the investigations.
- Scientists review and ask questions about the results of other scientists' work.

Grades 5-8

- Different kinds of questions suggest different kinds of scientific investigations.
- Current scientific knowledge and understanding guide scientific investigations.
- Mathematics is important in all aspects of scientific inquiry.
- Technology used to gather data enhances accuracy and allows scientists to analyze and quantify results of investigations.
- Scientific explanations emphasize evidence, have logically consistent arguments, and use scientific principles, models, and theories.
- Science advances through legitimate skepticism.
- Scientific investigations sometimes result in new ideas and phenomena for study, generate new methods or procedures for an investigation, or develop new technologies to improve the collection of data.

Grades 9-12

- Scientists usually inquire about how physical, living, or designed systems function.
- Scientists conduct investigations for a wide variety of reasons.
- Scientists rely on technology to enhance the gathering and manipulation of data.
- Mathematics is essential in scientific inquiry.
- Scientific explanations must adhere to criteria such as: a proposed explanation must be logically consistent; it must abide by the rules of evidence; it must be open to questions and possible modification; and it must be based on historical and current scientific knowledge.
- Results of scientific inquiry — new knowledge and methods — emerge from different types of investigations and public communication among scientists.

Table 2-3. Content Standard for Science as Inquiry: Fundamental Understandings About Scientific Inquiry

Grades K-4

- Scientific investigations involve asking and answering a question and comparing the answer with what scientists already know about the world.
- Scientists use different kinds of investigations depending on the questions they are trying to answer.
- Simple instruments, such as magnifiers, thermometers, and rulers, provide more information than scientists obtain using only their senses.
- Scientists develop explanations using observations (evidence) and what they already know about the world (scientific knowledge).
- Scientists make the results of their investigations public; they describe the investigations in ways that enable others to repeat the investigations.
- Scientists review and ask questions about the results of other scientists' work.

Grades 5-8

- Different kinds of questions suggest different kinds of scientific investigations.
- Current scientific knowledge and understanding guide scientific investigations.
- Mathematics is important in all aspects of scientific inquiry.
- Technology used to gather data enhances accuracy and allows scientists to analyze and quantify results of investigations.
- Scientific explanations emphasize evidence, have logically consistent arguments, and use scientific principles, models, and theories.
- Science advances through legitimate skepticism.
- Scientific investigations sometimes result in new ideas and phenomena for study, generate new methods or procedures for an investigation, or develop new technologies to improve the collection of data.

Grades 9-12

- Scientists usually inquire about how physical, living, or designed systems function.
- Scientists conduct investigations for a wide variety of reasons.
- Scientists rely on technology to enhance the gathering and manipulation of data.
- Mathematics is essential in scientific inquiry.
- Scientific explanations must adhere to criteria such as: a proposed explanation must be logically consistent; it must abide by the rules of evidence; it must be open to questions an possible modification; and it must be based on historical and current scientific knowledge.
- Results of scientific inquiry — new knowledge and methods — emerge from different types of investigations and public communication among scientists.

Appendix A-1, which is taken directly from the *Standards*, provides more elaboration for these abilities for each grade span.

Understandings About Scientific Inquiry

Table 2-3 presents the fundamental understandings about the nature of scientific inquiry from the *Standards*. Although in some cases these "understandings" appear parallel to the "abilities" displayed in Table 2-2, they actually represent much more. Understandings of scientific inquiry represent how and why scientific knowledge changes in response to new evidence, logical analysis, and modified explanations debated within a community of scientists. The work of the geologist described in Chapter 1, for example, was guided by his initial question and the evidence-to-explanation nature of scientific inquiry.

As with the abilities of inquiry, the understandings of inquiry are very similar from one grade to the next but increase in complexity. For example, K-4 students understand that "scientists develop explanations using observations (evidence) along with what they already know about the world (scientific knowledge)," while students in grades 5-8 know that "scientific explanations emphasize evidence, have logically consistent arguments, and use scientific principles, models, and theories." Students in grades 9-12 understand that scientific explanations must abide by the rules of evidence, be open to possible modifications, and satisfy other criteria.

Appendix A-2, taken directly from the *Standards*, provides more elaboration for these understandings for each grade span.

LEARNING THROUGH INQUIRY AND ITS IMPLICATIONS FOR TEACHING

Having defined inquiry in part as a set of student learning outcomes, the next question becomes: What is teaching through inquiry, and when and how should it be done?

The science teaching standards provide a comprehensive view of science teaching (Table 2-4). These standards apply to the many teaching strategies, including inquiry, that make up an effective teacher's repertoire. Although the teaching standards refer to inquiry, they are also clear that "inquiry is not the only strategy for teaching science" (p. 23). Nevertheless, inquiry is a central part of the teaching standards. The standards say, for example, that teachers of science "plan an 'inquiry-based' science program," "focus and support inquiries," and "encourage and model the skills of scientific inquiry."

Because the teaching standards are so broad, it is helpful for our purposes

Table 2-4. Science Teaching Standards

TEACHING STANDARD A:

Teachers of science plan an inquiry-based science program for their students. In doing this, teachers

- Develop a framework of yearlong and short-term goals for students.
- Select science content and adapt and design curricula to meet the interests, knowledge, understanding, abilities, and experiences of students.
- Select teaching and assessment strategies that support the development of student understanding and nurture a community of science learners.
- Work together as colleagues within and across disciplines and grade levels.

TEACHING STANDARD B:

Teachers of science guide and facilitate learning. In doing this, teachers

- Focus and support inquiries while interacting with students.
- Orchestrate discourse among students about scientific ideas.
- Challenge students to accept and share responsibility for their own learning.
- Recognize and respond to student diversity and encourage all students to participate fully in science learning.
- Encourage and model the skills of scientific inquiry, as well as the curiosity, openness to new ideas and data, and skepticism that characterize science.

TEACHING STANDARD C:

Teachers of science engage in ongoing assessment of their teaching and of student learning. In doing this, teachers

- Use multiple methods and systematically gather data about student understanding and ability.
- Analyze assessment data to guide teaching.
- Guide students in self-assessment.
- Use student data, observations of teaching, and interactions with colleagues to reflect on and improve teaching practice.
- Use student data, observations of teaching, and interactions with colleagues to report student achievement and opportunities to learn to students, teachers, parents, policymakers, and the general public.

TEACHING STANDARD D:
Teachers of science design and manage learning environments that provide students with the time, space, and resources needed for learning science. In doing this, teachers

- Structure the time available so that students are able to engage in extended investigations.
- Create a setting for student work that is flexible and supportive of science inquiry.
- Ensure a safe working environment.
- Make the available science tools, materials, media, and technological resources accessible to students.
- Identify and use resources outside the school.
- Engage students in designing the learning environment.

TEACHING STANDARD E:
Teachers of science develop communities of science learners that reflect the intellectual rigor of scientific inquiry and the attitudes and social values conducive to science learning. In doing this, teachers

- Display and demand respect for the diverse ideas, skills, and experiences of all students.
- Enable students to have a significant voice in decisions about the content and context of their work and require students to take responsibility for the learning of all members of the community.
- Nurture collaboration among students.
- Structure and facilitate ongoing formal and informal discussion based on a shared understanding of rules of scientific discourse.
- Model and emphasize the skills, attitudes, and values of scientific inquiry.

TEACHING STANDARD F:
Teachers of science actively participate in the ongoing planning and development of the school science program. In doing this, teachers

- Plan and develop the school science program.
- Participate in decisions concerning the allocation of time and other resources to the science program.
- Participate fully in planning and implementing professional growth and development strategies for themselves and their colleagues.

to focus more on inquiry in classrooms: to propose a working definition that distinguishes inquiry-based teaching and learning from inquiry in a general sense and from inquiry as practiced by scientists. The following definition is derived in part from the abilities of inquiry, emphasizing questions, evidence, and explanations within a learning context. Inquiry teaching and learning have five essential features that apply across all grade levels (see Table 2-5).

1. *Learners are engaged by scientifically oriented questions.* Scientifically oriented questions center on objects, organisms, and events in the natural world; they connect to the science concepts described in the content standards. They are questions that lend themselves to empirical investigation, and lead to gathering and using data to develop explanations for scientific phenomena. Scientists recognize two primary kinds of scientific questions (Malley, 1992). Existence questions probe origins and include many "why" questions. Why do objects fall towards the earth? Why do some rocks contain crystals? Why do humans have chambered hearts? Many "why" questions cannot be addressed by science. There are also causal/functional questions, which probe mechanisms and include most of the "how" questions. How does sunlight help plants to grow? How are crystals formed?

Students often ask "why" questions. In the context of school science, many of these questions can be changed into "how" questions and thus lend themselves to scientific inquiry. Such change narrows and sharpens the inquiry and contributes to its being scientific.

In the classroom, a question robust and fruitful enough to drive an inquiry generates a "need to know" in students, stimulating additional questions of "how" and "why" a phenomenon occurs. The initial question may originate from the learner, the teacher, the instructional materials, the Web, some other source, or some combination. The teacher plays a critical role in guiding the identification of questions, particularly when they come from students. Fruitful inquiries evolve from questions that are meaningful and relevant to students, but they also must be able to be answered by students' observations and scien-

Table 2-5. Essential Features of Classroom Inquiry

- Learners are engaged by scientifically oriented questions.
- Learners give priority to **evidence**, which allows them to develop and evaluate explanations that address scientifically oriented questions.
- Learners formulate **explanations** from evidence to address scientifically oriented questions.
- Learners evaluate their explanations in light of alternative explanations, particularly those reflecting scientific understanding.
- Learners communicate and justify their proposed explanations.

tific knowledge they obtain from reliable sources. The knowledge and procedures students use to answer the questions must be accessible and manageable, as well as appropriate to the students' developmental level. Skillful teachers help students focus their questions so that they can experience both interesting and productive investigations.

An example of a question that meets these criteria for young students is: how do mealworms respond to light? One for older students is: how do genes influence eye color? An example of an unproductive question for younger students is: why do people behave the way they do? This question is too open, lending itself to responses that may or may not have a scientific basis. It would be difficult to gather evidence supporting such proposed answers as, "it is human nature" or "some supernatural force wills people to behave the way they do." An example of an unproductive question for older students is: what will the global climate be like in 100 years? This question is scientific, but it is also very complex. It requires an answer that will almost assuredly not consider all the evidence and arguments that would go into a prediction. Students might consider individual factors, for example, how would increasing cloud cover influence climate change? Or they might consider causal relationships, for example, what effect would 5 degrees warmer (or cooler) temperatures have on plants? currents? weather?

2. *Learners give priority to* **evidence**, *which allows them to develop and evaluate explanations that address scientifically oriented questions.* As the *Standards* note, science distinguishes itself from other ways of knowing through use of empirical evidence as the basis for explanations about how the natural world works. Scientists concentrate on getting accurate data from observations of phenomena.

They obtain evidence from observations and measurements taken in natural settings such as oceans, or in contrived settings such as laboratories. They use their senses, instruments such as telescopes to enhance their senses, or instruments that measure characteristics that humans cannot sense, such as magnetic fields. In some instances, scientists can control conditions to obtain their evidence; in other instances they cannot control the conditions or control would distort the phenomena, so they gather data over a wide range of naturally occurring conditions and over a long enough period of time so that they can infer what the influence of different factors might be (AAAS, 1989). The accuracy of the evidence gathered is verified by checking measurements, repeating the observations, or gathering different kinds of data related to the same phenomenon. The evidence is subject to questioning and further investigation.

The above paragraph explains what counts as evidence in science. In their classroom inquiries, students use evidence to develop explanations for scientific phenomena. They observe plants, animal, and rocks, and carefully describe their characteristics. They take measurements of temperature, distances, and time, and carefully record them. They observe chemical reactions and moon phases and chart their progress. Or they obtain evidence from their teacher, instructional materials, the Web, or elsewhere, to "fuel" their inquiries. As the *Standards* note, "explanations of how the natural world changes based on myths, personal beliefs, religious values, mystical inspiration, superstition, or authority may be personally useful and socially relevant, but they are not scientific" (p. 201).

3. *Learners formulate explanations from evidence to address scientifically oriented questions.* Although similar to the previous feature, this aspect of inquiry emphasizes the path from evidence to explanation rather than the criteria for and characteristics of the evidence. Scientific explanations are based on reason. They provide causes for effects and establish relationships based on evidence and logical argument. They must be consistent with experimental and observational evidence about nature. They respect rules of evidence, are open to criticism, and require the use of various cognitive processes generally associated with science — for example, classification, analysis, inference, and prediction, and general processes such as critical reasoning and logic.

Explanations are ways to learn about what is unfamiliar by relating what is observed to what is already known. So, explanations go beyond current knowledge and propose some new understanding. For science, this means building upon the existing knowledge base. For students, this means building new ideas upon their current understandings. In both cases, the result is proposed new knowledge. For example, students may use observational and other evidence to propose an explanation for the phases of the moon; for why plants die under certain conditions and thrive in others; and for the relationship of diet to health.

4. *Learners evaluate their explanations in light of alternative explanations, particularly those reflecting scientific understanding.* Evaluation, and possible elimination or revision of explanations, is one feature that distinguishes scientific from other forms of inquiry and subsequent explanations. One can ask questions such as: Does the evidence support the proposed explanation? Does the explanation adequately answer the questions? Are there any apparent biases or flaws in the reasoning connecting evidence and explanation? Can other reasonable explanations be derived from the evidence?

Alternative explanations may be reviewed as students engage in dialogues, compare results, or check their results with those proposed by the teacher or instructional materials. An essential component of this characteristic is ensuring that students make the connection between their results and scientific knowledge appropriate to their level of development. That is, student explanations should ultimately be consistent with currently accepted scientific knowledge.

5. *Learners communicate and justify their proposed explanations.* Scientists communicate their explanations in such a way that their results can be reproduced. This requires clear articulation of the question, procedures, evidence, proposed explanation, and review of alternative explanations. It provides for further skeptical review and the opportunity for other scientists to use the explanation in work on new questions.

Having students share their explanations provides others the opportunity to ask questions, examine evidence, identify faulty reasoning, point out statements that go beyond the evidence, and suggest alternative explanations for the same observations. Sharing explanations can bring into question or fortify the connections students have made among the evidence, existing scientific knowledge, and their proposed explanations. As a result, students can resolve contradictions and solidify an empirically based argument.

Taken as a whole, these essential features introduce students to many important aspects of science while helping them develop a clearer and deeper knowledge of some particular science concepts and processes. The path from formulating scientific questions, to establishing criteria for evidence, to proposing, evaluating, and then communicating explanations is an important set of experiences for school science programs.

Teaching approaches and instructional materials that make full use of inquiry include all five of these essential features. Each of these essential features can vary, of course. These variations might include the amount of structure a teacher builds into an activity or the extent to which students initiate and design an investigation. For example, every inquiry engages students in scientifically oriented questions. However, in some inquiries students pose the initial question; in others students choose alternatives or sharpen the initial question; and in others the students are provided the question. Research demonstrates the importance of students' taking ownership of a task, which argues for engaging students in identifying or sharpening questions for inquiry. But all variations appropriate for the particular learning goal are acceptable, as long as the learning experience centers on scientifically oriented questions that engage students' thinking.

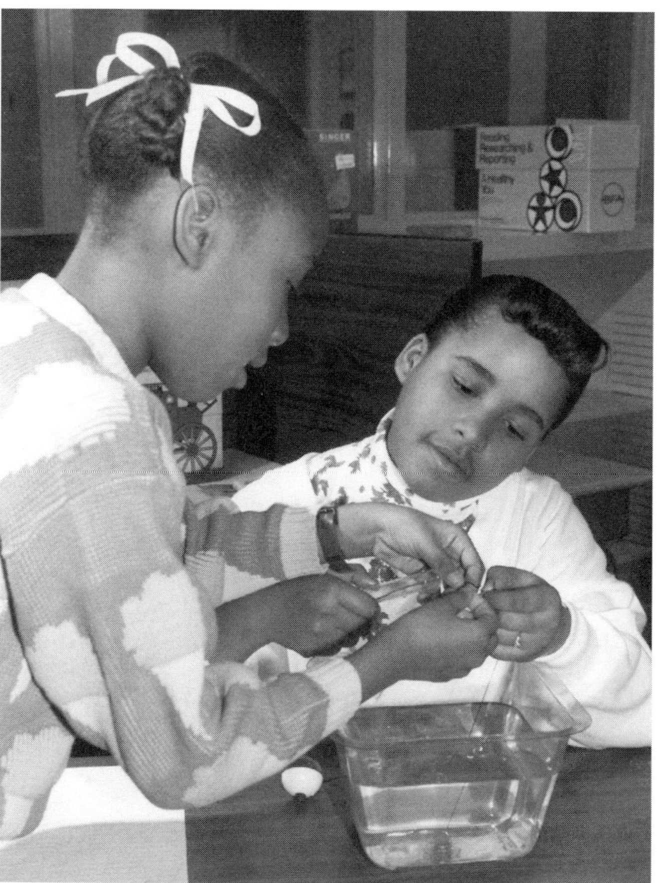

Sometimes inquiries are labeled as either "full" or "partial." These labels refer to the proportion of a sequence of learning experiences that is inquiry-based. For example, when a teacher or textbook does not engage students with a question but begins by assigning an experiment, an essential element of inquiry is missing and the inquiry is partial. Likewise, an inquiry is partial if a teacher chooses to demonstrate how something works rather than have students explore it and develop their own questions or explanations. If all five of the essential elements of classroom inquiry are present, the inquiry is said to be full.

Inquiry-based teaching can also vary in the amount of detailed guidance that the teacher provides. Table 2-6 describes variations in the amount of structure, guidance, and coaching the teacher provides for students engaged in inquiry, broken out for each of the five essential features. It could be said that most open form of inquiry-based teaching and learning occurs when students' experiences are described by the left-hand column in Table 2-6. However, students rarely have the abilities to begin here. They first have to learn to ask and evaluate questions that can be investigated, what the difference is between evidence and opinion, how to develop a defensible explanation, and so on. A more structured type of teaching develops students' abilities to inquire. It helps them learn how to determine what counts. The degree to which teachers structure what students do is sometimes referred to as "guided" versus "open" inquiry. (Note that this distinction has roots in the history recounted earlier in the chapter as Schwab's three approaches to "labora-

e 2-6. Essential Features of Classroom Inquiry and Their Variations

ial Feature	Variations			
ırner engages in entifically oriented estions	Learner poses a question	Learner selects among questions, poses new questions	Learner sharpens or clarifies question provided by teacher, materials, or other source	Learner engages in question provided by teacher, materials, or other source
ırner gives priority **evidence** in ponding to estions	Learner determines what constitutes evidence and collects it	Learner directed to collect certain data	Learner given data and asked to analyze	Learner given data and told how to analyze
ırner formulates **planations** from dence	Learner formulates explanation after summarizing evidence	Learner guided in process of formulating explanations from evidence	Learner given possible ways to use evidence to formulate explanation	Learner provided with evidence
ırner connects planations to entific knowledge	Learner independently examines other resources and forms the links to explanations	Learner directed toward areas and sources of scientific knowledge	Learner given possible connections	
ırner communicates d justifies planations	Learner forms reasonable and logical argument to communicate explanations	Learner coached in development of communication	Learner provided broad guidelines to sharpen communication	Learner given steps and procedures for communication

More ——— **Amount of Learner Self-Direction** ——— **Less**

Less ——— **Amount of Direction from Teacher or Material** ——— **More**

tories" which vary in their degree of structure and guidance by teachers or materials.) Table 2-6 illustrates that inquiry-based learning cannot simply be characterized as one or the other. Instead, the more responsibility learners have for posing and responding to questions, designing investigations, and extracting and communicating their learning, the more "open" the inquiry (that is, the closer to the left column in Table 2-6). The more responsibility the teacher takes, the more guided the inquiry (that is, the closer to the right column on Table 2-6).

Experiences that vary in "openness" are needed to develop the inquiry abilities in Table 2-2. Guided inquiry can best focus learning on the development of particular science concepts. More open inquiry will afford the best opportunities for cognitive development and scientific reasoning. Students should have opportunities to participate in all types of inquiries in the course of their science learning.

How does a teacher decide how much guidance to provide in an inquiry? In making this decision, a key element is the intended learning outcomes. Whether the teacher wants students to learn a particular science concept, acquire certain inquiry abilities, or develop understandings about scientific inquiry (or some combination) influences the nature of the inquiry.

Below are examples of learning experiences designed to incorporate some form of inquiry. (Note the emphasis on series of lessons or learning experiences, rather than single lessons, illustrating that inquiries require time to unfold and for students to learn.) Each example considers not only the learning outcomes and the teaching strategy but the way the teacher will assess whether students have achieved the intended outcome. Assessment is a critical aspect of inquiry because it sharpens and defines the design of learning experiences. When teachers know what they want students to demonstrate, they can better help them learn to do so.

As one example, consider a series of lessons in which the learning outcome is for students to strengthen all the fundamental abilities of inquiry. In Chapter 1, when Mrs. Graham was presented with an interesting question from her students, she recognized an opportunity for her students to engage in a learning activity where they could complete a full inquiry originating with their question about the trees and culminating in communication of scientific explanations based on evidence. The inquiry incorporated all five essential features, with student engagement described by the left column in Table 2-6. Through her assistance and coaching, Mrs. Graham helped the students learn how to clarify their questions and identify possible explanations that could be tested by scientific investigations. She helped them learn the importance of examining alternative explanations and comparing them with the evidence gathered. She helped students understand the relationship between

evidence and explanation. As a result, the students not only learned some science subject matter related to the growth of trees, they also developed specific inquiry abilities.

A second example focuses on developing student understandings about scientific inquiry. A high school biology teacher is planning student learning activities for a unit on biological evolution. Several of the classroom investigations and discussions focus on factors leading to adaptation in organisms. Because of the interesting historical development of these scientific ideas, the teacher decides to take advantage of the opportunity to develop students' understanding of how scientific inquiry works. The assessment for this learning outcome is for students to be able to describe the place of logic, evidence, criticism, and modification in the account of a scientific discovery. Based on readings about past and current investigations of evolution on the Galapagos Islands (including Darwin's *On the Origin of Species* and *The Beak of the Finch* by Jonathan Weiner), students discuss and answer the following

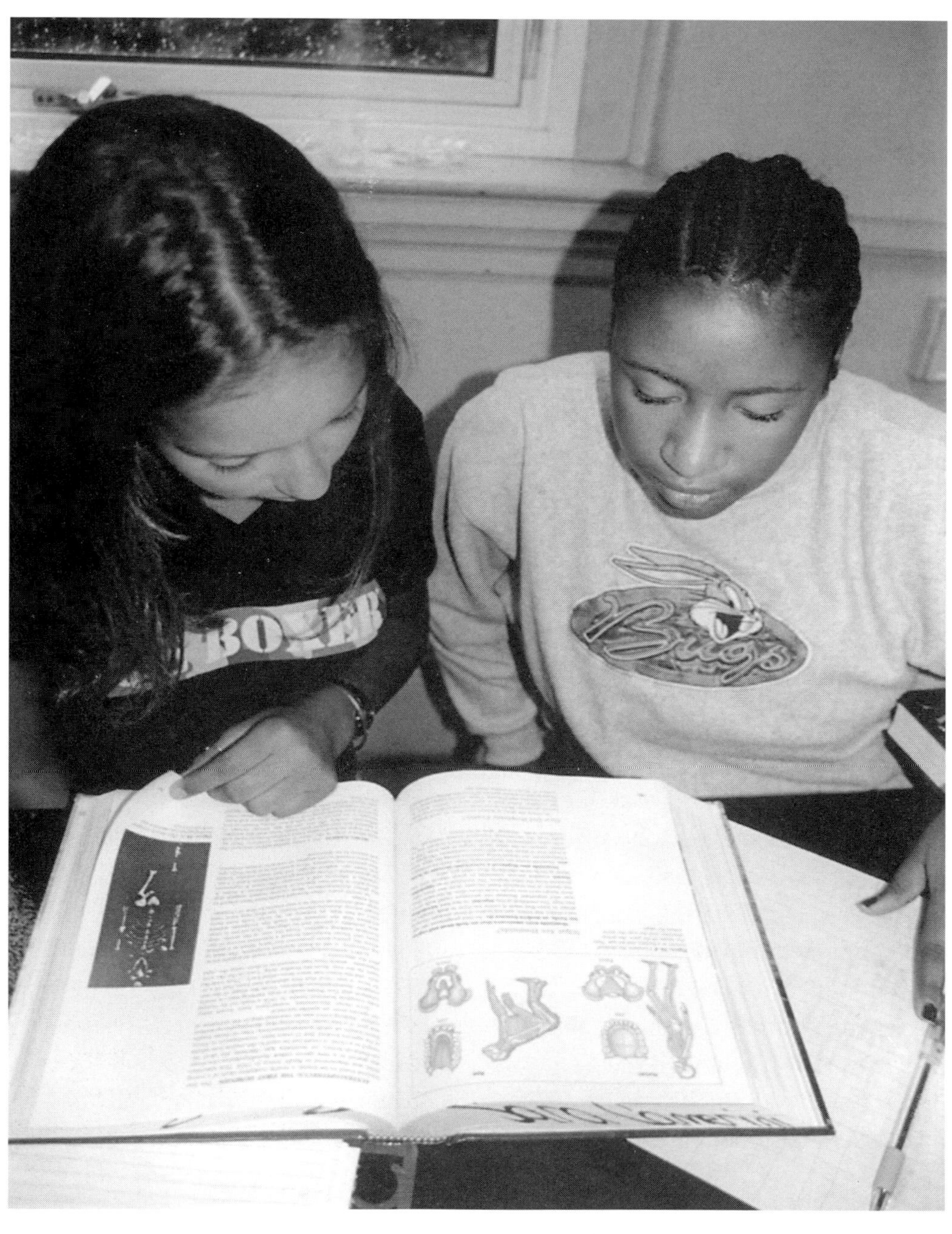

questions: What led to past and current investigation of the finches on the islands? How have investigations differed, and how have they been similar? Have the scientific explanations derived from these investigations been logically consistent? Based on evidence? Open to skeptical review? Built on a knowledge base of other experiments? Following the readings and discussion of the questions, the teacher would have student groups prepare oral reports on the topic "The Role of Inquiry in Science."

This learning activity does not contain all of the essential features of classroom inquiry, but many features are present. The activity engages students in scientifically oriented questions. It promotes discussion of the priority of evidence in developing scientific explanations. It connects those explanations to accepted scientific knowledge. And it requires students to communicate their understandings of scientific inquiry to others. This activity thus could be an integral part of a sequence of learning opportunities that in total contains all five essential features of inquiry.

As a final example, consider a series of lessons that seeks to have students develop an understanding of the concept of density. One way to determine the best teaching strategy for this particular outcome would be to think about how students might demonstrate that they understand density. One performance assessment for older elementary students might be to provide them with objects of different densities, a scale, and a water-filled flask with volume markings on the side. Students would then be asked to select objects and, using the scale and flask, determine their densities. Given this assessment, what kinds of inquiry learning experiences would help students understand density well enough to be successful? One teaching strategy would be a series of laboratory activities framed by questions requiring the gathering and use of evidence to develop explanations about mass and volume relationships. Students would connect their explanations to scientific explanations provided by the teacher and their text, so all five essential features of classroom inquiry would be incorporated.

PROVIDING COHERENT INQUIRY-BASED INSTRUCTION — INSTRUCTIONAL MODELS

How can the features of inquiry be combined in a series of coherent learning experiences that help students build new understandings over time? Instructional models offer a particularly useful way for teachers to improve their use of inquiry.

Instructional models originated in observations of how people learn. As early as the turn of the century, Herbart's (1901) ideas about teaching included starting with students' interest in the natural world and in interactions with others. The teacher crafted learning experiences that expanded concepts students already knew and explained others they could not be expected to discover. Students then applied the concepts to new situations. Later, Dewey (1910) built upon the idea of reflective experience in which students began with a perplexing situation, formulated a tentative interpretation or hypothesis, tested the hypothesis to arrive at a solution, and acted upon the solution. Dewey's prior experience as a science teacher explains the obvious connection between reflective thinking and scientific inquiry (Bybee, 1997).

Piaget's theory of development contributed much to the elaboration of instructional models (Piaget, 1975; Piaget and Inhelder, 1969). In his view, learning begins when individuals experience disequilibrium: a discrepancy between their ideas and ideas they encounter in their environments (that is, what they think they know and what they observe or experience). To bring their understanding back into equilibrium, they must adapt or change their cognitive structure through interaction with the environment.

Piaget's work was the basis for the learning cycle, an instructional model, proposed by Atkin and Karplus (1962) and used in the SCIS elementary science curriculum. Although the learning cycle has undergone elaboration and modification over time, its phases and normal sequence are typically represented as exploration, invention, and discovery. Exploration refers to relatively unstructured experiences when students gather new information. Invention refers to the formal statement of a new concept — often a definition — in which students interpret newly acquired information by restructuring their prior concepts. Discovery involves applying the new concept to a novel situation.

Research on how people learn (discussed in detail in Chapter 6) suggests a dynamic and interactive view of human learning. Students bring to a learning experience their current explanations, attitudes, and abilities. Through meaningful interactions with their environment, with their teachers, and among themselves, they reorganize, redefine, and replace their initial explanations, attitudes, and abilities. An instructional model incorporates the features of inquiry into a sequence of experiences designed to challenge students' current conceptions and provide time and opportunities for reconstruction, or learning, to occur (Bybee, 1997).

A number of different instructional models have been developed that can help teachers organize and sequence inquiry-oriented learning experiences for their students. All can incorporate the essential features of inquiry. They

Table 2-7. Common Components Shared by Instructional Models

- Phase 1: Students engage with a scientific question, event, or phenomenon. This connects with what they already know, creates dissonance with their own ideas, and/or motivates them to learn more.
- Phase 2: Students explore ideas though hands-on experiences, formulate and test hypotheses, solve problems, and create explanations for what they observe.
- Phase 3: Students analyze and interpret data, synthesize their ideas, build models, and clarify concepts and explanations with teachers and other sources of scientific knowledge.
- Phase 4: Students extend their new understanding and abilities and apply what they have learned to new situations.
- Phase 5: Students, with their teachers, review and assess what they have learned and how they have learned it.

seek to engage students in important scientific questions, give students opportunities to explore and create their own explanations, provide scientific explanations and help students connect these to their own ideas, and create opportunities for students to extend, apply, and evaluate what they have learned. Common components or phases that are shared by instructional models are shown in Table 2-7.

Instructional models have helped teachers and those who support them — in particular, curriculum developers — to design instruction in ways that attend to how learning occurs and afford students opportunities to engage in scientific inquiry. The primary disadvantage of instructional models applies to models in general: by definition, they simplify the world. Teachers and others can be misled into thinking of them as lockstep, prescriptive devices — rather than as general guides for designing instruction that help learning to unfold through inquiry, which must always be adapted to the needs of particular learners, the specific learning goals, and the context for learning.

SOME MYTHS ABOUT INQUIRY-BASED LEARNING AND TEACHING

A number of myths about inquiry-based learning and teaching have at times been wrongly attributed to the *National Science Education Standards*. These myths threaten to inhibit progress in science education reform either by characterizing inquiry as too difficult to achieve or by neglecting the essential features of inquiry-based learning. Listed below are responses to five of these mistaken beliefs.

Myth 1: All science subject matter should be taught through inquiry. Teaching science effectively requires a variety of approaches and strategies. It is not possible in practice to teach all science subject matter through inquiry, nor is it desirable to do so. Teaching all of science using only one method would be ineffective, and it would probably become boring for students.

Myth 2: True inquiry occurs only when students generate and pursue their own questions. For students to develop the ability to ask questions, they must "practice" asking questions. But if the desired outcome is learning science subject matter, the source of the question is less important that the nature of the question itself. It is important to note, however, that in today's science classrooms students rarely have opportunities to ask and pursue their own questions. Students will need some of these opportunities to develop advanced inquiry abilities and to understand how scientific knowledge is pursued.

Myth 3: Inquiry teaching occurs easily through use of hands-on or kit-based instructional materials. These materials can increase the probability that students' thinking will be focused on the right things and learning will occur in the right sequence. However, the use of even the best materials does not guarantee that students are engaged in rich inquiry, nor that they are learning as intended. A skilled teacher remains the key to effective instruction. He or she must pay careful attention to whether and how the materials incorporate the five essential features of inquiry. Using these five features to review materials as well as to assess classroom practice should enhance the kinds and depth of learning.

Myth 4: Student engagement in hands-on activities guarantees that inquiry teaching and learning are occurring. Although participation by students in activities is desirable, it is not sufficient to guarantee their mental engagement in any of the essential features of inquiry.

Myth 5: Inquiry can be taught without attention to subject matter. Some of the rhetoric of the 1960s was used to promote the idea that learning science processes should be the only meaningful outcome of science education. Today, there are educators who still maintain that if students learn the processes of science, they can learn any content they need by applying these processes. But as stated at the beginning of this chapter, student understanding of inquiry does not, and cannot, develop in isolation from science subject matter. Rather, students start from what they know and inquire into things they do not know. If, in some instances, a teacher's desired primary outcome is that students learn to conduct an inquiry, science subject matter serves as a means to that end. Scientific knowledge remains important. The abilities and understandings outlined in the *Standards* extend beyond the processes of science to engage students in a full complement of thinking and learning science.

CONCLUSION

This chapter has provided the definitions of inquiry and inquiry-based teaching that undergird the Standards. Chapter 3 will present a series of classroom vignettes that illustrate how elementary, middle, and high school teachers design different kinds of inquiries to achieve diff¡erent learning outcomes. Chapter 4 will look at assessment: within the context of good instruction, how can the achievement of different learning outcomes best be assessed? Subsequent chapters then turn to how teachers can be prepared and supported to use these strategies in their classrooms.

3
Images of Inquiry in K-12 Classrooms

From the earliest grades, students should experience science in a form that engages them in the active construction of ideas and explanations and enhances their opportunities to develop the abilities of doing science. (National Research Council, 1996, p.121)

Chapter 2 introduced the fundamental concepts that underlie inquiry in science classrooms. It described inquiry not only as a means to learn science content but as a set of skills that students need to master and as a body of understanding that students need to learn. It detailed the five essential elements of classroom inquiry, from engaging with a scientifically oriented question to communicating and justifying explanations (Table 2-5). And it discussed the use of instructional models to organize and sequence inquiry-based experiences.

This chapter looks at the concepts introduced in Chapter 2 in practice. It consists largely of classroom vignettes that show how teachers create learning opportunities to help students achieve science standards that incorporate the essential features of inquiry and are supported by instructional models. In the first vignette, a class of third graders learns basic ideas from the life science standards, several of the abilities of inquiry, and aspects of technological design from a study of earthworms. In the second vignette, a class of eighth graders learn content from the earth and space science standard and strengthen their inquiry abilities through an investigation of the phases of the moon. In the final two vignettes, classes of high school students engage in inquiry-based units involving forces (included in the physical science standards) and environmental issues (from the life science and science in personal and social perspectives standards).

These vignettes — each of which is a composite of classroom experiences — provide many opportunities to reflect on the complexity inherent in classroom teaching. In each, inquiry serves both as an outcome and as a means of learning. Different teachers pursue multiple outcomes depending on the nature of the lesson and the teacher's intentions. Analyses of these examples demonstrate how learning outcomes, the essential features of classroom inquiry, and learning models fit together in real classrooms.

The vignettes can be read in any order, depending on a reader's interest. However, each vignette should be read in the context of the following three questions:

- What are the outcomes that the teacher is striving to achieve?
- How are the five essential features of classroom inquiry incorporated into students' learning experiences?
- What is the teacher's instructional model, and what does he or she do to help students achieve the desired outcomes?

Discussions following each vignette address these three questions.

IMAGES OF INQUIRY IN K-4 CLASSROOMS

Ms. Flores's third-grade class was engaged in a field study in a vacant lot near the school. In teams of three, the students had measured off a square meter and marked it with popsicle sticks and string. The purpose of the study was to recognize the diversity of organisms that occupy the same environment and understand how that environment meets all of their needs.

During the investigation several students found earthworms in their square meter and became fascinated with earthworm behavior. Some of the other students wanted to know why they did not find earthworms in their study areas. Others wanted to know why the worms were different sizes. One student suggested that worms "liked" to live near some kind of plants and not others, since when she and her dad went fishing they always dug for worms where there was grass.

Table 3-1. Excerpts from Life Science Standard, K-4

As a result of activities in grades K-4, all students should develop understanding of

The characteristics of organisms

- Organisms have basic needs. Organisms can survive only in environments in which their needs can be met. The world has many different environments, and distinct environments support the life of different types of organisms.
- Each plant or animal has different structures that serve different functions in growth, survival, and reproduction.
- The behavior of individual organisms is influenced by internal cues (such as hunger) and by external cues (such as a change in the environment). Humans and other organisms have senses that help them detect internal and external cues.

Life cycles of organisms

- Plants and animals have life cycles that include being born, developing into adults, reproducing, and eventually dying. The details of this life cycle are different for different organisms.
- Plants and animals closely resemble their parents.
- Many characteristics of an organism are inherited from the parents of the organism, but other characteristics result from an individual's interactions with the environment.

Organisms and their environments

- All animals depend on plants. Some animals eat plants for food. Other animals eat animals that eat the plants.
- An organism's patterns of behavior are related to the nature of that organism's environment, including the kinds and numbers of other organisms present, the availability of food and resources, and the physical characteristics of the environment. When the environment changes, some plants and animals survive and reproduce, and others die or move to new locations.
- All organisms cause changes in the environment where they live. Some of these changes are detrimental to the organism or other organisms, whereas others are beneficial (p. 129).

The discussion about worms could not have come at a better time, because Mrs. Flores was anticipating a series of lessons to help her students learn some of the basic ideas in the life science standard: characteristics of organisms, life cycles of organisms, and organisms and their environments (Table 3-1). Here was a context for doing so. She contacted a biological supply house and learned that she could order supplies of earthworms with egg cases and immature earthworms. Ms. Flores was delighted because this would enable the children to observe all stages in the worm's life cycle and some of their habits.

She realized that it would take considerable time for the earthworms to grow, so she decided to include other learning outcomes as well. Her assessments of her students indicated that they needed to work on several of the abilities of inquiry, such as refining a question for investigation and designing an investigation (the abilities of inquiry are listed in Table 2-2 in the previous chapter). She also decided to incorporate some abilities of technological design from the science and technology standard, since she thought it would be useful for her students to think about designing "homes" for their worms (Table 3-2). And she knew that a full inquiry would allow her to weave in attention to understandings of inquiry. Perhaps she would invite some local scientists into the classroom to point out similarities between what the students were doing and how the scientists worked.

Anticipating the shipment of worms, Ms. Flores suggested to the children that they build a place for the worms to live. They returned to the vacant lot so

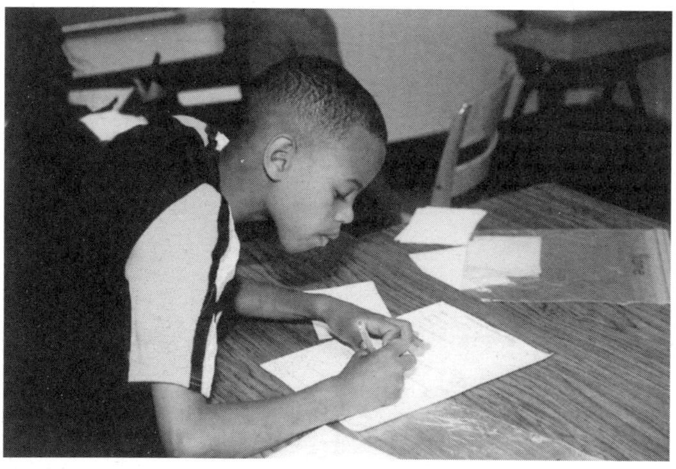

the children could explore where they had originally found worms and study the nature of the soil where they lived. The groups returned to their square meter plots and made notes and drawings of where worms were and were not found. Ms. Flores also asked students to talk to their parents and relatives about where they thought worms lived.

The next day in class the students generated a list of places where they found worms and other places worms might be found. Students suggested looking in wet dirt, under logs, in the roots of plants, and in a compost pile. Ms. Flores then asked them what these places could tell them about how to build a home for worms. In groups of four, the students were asked to design a home for worms using an empty two-liter plastic soda bottle with the top section removed.

The students presented their initial designs before they started building. Students from other groups listened carefully and asked lots of questions since they knew that they could revise their designs after the presentations.

Some students built their worm homes from soil and leaves and put grass on top. Others covered the sides with black paper "so it is like underground." Others used just soil and placed their bottle sideways. One group punched tiny holes in the side to let air into the soil and to let extra water out.

When the worm shipment arrived, Ms. Flores gave each group a handful of worms and instructed them to observe each worm carefully and draw a picture of it. Drawing provoked many questions, including "What kind of an animal is a worm?" Knowing that children typically have different conceptions of animals, Ms. Flores had them add to their drawings some sentences describing what kind of animal they thought it was and why. Some said snakes; some said insects;

Table 3-2. Excerpts from Science and Technology Standard, K-4

As a result of activities in grades K-4, all students should develop:

Abilities of technological design
- identify a simple problem
- propose a solution
- implement proposed solutions
- evaluate a product or design
- communicate a problem, design, and solution

Understanding about science and technology
- People have always had problems and invented tools and techniques (ways of doing something) to solve problems. Trying to determine the effects of solutions helps people avoid some new problems.
- Tools help scientists make better observations, measurements, and equipment for investigations. They help scientists see, measure, and do things that they could not otherwise see, measure, and do.

Abilities to distinguish between natural objects and objects made by humans
- Some objects occur in nature; others have been designed and made by people to solve human problems and enhance the quality of life.
- Objects can be categorized into two groups, natural and designed (pp. 137-138).

some had no idea; some said a worm is a worm.

Next, Ms. Flores asked students what questions they had about worms and recorded their responses on a large chart. The questions included: "How do earthworms have babies?" "Do they like to live in some kinds of soil better than others?" "Do they really like the dark?" "How do they go through the dirt?" "How big can an earthworm get?"

Ms. Flores divided the class into groups and asked each group to choose a question that they would like to investigate and develop a plan for how to do so. The next day the groups reported plans for their investigations, which they had recorded in lab notebooks. Ms. Flores asked the group how they could

devise tests that she called "fair." For example, one group wanted to investigate how much water worms like. Ms. Flores asked, "If you wanted to find out if worms like very wet, wet, medium wet, or dry soil conditions, would it be a 'fair test' if you put a worm with very wet soil in a bottle, another worm with wet soil in another bottle, and a third worm with medium wet soil in another bottle, then put one bottle in the sun and the other two in the shade?" "No," called out a student, "because the bottles in the sun would get hot and worms don't like hot, that's why they live underground, and you couldn't tell whether it was the hot they didn't like or how wet the soil was." Ms. Flores used another group's design for an investigation to assess whether other students understood this idea of a fair test.

Ms. Flores then asked the groups how they would know which place a worm "liked" the best. Students' answers varied. One said if the worms grew bigger and had babies that was a sign they "liked" a place. Several said that if the worms died it meant they didn't like something. Another suggested that if they set up an experiment where there were different options for the worms, where the worms crawled would tell you what they liked.

With a better understanding of what evidence to look for and how to prepare a fair test, the students were soon deep into their investigations. One group was studying the question of how earthworms have babies. They were busy examining the egg cases that they found in the soil using hand lenses and making drawings. They compared their drawings to those in books the librarian had brought to class for them and read about other characteristics of earthworms.

Two groups were exploring how the worms reacted to changes in their environment. They were struggling with how to deal with moisture, light, and temperature all at once. Ms. Flores asked some leading questions beginning with "what would happen if?" in the hope that the students would discover the value of studying one variable at a time. She would check on them later.

Another group wanted to know about the eating habits of worms. They decided to put slices of different fruits and vegetables into the soil and count the number of worm holes as evidence of what worms liked best. The two other groups set up a discarded ant farm with glass sides to observe the movement of worms in different kinds of soil.

Through the investigations and discussions of their observations, measurements, and library research, Ms. Flores's students came to know more about the characteristics of worms, for example how they move, their eating habits, their life cycles, the characteristics of their environments, and their relationship to their environments. Their observations, combined with the research they did in library books, helped them understand why worms were not snakes or insects, but members of a phylum called annelid. They used the drawings and information in their lab notebooks to produce their own books, illustrated with drawings and

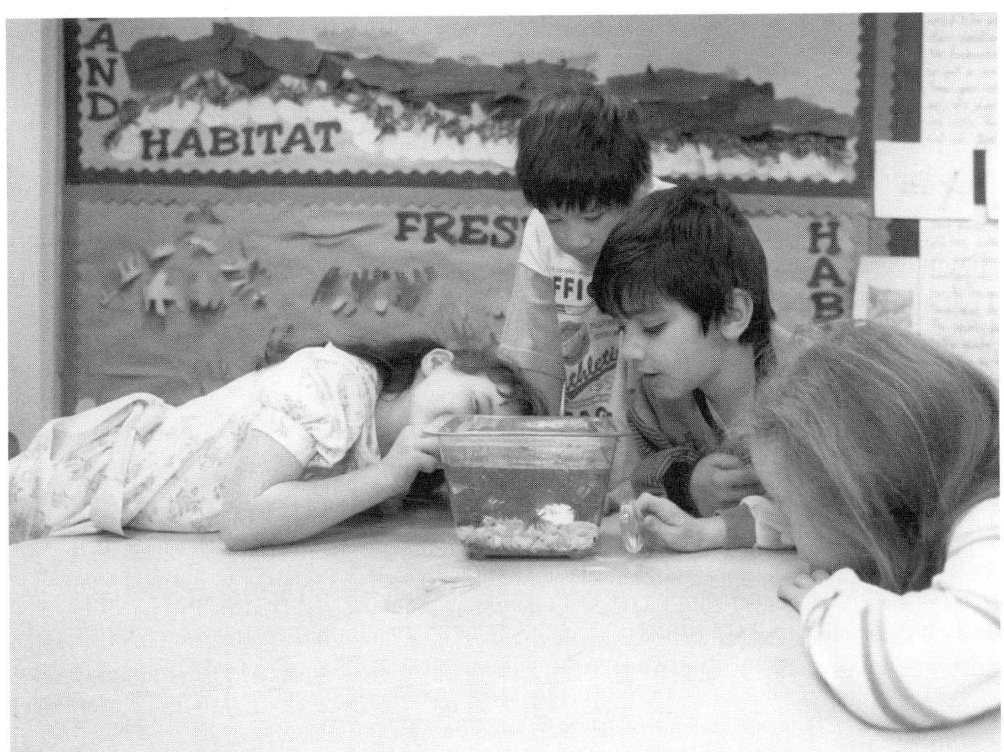

diagrams. They also revisited their designs for worm homes, given the evidence they had gathered over the past several weeks, and talked about how they could redesign them to work better.

During the final days of the study, Ms. Flores focused discussions on the ways of thinking and actions taken during the course of their investigations. The students learned to limit their explanations to ones that they could support with evidence from their own observations. Ms. Flores demonstrated how they could check their explanations against scientific reports in books and with the observations of others. They discussed how conducting a fair test helped them be certain that the answers and explanations they proposed were reasonable. They reviewed how they learned to make observations and measurements using hand lenses, rulers, and balances.

For the final section of their books, Ms. Flores asked the students to write a short explanation of what they would tell another student if that student wanted to study worms. She also asked them to write what they would do differently if they had the project to do over again. Finally, each group assembled their drawings, photographs, data tables, and notes of their observations into books and presented the results of their investigation to the class. They shared the books with the kindergarten and first-grade students and also took them home for their parents and others to read. Ms. Flores also used their books as a form of assessment and analyzed them for the extent to which students demonstrated understanding of the science concepts and their abilities to think scientifically.

As a culminating activity, Ms. Flores invited two scientists to visit her classroom. To prepare the visiting scientists, she loaned each several of the students' research report books and she gave them a list of the fundamental concepts for the standard on understanding scientific inquiry. The scientists intrigued the students with their personal stories of investigations that produced evidence similar to observations made by the students. Students were especially interested in the last stage: how the scientists needed to make their results public, which meant that they were often criticized and challenged as part of building a strong base of scientific knowledge.

ANALYSIS OF K-4 IMAGE OF INQUIRY

Learning Outcomes. Ms. Flores sought to help her students achieve several abilities and understandings specified in the *National Science Education Standards*, including understandings of the characteristics of organisms, their life cycles, and living environments; abilities and understandings of scientific inquiry; and the science and technology standard on technological design. Ms. Flores decided to work especially hard to help her students develop each of the abilities of inquiry — from posing and honing a good question, to conducting a "fair test," to communicating explanations in different and meaningful ways. Finally, she helped her students understand what scientists do by linking their own inquiries to those of scientists.

In an elementary classroom such as Ms. Flores', science activities can also help students develop language and mathematics skills — an important concern for young children. In her class, students were developing abilities to communicate their observations in writing and orally, to craft and share their explanations using logical reasoning, and to measure, display, and interpret data. This demonstrates the integrative potential of science activities for elementary school classrooms.

Essential Features of Classroom Inquiry. Ms. Flores's unit had all of the essential features of classroom inquiry. Her students identified a question of their own interest about earthworms around which to design an investigation. The question derived from their own understanding of the characteristics and environments of earthworms and their curiosity about these animals, and so the question they chose engaged them thoroughly. As they developed answers to their questions, Ms. Flores helped them understand that they needed evidence and what the nature of that evidence needed to be. They looked for evidence through their careful observations and what they read in scientific books. Learning about fair tests increased the likelihood that their evidence would be sound. As they collected their evidence, they built their cases for explanations that addressed their questions. The group looking for favorable environments, observed how the earthworms behaved in "homes" with varying amounts of moisture, and arrived at their explanation of just the right amount; the group examining eating habits observed the numbers of worm holes in different fruits and vegetables and explained worm "preferences" through those data. Throughout the investigations, students developed their own explanations using the evidence they collected and compared them with published scientific explanations from their text books, library books, and the Web. Finally, the students communicated their learning in a variety of ways, clarifying what they did, what results they achieved, and how they knew the results were correct. This communication also served Ms. Flores as an assessment of her students' understanding of life cycles and their abilities of inquiry. As third graders, Ms. Flores's students did not begin with well-developed inquiry abilities. But because Ms. Flores realized that using earthworms would involve an investigation extending over several weeks, she took advantage of the fact that she could pay a great deal of attention to developing her students' inquiry abilities as they learned the subject matter content. Therefore, her students' inquiry was relatively open, with as much coaching as necessary to make sure that the class had many choices for research questions, had a variety of designs for their investigations, and clearly communicated their results.

Instructional Model. Ms. Flores's unit illustrates an interesting and complex sequence of learning activities. Early in the unit, she engaged the students repeatedly in direct, firsthand experience, first almost by accident as they stumbled upon the earthworms in their study of the vacant lot. Later Ms. Flores involved them again in examining the area where they originally found the worms so that they could think about what kind of "home" they would build for their worms.

As Ms. Flores focused the students on the questions they generated and the ideas they had about worms, they began to explore the worms' characteristics, their environments, and their life cycles. They made observations over days and weeks; tried out their ideas; proposed explanations; and shared what they were learning with others. Ms. Flores called them together on a regular basis to help them synthesize what they were learning and create explanations. She supplemented their explanations with scientific information in library books.

Towards the end of the unit, Ms. Flores gave her students opportunities to elaborate on what they were learning. The visit from the scientists deepened their understanding of how their investigations resembled those of scientists. Finally, Ms. Flores's continual questioning and coaching gave both Ms. Flores and the students opportunities to evaluate their progress in an ongoing way. The assignment to speculate on what they would do differently were they to repeat their investigation, with some reasons why, allowed them to reflect back and assess the process and value of their work.

An instructional model must not be used as a "lockstep" device that limits the flexibility of a teacher to facilitate an inquiry that is sensitive to students' needs and interests. This is illustrated by the impossibility of saying where one stage of the instructional model stopped in Ms. Flores's unit and the other began: students were engaging, exploring, explaining, elaborating, and evaluating throughout the several weeks they spent studying worms. However, her instructional model helped Ms. Flores lay out the unit initially and monitor and assess her students' learning and development as it proceeded.

IMAGES OF INQUIRY IN 5-8 CLASSROOMS

Each year Mr. Gilbert looks forward to teaching the solar system unit, especially when they get to the moon (see Table 3-3). From past experience, Mr. Gilbert knew that most middle school students have difficulty finding an explanation for the moon's phases consistent with their direct observations, which always made the unit challenging as well as exciting. Further, learning about the moon's phases also provided many opportunities for his students to develop critical inquiry abilities: to use scientific instrumentation to increase and

Table 3-3. Excerpts from Earth and Space Science Standard, 5-8

As a result of activities in grades 5-8, all students should develop understanding of

Earth in the solar system

- Most objects in the solar system are in regular and predictable motion. Those motions explain such phenomena as the day, the year, phases of the moon, and eclipses (p. 160).

evaluate the accuracy of their observations, to design and conduct investigations to test their conjectures, and to think critically and logically about the relationships between evidence and explanations.

Earlier in the solar system unit, Mr. Gilbert emphasized the importance and technique of gathering evidence about the world and recording it in a notebook. For example, when he challenged the students in his science classes several weeks ago to create sun clocks using sun shadows, he encouraged them to record data about the position, size, and orientation of the shadows that they studied, and to note the rate at which the shadows moved. He also asked them to include a detailed description and sketches of the way in which the shadows were observed to change. They had carefully carried out his instructions, recording their results in their science notebooks.

In earlier class sessions, Mr. Gilbert's students learned how to construct and use several simple tools that helped them make their data and evidence gathering more accurate. One they would use in their study of the moon was a simple sextant constructed from a protractor, a plastic drinking straw, and a string with a metal washer attached to it. They had taped the string with the washer on the end to the bottom of the protractor at the 90° line. Then they taped the straw along the straight edge of the

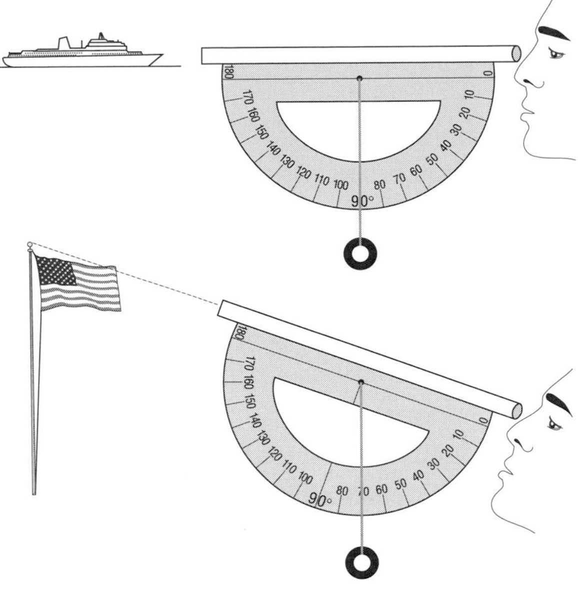

In the illustration above, a simple sextant (as described in the text) is being used to determine the angle of inclination of the top of a flagpole. The student first sights the horizon, a 90° reading on the sextant. Then she sights the top of the flagpole, which gives a 70° reading. To determine the angle of inclination, the student must determine the difference between the sextant reading for the top of the flagpole, 70°, and the reading for the horizon, 90°. Therefore, the angle of inclination of the top of the flagpole from the student's vantagepoint is 20°. The height of the flagpole can be determined once the distance of the student from the flagpole is measured. When observing celestial objects, the apparent angle of elevation above the horizon is found by determining the difference between 90° (the horizon) and the sextant reading when the object is sighted through the straw. For printed clarity, the protractor above contains only one scale, 180°–0°, unlike a real protractor which will also have a scale from 0°–180°. The difference between 90° and the sextant reading will always be the same on either scale.

protractor (the 0°–180° line). When they located an object on the horizon by sighting through the straw, the weighted string hung straight down the 90° line. As they rotated the straw to observe an object directly overhead, the weighted string hung along the 0°-180° line of the protractor. When the students sighted an object in the sky through the straw, the string would hang straight down and hit the protractor at a point that would indicate at what angle the object appeared above the horizon in the sky. For example, an object overhead would be 90° above the horizon. The students also learned to use a compass to measure an object's "azimuth" — that is, its distance along the north/south plane of the horizon, an orientation such as N 30 degrees E. With angular elevation plus azimuth, the students could completely describe an object's location: azimuth told them what direction to look in and angular elevation told they how high above the horizon to look in that direction. Students had practiced using the sextant and compass by determining the angular elevation and azimuth of trees, the school flagpole, telephone poles, tops of buildings, and airplanes in the sky. Group data had been posted on a class data chart in order to identify outliers (data that don't fit), as well as to determine the acceptable range of values (error bars) for measurements. Mr. Gilbert found that such inquiry lessons about the use of tools, coupled with a public sharing and discussion of data, was extremely helpful in getting students to evaluate data and to improve the accuracy of obtaining and reporting it.

Introductory Lesson. Today Mr. Gilbert plans to introduce his students to the study of the phases of the moon. He knows from conducting his own observations that tracking the moon's phases can be challenging because of the possibility of occasional intervening clouds, but he feels that students will be able to learn more deeply from the opportunity to conduct an investigation of this phenomenon firsthand. He has decided to begin this lesson today because the moon is currently two days past new and, for the next two weeks, it will be visible in the afternoon and early evening.

He begins the lesson by asking his students to write down everything they know about the moon, together with the questions that they have about the moon. He then asks them to discuss their lists with a partner, making note of the items that are included on both lists. Following these discussions, Mr. Gilbert asks his students to compile their lists into one class list of what they know about the moon, and another class list of questions they have about the moon. Mr. Gilbert identifies six items on the students' list that he knows are crucial to their understanding of the moon's phases:

Things We Know About the Moon	*Questions We Have About the Moon*
The moon changes shape.	How can the moon be visible during the day?
The moon is smaller than the earth.	Why don't eclipses happen more often?
People have walked on the moon.	What causes the moon's phases?

He asks several students how they know that the three items in the left column are true. Their responses include "Because I saw it on TV," "My mother told me," "I read about it in a book that my aunt gave me," and "my fourth grade teacher showed us a video." As the discussion proceeds, students recognize that these explanations are shallow compared to what they could learn from observing and collecting data over time about the changing shape of the moon.

Carrying Out the Investigation. Mr. Gilbert then invites the students to undertake a five-week-long investigation of the behavior of the moon, which will help them answer most of the questions they generated. They will begin by observing the moon and gathering evidence about its position, shape, and motion. He asks students to divide up the responsibilities for data gathering among members of their four-person groups, suggesting that during the first week they will all observe, and after that each student will be responsible for one week of observations and data gathering. The assignment is to make at least one observation and data entry of the moon each day and complete a chart on which they will record the date, time, and sky conditions; measure the angular elevation of the moon with their sextant and the moon's azimuth with a compass; indicate (if observed at night) the constellation the moon is

closest to; and sketch the moon's appearance.

"But what will we do if it is cloudy?" asks one of the students. They discuss this and agree that they will make note of the weather conditions, predict where the moon would have appeared, and what they think it might have looked like. Mr. Gilbert agrees that, if direct observation fails, they should consult other resources, including the newspaper or the Internet, to verify their predictions and to create the most accurate record possible over the next 35 consecutive days.

The next day Mr. Gilbert takes the class outside to make their first observation of the moon and to ensure that they understand how to keep the daily record, including measuring angular elevation and azimuth. Each day afterwards for the next five weeks each group posts its data on a wall chart similar to the one they are using for individual record keeping. The class works on other areas of the science curriculum as the data-gathering progresses.

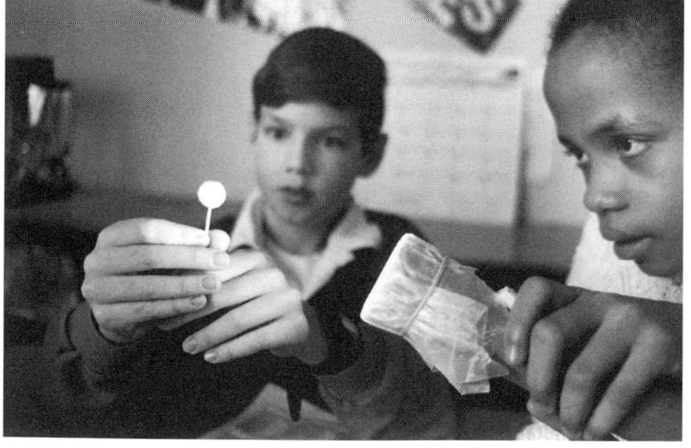

On the last day of the five-week observation period, the class returns to the moon unit, beginning a transition from collecting and analyzing data to developing new concepts about the phases of the moon.

As groups review their observational data on their charts, interesting discussions begin to occur. With some prompting from Mr. Gilbert, students begin talking about models that might account for the data they have collected — an important aspect of doing science. Mr. Gilbert decides to begin with a model that explains the phases of the moon recorded by students. He provides students with a toothpick and a small bead and then invites them to consider this thought experiment: "If you were to put the bead at the end of the toothpick and then hold it up at arm's length between your eye and the moon, how much of the moon's surface do you think the bead would cover?" Mr. Gilbert asks the students to draw their predictions. He then asks them to go outside to test their predictions. As he moves from group to group, he asks the students to perform another observation. "Try holding the toothpick and bead out to the side. Now look at the shape of the moon and then look at the shape of sunlight you see on the bead." They are amazed to discover that the moon's appearance and the bead's appearance are the same. Mr. Gilbert knows that this experience will give students an opportunity to get a sense of what causes the phases of the moon. He also knows that it will help them understand something about the use and limits of models, helping them not only to learn about the moon, but to understand that models are tools that scientists often use to build and test new knowledge.

Constructing a Model. The next day, the end of the observations, Mr. Gilbert asks his students to look closely at their posted charts of the moon's phases over the past five weeks. Mr. Gilbert asks: "What do you think causes this repeated monthly pattern of moon phases?" He asks the students to work in groups of three and after about 10 minutes, two different explanations emerge. Some of the students suggest that the earth's shadow covers different amounts of the moon's surface at different times of the month, resulting in the moon's pattern of phases. Others propose that as the moon moves through its orbit around the earth, we see different amounts of the side of the moon that is lighted by the sun. Next Mr. Gilbert asks the students to form small groups based upon the different explanations. He asks each group to make a labeled drawing that would support its explanation for why the moon changes shape. Mr. Gilbert can tell from the discussion of their drawings that many of the students are not particularly confident about their explanations. For some, different explanations seem to make sense. Before dismissing them, Mr. Gilbert asks the students to think about how they might use models to test the two different explanations.

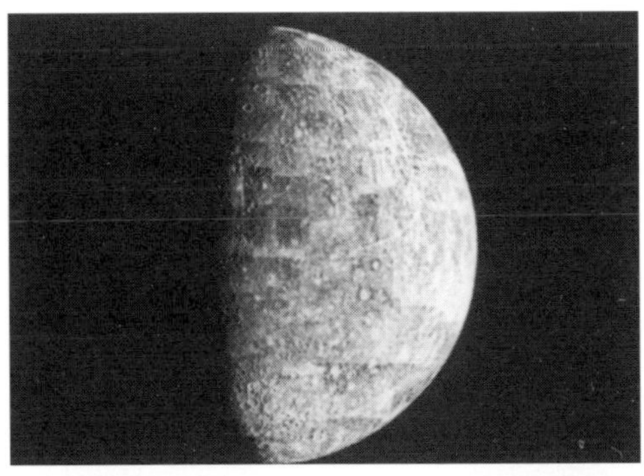

The next day, the students design an investigation to test each explanation. Using globes for the earth, tennis balls for the moon, and the light from an overhead projector for the sun, each group is ready to manipulate the materials in a darkened room to explore relationships between the relative positions and motions of the objects and the resulting pattern of phases. The exploration gives students opportunities to clarify the question about moon phases, determine what would constitute evidence to support each explanation, model each of the alternative explanations, and then determine which explanation for moon phases is supported by the evidence they personally gathered earlier in the unit.

To assess what they already know before beginning the activity, Mr. Gilbert asks the students what they think their drawings should show. The students agree they should show: 1) the position of the earth and moon when looking down at the North Pole, 2) the source and path of sunlight using arrows and, 3) the shadows for the earth/globe and moon/balls. They also agree that the positions of earth and moon shadows are critical. With these consistent conditions in their drawings, it will be easier to compare findings and explanations for moon phases. Mr. Gilbert encourages them to show the moon in many different positions in its orbit around the earth.

Mr. Gilbert circulates among the groups, checking how they are setting up their materials and listening to the students' conversations. He also makes sure to look at their drawings. From time to time he asks questions to probe students' understandings and refocus their thinking about the relationship between evidence and explanation. "What moon shape would you see if the earth, sun, and moon were positioned as you have them now? Where would the moon have to be in your model to result in a quarter moon? Show me where the earth's shadow would be. What evidence do you have that supports your conclusion or causes you to change your mind?" He asks students to show him the direction in which the moon moves around the earth in their model. Then he asks: "How do you know? What evidence led you to this conclusion?" When needed, Mr. Gilbert reminds students to look at the class data table: "A good model will explain the data." Listening to student conversations and coaching with questions allows him to assess student progress in understanding the cause of moon phases. It also allows him to assess how well students are using certain inquiry abilities such as thinking critically and logically about the relationship between the evidence they gathered in earlier lessons and explanations.

Mr. Gilbert begins the next class by asking each group to post their model drawings and then invites the rest of the class to examine the results. Then Mr. Gilbert asks each group to describe their conclusions about the different explanations for moon phases. Their observations and interpretations seem to support the explanation that, as the moon moves in its orbit around the earth, the amount of the lighted side of the moon that can be seen from earth changes.

The students agree that comparing the order of phases in their model to the order of moon phases shown on a calendar helps them assess the apparent relationship between the earth, sun, and moon. Mr. Gilbert asks what evidence seems to be most helpful in testing the different explanations. Some of the groups agree that the position of the earth's shadow during the month is critical evidence. Mr. Gilbert asks them to explain why.

The students explain that the orientation of the earth's shadow brings it in contact with the moon in various ways during the month. One team points out that, during the first quarter phase of the moon, the earth's shadow would have to turn a right corner in order to fall on the moon. "That is not the way that light and shadows work." Based upon such evidence, even the students who proposed the "earth's shadow" model decide to reject it. To check for understanding, Mr. Gilbert asks, "How would the sequence of moon phases be affected if the moon moved around the earth in the opposite direction?" The investigations raise a problem for several groups. Students are confused because, in some of the drawings, it looks like there should be an eclipse of the moon and an eclipse of the sun every month. "Something must be wrong with our model because we know that doesn't happen." "Good observation," remarks Mr. Gilbert "What modifications would you need to make in your models so that the cycle of moon phases does not produce these eclipses every month? What additional information might help you? What reference materials might you use?" The class decides to consult their textbook and references from the media resource center.

As the class discusses their readings, Mr. Gilbert questions them about the plane of the moon's orbit around the earth, compared to the plane of earth's orbit around the sun, and how it changes during the year. The student teams then modify their earth, sun, and moon models and alter their drawings to apply this new information. At this point Mr. Gilbert asks them to step back from their work to reflect on the models of the balls and light source they are using, as they had with the beads on the toothpicks. Again he poses the questions, "What features of the models work well? What features don't?" Students respond that the model does not do a good job at explaining the changes in the height of the moon above the horizon, but it does show how the phases of the moon occur.

After this discussion, Mr. Gilbert notes that, historically, models have played a role in understanding the "heavens." He asks them to recall what they remember about the early historical explanations for the motions of bodies in the night sky. Together, Mr. Gilbert and the students recall that, prior to the time of Copernicus and Galileo, the accepted model of the heavens was that all the planets and stars revolved around the earth, which was located in the center of the universe. They discuss how the predictable patterns of stars moving across the night sky were used as evidence to support this early explanation. "What evidence did Galileo uncover that caused him to question the earth-centered explanation?" Mr. Gilbert asks. The students use this question to focus their reading in their reference materials. During the ensuing discussion, Mr. Gilbert asks the students to compare the evidence-to-explanation thinking they used in their testing of the two different explanations for Moon phases to the scientific work that Galileo conducted – in which he observed the phases of the moons of Jupiter and then constructed an explanation to account for the evidence. For Galileo the explanation required placing the sun and not the earth to be at the center of the heavens. From their investigations, readings, and discussions, the students begin to understand how scientific explanations are formulated and evaluated with evidence, and to understand that the scientific community accepts and uses various explanations until they are displaced by better

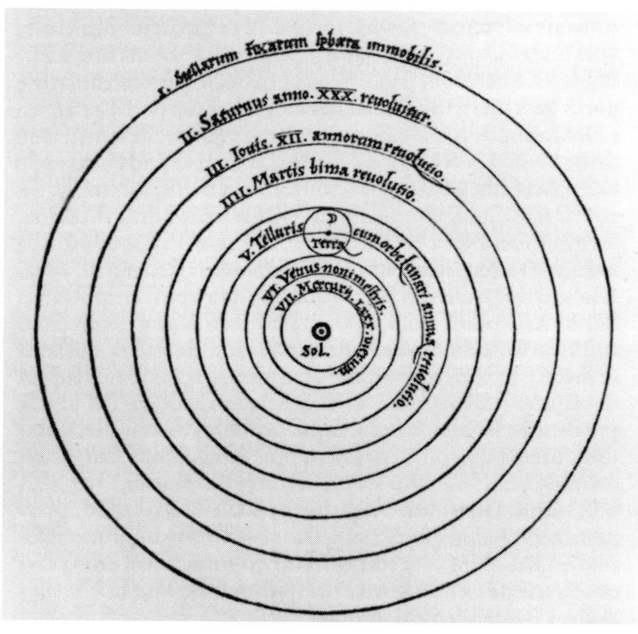

The Copernican Universe
"In the midst of all dwells the sun," said Copernicus. To him, the universe was systematic, mathematical, knowable, and above all, simple. In this diagram from *De revolutionibus* the Earth is number v, "Telluris," counting from the outermost ring of stars. Copernicus was not entirely liberated from Aristotle and Ptolemy, however, for he too believed the orbits to be circular and uniform.
—Bruno, L.C. (1987). *The Tradition of Science.*

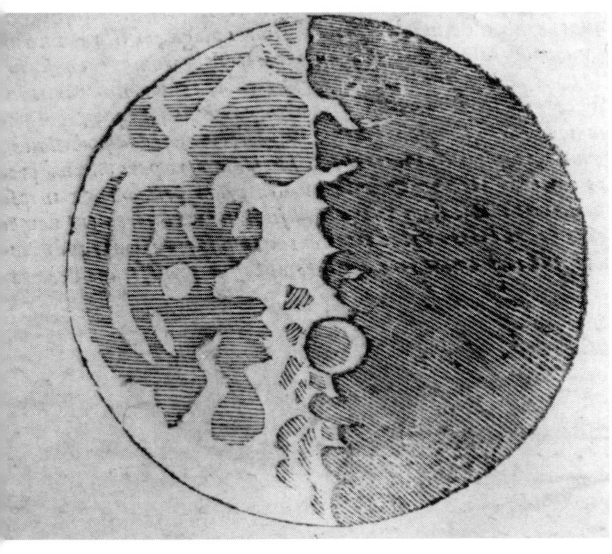

Page from Galileo's "Starry Messenger"
Galileo's "Starry Messenger" contained the first telescopic drawings of the moon to be published. Galileo showed the moon to be a solid body with irregular surface features. This drawing correctly shows mountain tops catching the sunlight and casting shadows, the length of which Galileo used to estimate the mountains' height.
—Bruno, L.C. (1987). *The Tradition of Science.*

ones. The students recognize that each of their explanations may have seemed plausible until all the evidence was brought into play. Moreover, they were not embarrassed to give up an explanation that did not work when the evidence pointed in another direction. When such displacement occurs, scientific understanding advances.

At this point in the unit, Mr. Gilbert finds it very helpful to assign a take-home exam. Each student is asked to look at all the activities the class has completed thus far. The assignment is to select and then record in a summary table all the evidence that supports or refutes the class' model of the phases of the moon. "You should consider each and every activity we have completed. Your job is to construct an argument for either the acceptance or rejection of your model. Pay particular attention to the data we gathered during our observations of the moon. What patterns in the data support or refute your model?"

Mr. Gilbert writes the assignment on the board:

- Part 1: draw and label your model.
- Part 2: list the evidence that supports your model.
- Part 3: list the evidence that refutes your model.
- Part 4: write 1) an explanation using science concepts for the phases of the moon; 2) a list of questions you now have about the motion of the moon.
- Total: no more than 10 pages. It will be a major part of your grade for the unit.

ANALYSIS OF 5-8 IMAGE OF INQUIRY

This vignette illustrates how a wide variety of learning outcomes can result through different kinds of investigations by students. It also shows how a sequence of learning experiences that are carefully crafted by a teacher can build and deepen understanding gradually, through motivating and engaging activities.

Learning Outcomes. Mr. Gilbert used students' study of moon phases to help them learn both science subject matter and inquiry — learning both how to conduct inquiries and what inquiry is. His subject matter outcomes were drawn directly from the earth and space science standards of the *National Science Education Standards*: the regular and predictable motion of objects in the solar system explains such phenomena as the phases of the moon and eclipses. Mr. Gilbert found he could also use the sequence of instructional activities to help students develop many inquiry abilities. They began by collecting data about the moon's phases through direct observation, using some tools to increase the precision of their observations, and supplementing direct observation with data from sources such as newspapers and the Internet. Their inquiry also helped them learn to use models to construct explanations for natural phenomena, to evaluate the models they were using for their benefits and shortcomings, and to gather an array of evidence to analyze alternative explanations and determine which best fits the evidence.

Mr. Gilbert's students also deepened their understanding of scientific inquiry, when they discussed how Galileo's study of moon's phases helped people understand the configuration of different bodies in the universe. This opportunity helped them to understand the role that scientific inquiry has played over the centuries — how scientists think and work to formulate and advance scientific knowledge, as well as how profound new understandings have come from investigations of the natural world.

Essential Features of Classroom Inquiry. The sequence of learning activities just described contained all five essential features of classroom inquiry that were displayed on pages 24-27 of Chapter 2. Some of these features appeared several times throughout the sequence of lessons. Mr. Gilbert engaged the learners in scientifically oriented questions about moon phases. Although Mr. Gilbert proposed some of the questions, the students became mentally engaged and took ownership of the problems they posed. Assisted by Mr. Gilbert's questioning, the students identified two different explanations for what causes moon phases. They produced drawings representing the relative positions and motions of the earth, sun, and moon for each explanation. Mr. Gilbert helped the students to determine what would constitute evidence to support each explanation. The students then manipulated models to explore each explanation, gathering evidence to either support or reject each in turn. They drew liberally on the scientific literature as their understanding and, consequently, their questions, became more complicated. Each student group presented and defended its findings, resulting in a final class consensus about which explanation for moon phases could logically be supported by evidence.

It is reasonable to assume that all of Mr. Gilbert's students did not begin the unit of study with fully developed inquiry abilities. Knowing that the sequence of learning activities to help students understand moon phases would require them to use all of the inquiry abilities to some degree, Mr. Gilbert decided to take this opportunity to help his students reflect specifically on how one constructs and evaluates explanations from evidence. His goal was to help his students improve these abilities, becoming more independent and skilled in their use and application to learn science content. He introduced the important idea that although models can be helpful to both their learning and to the development of scientific knowledge, every model has its limits. Evaluating and communicating the advantages and disadvantages of the specific models they used in their study of moon phases reinforced this need to be always critical of their tools and methods, and to take those into account when reflecting on what they learned and the confidence they have in that learning, much like scientists do. Further, Mr. Gilbert took advantage of the interesting historical context to broaden his students' understanding of scientific inquiry and how scientists have used inquiry to advance our scientific knowledge of nature.

Instructional Sequence. The example just given of Mr. Gilbert and his students illustrates a way of sequencing learning and teaching activities that is consistent with the features of inquiry. The unit evolved from data collection, then using those data for concept development and the evaluation of models and explanations. And when students were asked to deal with eclipse frequency, they applied their knowledge to a new scientific challenge. Early in the sequence Mr. Gilbert helped his students become engaged in thinking about moon phases by probing what they thought they knew about the moon and what they wondered about. Their study proceeded through a long period of observation and data gathering during which they recorded and then explored the patterns they observed in the moon's behavior. Students created their own explanations of the moon's phases and then tested their explanations and those of other students using models that they could manipulate and continue to explore.

Table 3-4. Excerpts from Physical Science Standard, 9-12

As a result of activities in grades 9-12, all students should develop understanding of

Motion and forces

- Objects change their motion only when a net force is applied. Laws of motion are used to calculate precisely the effects of forces on the motion of objects. The magnitude of the change in motion can be calculated using the relationship F=ma, which is independent of the nature of the force. Whenever one object exerts force on another, a force equal in magnitude and opposite in direction is exerted on the first object.
- Gravitation is a universal force that each mass exerts on any other mass. The strength of the gravitational attractive force between two masses is proportional to the masses and inversely proportional to the square of the distance between them (pp. 179-180).

IMAGES OF INQUIRY IN 9-12 CLASSROOMS

The lesson described in the following vignette begins a physics unit on force and motion. According to district curriculum guidelines, by the end of this high school physics unit, students should be able to use Newton's Laws and explain the forces acting on objects in various states of motion. In addition, the state and district learning outcomes include helping students develop abilities to do scientific inquiry and to understand the nature of scientific inquiry. (See Table 3-4.)

Mr. Hull begins most units with one or more short survey questions to get students to think about the kinds of situations, issues, and ideas they will be investigating for the next few days. Today, at the opening of class, he asked his students: "What do you think about when you hear the word *force*?" Among the responses were: "gravity is a force," "pushing, like when I push a car," "a push or a pull on something," and "making somebody do something they don't want to."

While students continued sharing their initial ideas, Mr. Hull wrote the ideas on the board. As he wrote, he organized the ideas into two categories: kinds of forces, and definitions of force (i.e.,"force is…"). Both of these categories would be important in their unit on Explanation of Motion.

Mr. Hull wanted his students to be able to represent their understanding of forces, so he guided them in crafting their representations. He said: "It sounds like several of you are thinking of force as a push or pull. What are some properties of pushes and pulls?" A student noted, "They are in a certain direction and they have a certain size." "So a force is a vector," said another student. Vector representation had been part of an earlier unit on describing motion, and the students recognized a new context in which the idea applies.

Mr. Hull queried, "It sounds like vectors might be useful for representing force? How would you use them to represent forces?" A student responded, "Well, a longer arrow would represent a bigger force, and the direction of the arrow would represent the direction of the force."

Mr. Hull waited while the students talked about this representation for a while. He then placed a book on the demonstration table in the front of the room and asked students to use vector arrows to represent the forces on the book, while it remained at rest on the table. He also asked students to pay attention to both the length and direction aspects of the vector representation and to add a label to each force arrow stating what exerts it. While each student drew and labeled his or her own representation of the situation, Mr. Hull walked around the room observing to get some idea of which students were suggesting what forces.

Although there were several variations in the students' representations, there was one main difference between the representations that he knew would occur. Some students had drawn and labeled an upward force by the table and others had not. From his experience in the workshops run by the local university, he had learned that this difference is evidence that the students have very different conceptions of force. After the students had finished their representations, Mr. Hull drew two books on the front blackboard. On one he drew only a downward arrow. On the other he drew both an upward arrow and a downward arrow. Between the two diagrams he drew a large question mark.

"I noticed one big difference in the diagrams," he said. "About half the class had an upward force by the table and half did not. That suggests a difference in the ways you are conceptualizing force. Since we are just beginning a unit on force, we'd better resolve this difference. So, why do some of you think we need to include an upward force by the table? And, why do others of you think we should not include an upward force by the table?"

Some students shared their ideas, suggesting that if the table did not exert a force on the book, it would fall. Others said there only needed to be a downward force in order to hold the book to the table. Still others argued that the table could not push or pull anything because it was not alive; it did not have any energy. Mr. Hull recognized that many of the students were thinking that force can be exerted only by active agents, so that passive agents, like tables, cannot exert force.

Mr. Hull asked the students to each pick up a book and hold it in an outstretched hand. He then asked the class to add a second diagram on their paper, a diagram of the forces acting on the book while the book is at rest on the hand.

In this case, most of the students who did not show an upward force in the first diagram now showed an upward force. A few students still did not show an upward force. When asked why they had not shown such a force, most said that since they had not put in an upward force when the book was on the table, they did not feel they needed to do so here. Mr. Hull pointed out that their attempt to have consistent reasoning across situations was commendable and important in science and in other subjects.

"Is there an upward force on the book?" he asked. Then, to increase the salience of the experience, he asked students to add additional books to their outstretched hands. Nearly all were willing to say there was an upward force by the hand. Still some students were concerned about the need to be consistent across situations, which Mr. Hull acknowledged by noting on the board the "need to have the same explanation across 'at rest' situations, if possible." Consistency in explanations is an important aspect of science that Mr. Hull wanted his students to incorporate into their thinking.

Next, Mr. Hull hung a book from a spring and asked students to draw a third diagram of the book on the spring and the forces that kept the

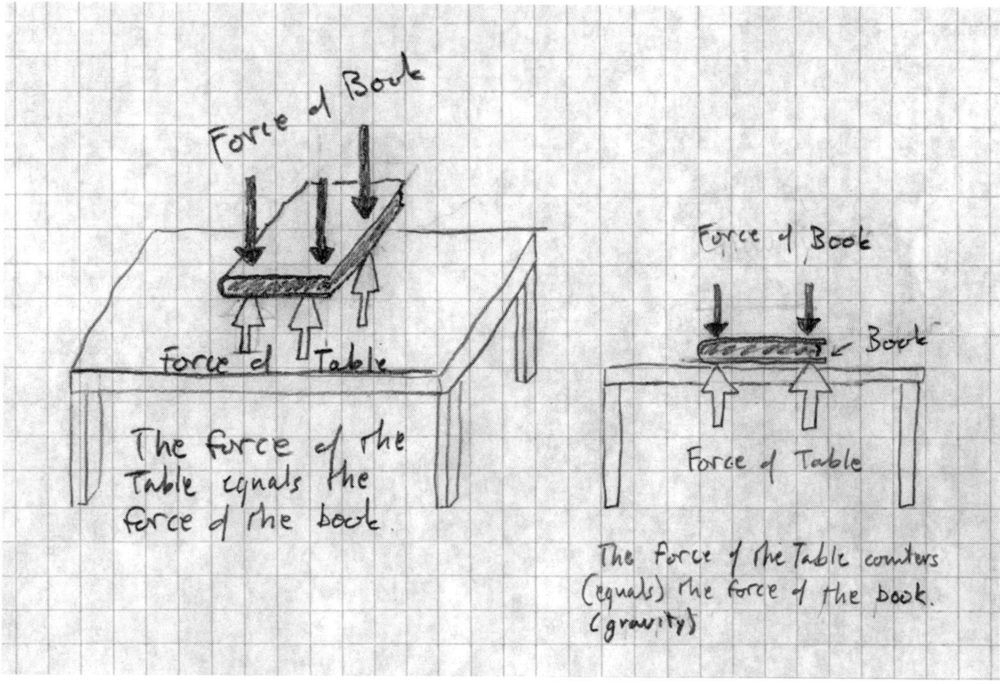

book at rest. Most of the class included an upward force by the spring in their diagrams. A few others argued that because the spring was not alive, it could not "exert" a force.

Mr. Hull asked, "So, how come many of you who said the table does not exert a force are now saying that the spring does exert an upward force? The spring isn't alive." The students responded, "The spring moves." "The spring compresses or extends."

The teacher asked the students to think about what was similar about the situations in which they were willing to say there was an upward force. They suggested that when the book was on the hand, one could see or feel the muscular activity in order to support the book, and when the book was on the spring one could see the change in the length of the spring. Mr. Hull pointed out that they were responding to evidence for a force by looking at some change in the "thing" that is doing the supporting. He wanted his students to be seeking observational evidence in support of their ideas and inferences.

Mr. Hull: "How about those of you who suggest the table does exert an upward force. In what way does that make sense to you?" While gesturing sideways, one student said, "Whenever anything stays still, if there is a force on one side, there has to be a force on the other side to keep it stopped." Mr. Hull: " I see you are talking about horizontal forces, does that also work with vertical forces?" Again, he guided his students to see the consistency across contexts, in this case, explanations of the at-rest condition should be the same whether considering horizontal forces or vertical forces. This gave some rational argument for an upward force.

Mr. Hull asked his students to think about evidence. "What observable evidence do you have that the table exerts an upward force?" A few students suggested the table bent like the spring. Others countered, arguing that the table was a heavy, solid demonstration table, that it was rigid and therefore could not bend. The students suggested the need for a critical experiment. "How could we see whether the table bends at all?" asked the teacher. Not hearing any suggestions, Mr. Hull proposed that they use a "light lever." Bringing out a light source (in this case a laser pointer), he placed it so that the light hit the shiny table top at a low glancing angle. With the room lights off, one could see where the reflected light hit the far wall. The teacher checked to be sure that the students knew that if the table bends, the light on the wall should move. Although the movement was not readily noticeable with one book placed on the table, as the stack got larger and was taken off and back on, the light could be seen to move.

After exploring ideas about force

through questions, discussion, and observations for much of the class period, the students were ready to summarize their class experience and its implications for the meaning of force. One said: "Since the table bent, like a stiff spring, all things had to deform some to support the book. Deformation was one sort of evidence we could look for when we considered forces." Another added, "That meant we could give the same explanation [involving an upward force] across several different 'at rest' systems." Another said: "That also meant we didn't need to worry about whether the supporting object was alive, awake, active, or passive. We could just focus on the observable evidence of deformation, although sometimes we might need more sensitive instruments [like a light lever] to detect the deformation." Mr. Hull pointed out that that was one of the "rules" of science: "If a simple, consistent explanation would work across several situations, then use the simpler explanation rather than needing to rely on use of different explanations depending on some non-observable characteristic like whether the object was actively or passively supporting the book." Mr. Hull further validated the work of the students, suggesting "that force could have been defined by incorporating the active/passive distinction, but for reasons like consistency and tying our ideas to observable evidence, the scientists' conception of force is more like the one our class has derived. Also, we now know that this conception has worked well for scientists for a long time. Like scientists, we will take our present idea of force as tentative and use it until new evidence suggests we might need to revise it."

The inquiry does not end here. In subsequent lessons focusing on forces on moving objects, students further develop their understanding of force and of the nature and processes of science. The preceding lesson is but one short inquiry allowing students to begin to understand the complex ideas that science has developed related to force and motion.

ANALYSIS OF 9-12 IMAGE OF INQUIRY

This example represents one lesson conducted in a single class period. Nevertheless, it demonstrates how a teacher can seamlessly interweave science subject matter, inquiry abilities, and understandings of scientific inquiry.

Learning Outcomes. Mr. Hull used three learning outcomes from his local school district curriculum and state standards to help him plan what and how to teach. Each of these three outcomes is also found in the *National Science Education Standards.* First, his lesson provided opportunities for his students to understand and apply the concept from physics of forces acting on objects in various states of motion. The students' prior understandings were challenged by questions about objects and forces in different contexts; this caused them to look for evidence to build improved explanations. Second, he helped his students develop abilities to do scientific inquiry, attending, in particular, to determining what constituted evidence of forces acting on objects in various conditions, and building evidence-based explanations that would apply across different contexts. Finally, Mr. Hull shared aspects of the nature of scientific inquiry with the students and drew on their ideas to show how scientists think and work.

Essential Features of Classroom Inquiry. This lesson includes a number of the essential features of classroom inquiry described in Chapter 2. Scientific questions focused students' thinking about the forces acting on objects in various states of motion. The students gathered observable evidence to develop explanations and gain a deeper understanding of the concept of force. They also questioned proposed explanations, focusing on the search for observable evidence. Mr. Hull guided the building of explanations from the evidence gathered. At the conclusion of the lesson, he helped the students make connections from their experiences to current scientific thinking about forces and motion.

Instructional Model. The example of Mr. Hull and his students illustrates one way of organizing and sequencing learning and teaching activities consistent with inquiry. Through questioning, Mr. Hull actively engaged his students in thinking about the existence of an upward force on an object at rest on a table. He used student-generated drawings to find out more about their current understanding of whether objects, such as a table or hand, can exert an upward force on an object at rest. Mr. Hull drew on the prior knowledge of the students to pose questions that motivated them to explore whether other types of objects, such as springs, can exert an upward force. The students developed explanations about how a stationary object could exert an upward force. Mr. Hull explained how scientists think about forces and helped the students elaborate their explanations across different contexts. The students critiqued their ideas on the basis of evidence. Through class discussion, Mr. Hull was able to evaluate student thinking and use this information to help structure the flow of the lesson.

In this vignette the teacher clearly guided the inquiry. Yet, stimulated by an initial question from the teacher, students asked their own questions, voiced their concerns, and shared their ideas. They also critiqued ideas focusing on the search for evidence.

ANOTHER IMAGE OF INQUIRY IN GRADES 9-12

Every year in the spring, Ms. Idoni's biology class conducts a full and open inquiry. The inquiry takes several weeks of class during the semester, so students have ample time to conduct their investigation. Ms. Idoni begins the inquiry by taking the students on a field trip to an environment where she is relatively certain their interest will be engaged. All year, students look forward to this experience. It is a tradition with Ms. Idoni and the students have heard that it is hard work, but something they will really find interesting.

Earlier in the school year the students have had many opportunities to learn and practice the inquiry skills they will need to conduct a full inquiry. Ms. Idoni has used a series of "invitations to inquiry" (Mayer, 1978), which are short teaching units designed to give students small samples of the process of inquiry. Each sample has a blank the students are invited to fill, for example, the plan of an investigation, a way to control one factor in an experiment, or the conclusion to be drawn from a set of data. Each "invitation" focuses student learning on one or two abilities of inquiry. Participating in the series of invitations over the year has equipped Ms. Idoni's students to identify questions that can be investigated, design appropriate investigations, gather data, interpret data, consult sources such as the Web for additional information, and draw definable conclusions — all of which will be called on in the full inquiry they are now beginning.

Before starting inquiry, Ms. Idoni makes plans for how to assess students' learning on an ongoing basis. She will ask each student to keep a journal through the inquiry. Because she is most interested in emphasizing the development of inquiry abilities, Ms. Idoni will have the students organize their journals according to a slightly modified form of the fundamental abilities as described in the *Standards*. The categories Ms. Idoni will use are:

- Questions and scientific ideas that guide the investigation
- Design of the investigation
- Technology and mathematics for the investigation
- Use of evidence to present explanations
- Alternative explanations
- Conclusions and defense of explanations

As students record their observations, Ms. Idoni will review their journals and ask more specific questions about scientific concepts that underlie their explanations, how technology helps them, what evidence they are collecting, if they have the best evidence and explanation, what other ideas they have heard, and if they have the strongest conclusions.

Ms. Idoni sets the stage for the field trip by explaining to the students that for most of the year their biology class has studied ideas and conducted laboratories that scientists and educators think that all students should know and experience. Although these experiences provide a foundation, now the approach will be different. They will have the opportunity to study something about the environment that they find interesting. "The field trip will help you decide what question you want to pursue." This year, Ms. Idoni has decided to take the students to a lake in the city park. When they arrive at the lake, Ms. Idoni asks the students to simply walk around the lake, to observe the lake, and to think about questions that they may be interested in answering. She asks them to record the observations and questions in their journal.

The next day's activity centers on the students' observations and questions. Ms. Idoni approaches these discussions with caution. She is sensitive to the balance between sustaining the students' interest and enthusiasm and the critical elements of a successful scientific inquiry for 10th graders. A critical aspect of successful inquiry is having students reflect on the ideas and scientific concepts that guide the inquiry. Also important is a knowledge base to support the investigation and help students to formulate an appropriate scientific explanation. Students'

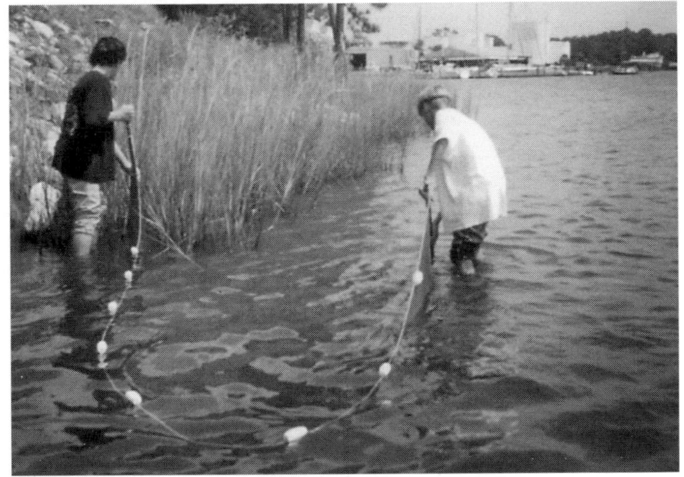

current concepts of the aquatic environment will shape, and may limit, their questions and ultimately their inquiry. So, after an initial class discussion, Ms. Idoni knows she will rely on small groups, brief reports on progress, and cooperative learning for the investigations.

Student questions begin with issues such as: Is the lake water safe to drink? Can people swim in the lake? What kinds of plants and animals live in the lake? How have humans changed the lake? As the discussion continues, it becomes clear to Ms. Idoni that the students are most interested in change and stability in the lake and, in particular, the influence humans have had on this environment. It also is clear that students have ideas about how the lake changes: the temperature changes daily and with seasons; there was more dirt since a recent rain; some small organisms could be seen; and, in some places, there were different

smells associated with the water. Ms. Idoni probes the students about their observations and reminds them to make entries in their journals. What important aspect of the lake do they want to investigate? What kinds of human influences are of most interest? "Pollution" is the term Ms. Idoni hears first and most consistently. She thinks it is essential to clarify the students' understanding of pollution and in particular the possible sources of human pollution in the city lake. She asks the students to discuss in small groups what they mean by pollution for the city lake.

Over several class periods, they struggle with the issue of normal change, what counts as pollution, and possible human influences. Ms. Idoni lets the students grapple with these issues, which seem to center on one major idea: as living and non-living elements of an ecosystem interact, they change. Any study of changes in an environment, such as the city lake, must begin with an analysis of the patterns of change under normal circumstances. Students realize they have to understand the natural functions of the interactive system before tackling the more complex question of the impact of human actions, in particular, their notion of pollution. At this point Ms. Idoni realizes she already has her final assessment: she will suggest that something has polluted the lake and the students will have to apply what they have learned to this new problem. But, for the time being, she must wait and let the students pursue their questions and investigations.

After hearing the results of small group discussions, Ms. Idoni facilitates a large group review of ideas and helps students identify an overarching question for the class to pursue in the investigation. The class decides on a general question: *Is city park lake polluted? If so, how have humans influenced the pollution?* The class decides to approach the inquiry by first establishing a baseline of data about city lake and then determine if the lake is polluted. Students realize that many factors affect water quality. With help from Ms. Idoni, they decide to organize their work, and so themselves, to focus on three kinds of factors: physical, chemical, and biological. The group investigating physical factors is interested in temperature, color, limits of light penetration, and amounts and types of suspended particles. The chemical factors group wants to learn about pH (which they have measured in various classes in past years and suspect might have something to do with a lake's "condition"), and amounts of oxygen, carbon dioxide, phosphates, and nitrates. The biological group wants to investigate the numbers and kinds of organisms.

Students decide to design the inquiry as follows. Each group will gather data for a period of two months, reporting all results to the other groups on a regular basis. Each group also will report about their ideas and what their library and computer searches suggest about the potential influence of the factors they are studying on the quality of city lake.

Ms. Idoni is very pleased with the way the class investigation is taking shape. Although she knows the students will still struggle with the question of how to determine what counts as pollution, and especially the human influence, she lets this issue remain unresolved. In fact, knowing it will emerge on its own, she doesn't bring it up.

Ms. Idoni is especially aware of three things. First, she keeps a mental list of the inquiry abilities for grades 9-12 and notes which abilities the students are engaged in as the inquiry progresses. Second, she recognizes that students are using what they have learned of physical and life sciences earlier in the year, especially the fundamental understandings associated with the life science standard on the interdependence of organisms (see Table 3-5). Finally, Ms. Idoni sees that this entire inquiry is providing ample opportunities for all students to understand several parts of the standard on science in personal and social perspectives, especially those associated with natural resources and environmental quality (see Table 3-6).

As the students begin organizing their group investigations, they easily and quickly recognize that the use of various technologies will improve data gathering and mathematics will improve the summary and presentation of data. For example, they decide to set up temperature probes and record data directly into computers, and to use Hach oxygen test kits, a pH meter, a Millipore environmental microbiology kit, and common items that help them gather samples for examination in the science classroom.

Ms. Idoni schedules periodic meetings in which the students share data they have collected and present what they understand about the influence of various factors. With time, students begin to realize that the

Table 3-5. Excerpt from Life Science Standard, 9-12

As a result of activities in grades 9-12, all students should develop understanding of:

Interdependence of organisms

- Energy flows through ecosystems in one direction, from photosynthetic organisms to herbivores to carnivores and decomposers.
- Organisms both cooperate and compete in ecosystems.
- Living organisms have the capacity to produce populations of infinite size, but environments and resources are finite. This fundamental tension has profound effects on the interactions between organisms.
- Human beings live within the world's ecosystems. Increasingly, humans modify ecosystems as a result of population growth, technology, and consumption. Human destruction of habitats through direct harvesting, pollution, atmospheric changes, and other factors is threatening current global stability, and if not addressed, ecosystems will be irreversibly affected.

Matter, energy, and organization in living systems

- The distribution and abundance of organisms and populations in ecosystems are limited by the availability of matter and energy and the ability of the ecosystem to recycle materials (p. 186).

Table 3-6. Excerpt from Science in Personal and Social Perspectives Standard, 9-12

As a result of activities in grades 9-12, all students should develop understanding of

Environmental quality

- Natural ecosystems provide an array of basic processes that affect humans. Those processes include maintenance of the quality of the atmosphere, generation of soils, control of the hydrologic cycle, disposal of wastes, and recycling of nutrients. Humans are changing many of these basic processes, and the changes may be detrimental to humans.
- Materials from human societies affect both physical and chemical cycles of the earth.
- Many factors influence environmental quality, including population growth, resource use, population distribution, overconsumption, the capacity of technology to solve problems, poverty, the roles of economic, political, and religious views, and different ways humans view the earth (p. 198).

factors interact. In one discussion, for example, the physical factors team suggests that temperature determines the number and kinds of organisms. The chemical factors team reports that the numbers and kinds of organisms influence how much oxygen and carbon dioxide are present. In one highly energized session, the students realize that an investigation of water quality is a search for relationships among physical, chemical, and biological factors.

In the process of data analysis, student teams review their findings, look at ranges of data and trends over the period of study (it is spring), and determine what is appropriate to consider and how to deal with anomalous data. During their group work, Ms. Idoni moves from group to group and asks questions, such as "What explanation did you expect to develop from the data?" "Where there any surprises in the data?" "How confident do you feel about the accuracy of the data?"

After two months, the groups present their data and their explanation of the specific effect the factors they studied have on the lake and if the effect would count as pollution. As students listen to the different groups, they recognize and analyze alternative explanations and models for understanding stability, change, and the potential of pollution in the city lake. They review what they know, weigh the evidence for different explanations, and examine the logic of the different group presentations. They challenge each others' findings, elaborating on their own knowledge as they help each other learn more about their particular factors. Slowly, they form the view that all factors have to be considered in any explanation for pollution of the lake.

To Ms. Idoni's surprise and pleasure, the students decide that they want to synthesize the data and formulate an answer to their guiding question. Their observations and explanations continually expand; they find they have to consider factors they did not originally think were important, such as season, rainfall, and the activities of domestic animals.

As they compile all of the evidence and begin the difficult task of answering their question, they realize they must first address the question: "What counts as pollution?" The students decide that they will use coliform bacteria because of what they learn in their reading. The literature points out that water can look, taste, and smell perfectly clean and yet be unsafe to drink because it contains bacteria. This eventually becomes the students' operational definition of pollution. They learn that coliform bacteria live longer and are easier to detect in water than bacteria that cause disease. Their presence is considered a real warning signal of sewage pollution. If coliform bacteria are *not* present in city lake, then, the students reason, the answer to their question is that the lake is free of pollution — at least by their operational definition of human pollution.

Working across groups, the class compiles their respective reports and prepares one major summary of their inquiry. They also include summaries of their respective results. The reports are excellent. Students capably describe procedures, express scientific concepts, review information, summarize data, develop charts and data, explain statistical procedures they used, and construct a reasonable and logical argument for their answer to the question, "Is city park lake polluted?" "And, if so, what is the human influence on the pollution?" The class concludes that, even though city park lake experiences variations and changes in many factors, it is not polluted.

For the final assessment, Ms. Idoni presents a new problem and asks each student to prepare a report describing how he or she would investigate the problem. Here is the problem: over several weeks there is a massive fish kill in the lake. Everyone suspects pollution — of some sort. But, no one knows exactly how to investigate the problem. The one thing they have discovered is that coliform bacteria have *not* been found in the lake. Students are to propose an inquiry that might be used by the City Council to address this problem.

ANALYSIS OF ANOTHER 9-12 IMAGE OF INQUIRY

Ms. Idoni is pleased with the student work and certain that it demonstrates significant learning. Their work has provided opportunities for all students to develop the abilities of scientific inquiry described in the *National Science Education Standards* — her primary learning goal for the full inquiry. She also realizes that the experiences provided students with the background they need to develop deeper understanding of many science concepts and the connections between science and personal and social issues. Finally, Ms. Idoni uses the experience of doing a full inquiry to review and strengthen students' understandings about scientific inquiry.

Ms. Idoni thinks the experience is important because it provides students with an understanding of the ways that scientists pursue questions that they identify as important. It also gives students one opportunity to use all of the abilities described for the Science as Inquiry standard in the *National Science Education Standards.* She knows that for students to develop these abilities, they must actively participate in scientific investigations and use the cognitive and manipulative skills associated with the formulation of scientific explanations.

As she initiates the activity, Ms. Idoni knows that some students will have trouble with variables and controls in experiments. Further, students often have trouble with data that seem anomalous and in proposing explanations based on evidence and logic rather than on their beliefs about the natural world.

Ms. Idoni uses the initial field experience as a way to make the investigation meaningful to students. She understands there are several

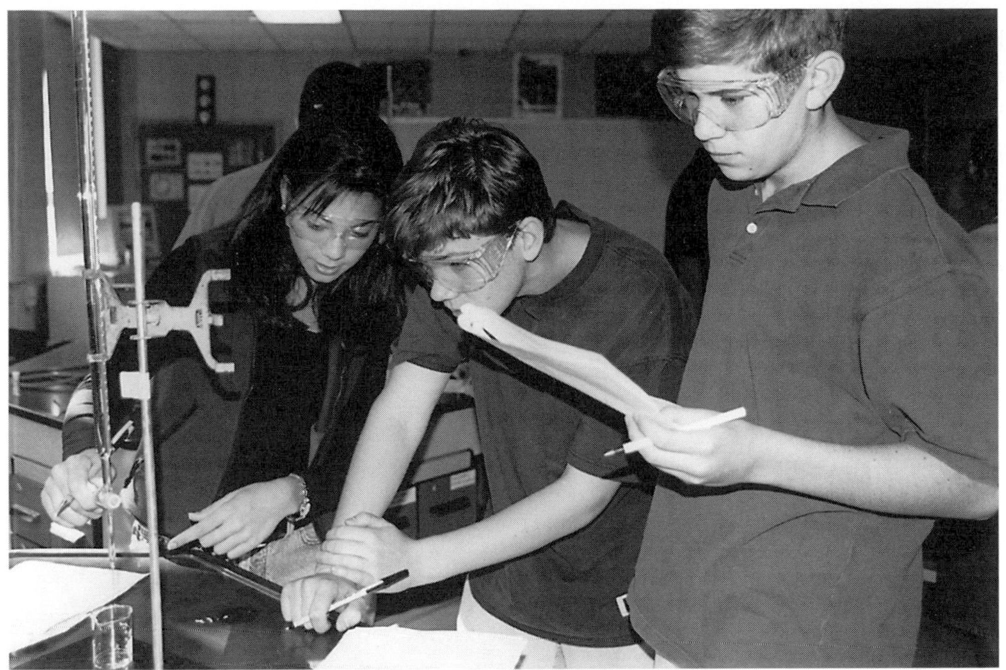

ways that students may find meaningful topics to pursue, for example, current topics in the media, local problems, and personal experiences. She also knows that initially some experiences may not be highly engaging, but active involvement by its very nature has some meaning. Over several years of teaching experience, Ms. Idoni has decided that for a majority of students an initial field trip provides the most meaningful context for beginning the inquiry.

CONCLUSION

Inquiry-based teaching requires careful attention to creating learning environments and experiences where students can confront new ideas, deepen their understandings, and learn to think logically and critically about the world around them. This chapter has suggested some ways to "see" inquiry in classrooms. The next chapter turns to how teachers learn to achieve and assess the wide range of outcomes they strive for in their use of inquiry.

FRESH BONES

Team Hanna
Vanessa

PART A: FRESH BONE SECTIONS

What bone do you think they sliced to make this section?
A femur

Why do you think so? We at least know it is a long bone because it has marrow. We think it is a femur because it is very large.

Sketch the cut end of the bone. Use labels.

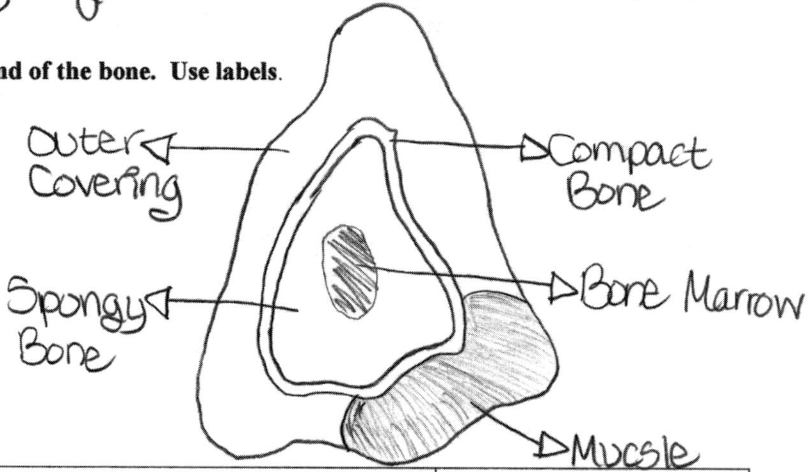

Outer Covering
Compact Bone
Spongy Bone
Bone Marrow
Mucsle

Describe the bone (feel, color, smell, texture, and so on)		Do you think there is a blood supply? Why?
Compact bone	hard, smooth but a little rough, offwhite or tan, smells like blood.	No, Because it is hard.
Spongy bone	Bloody, rough, reddish brown, lots of pores, smells like blood.	Yes, because it needs blood to carry away red blood cells that it makes, and it's bloody.
Marrow	Pink, soft, graing, does not smell.	Yes, It needs blood to carry away red blood cells, has blood vessels in it.
Outer covering	fatty, elastic, wet, has stringy webs in it.	It's a connective tissue so it needs a blood supply.

4
Classroom Assessment and Inquiry

The *National Science Education Standards* point out that "assessments provide an operational definition of standards, in that they define in measurable terms what teachers should teach and students should learn" (NRC, 1996, pp. 5-6). In the context of inquiry, assessments therefore need to gauge the progress of students in achieving the three major learning outcomes of inquiry-based science teaching: conceptual understandings in science, abilities to perform scientific inquiry, and understandings about inquiry.

Just as these objectives differ from those of other approaches to science education, so assessments of inquiry-based science education differ from more traditional assessments. Conventional multiple-choice or short-answer questions typically ask students to identify facts, concepts, or vocabulary. Such tests have proven too broad in their coverage, too shallow in the depth of reasoning required, and too narrow when it comes to measuring outcomes like "understanding the nature of science and the work of scientists." These tests are more likely to require recognition and recall rather than in-depth reasoning and application of underlying concepts. As such, they can pose a serious obstacle to inquiry-based science teaching. Teachers are less likely to focus on the goals of inquiry if their students' performance is evaluated on district or state-wide tests that assess isolated facts (Neill and Medina, 1989). Furthermore, when large-scale external examinations take these forms, teachers tend to create similar assessments for their classes (Raizen and Kaser, 1989; Baron, 1990).

Assessment in inquiry-based classrooms takes a broader perspective on the rich learning called for by the *Standards*. It asks what each student knows and understands, what is fuzzy or missing, and what students can do with what they know. Assessment determines whether students can generate or clarify questions, develop possible explanations, design and conduct investigations, and use data as evidence to support or reject their own explanations. At the broadest level, it measures the capacity of students to evaluate the kinds of questions that scientists investigate, understand the purposes of investigations, and assess the qualities of data, explanations, and arguments.

Assessment can take many forms in inquiry-based classrooms, and it serves many purposes. Assessments can range from the questions teachers ask during a lesson to end-of-unit tests and statewide and national examinations. Assessment data can be used to plan a lesson, guide a student's learning, calculate grades, determine access to special programs, inform policy, allocate resources, or evaluate the quality of a curriculum or instruction. In the breadth of its application, assessment merges seamlessly into considerations of the curriculum and teaching.

An important distinction needs to be made between formative assessment and summative assessment. Formative assessments can occur at any time and are used to influence a teacher's plans to meet specific student learning experiences and needs. Summative assessments typically occur at the end of a learning activity to determine its impact on student learning.

The vignettes in the previous chapter included many examples of formative assessments. For example, Ms. Flores asked her students where they might find worms and how they could build homes for their worms. Mr. Gilbert listened as his students constructed their models of the earth-moon-sun system and asked questions to assess and further their understanding. Similarly, Mr. Hull observed his students' drawings of forces to gauge their understanding. In general, teachers in inquiry-based classrooms are continually assessing to know what to do next, what abilities are developing, which are still underdeveloped, and whether the objectives of a particular lesson or unit are being achieved.

Formative assessments are important for general planning and guidance, but they generally are too informal and insufficiently documented to answer many of the hard questions posed by parents, principals, and teachers: What have students actually learned? What evidence demonstrates that they are learning? How well are they learning it, and at what level of competence?

Formative assessments also are not sufficient to support high-stakes decisions about an individual or changes in policy or professional development designs. Such decisions require summative assessments that provide evidence to parents, teachers, and policy-makers that a student or class is progressing toward meeting the standards for inquiry or falling behind. Such assessments require more standardized instruments and a way of recording student responses, whether a test, interview protocol, or observation guide for a performance assessment. Stable, quantifiable ways of converting student responses to numbers and averages can better support accountability decisions.

The results of summative assessments of student learning can take many forms, from descriptions of individual achievement to formal comparisons across time or with other students. For example, Mr. Gilbert assigned a take-home exam at the end of his session on phases of the moon in which he asked students to summarize all of their evidence that supported or refuted their understanding of the phases of the moon. Ms. Idoni assigned as a final assessment a report describing how each student would investigate an unexpected phenomenon in the lake they had studied. In general, the results of such assessments need to be presented in such a way that they can be summarized and compared with other evidence so that judgments can be made.

This chapter describes features of classroom assessments that support inquiry and the *National Science Education Standards*. It first discusses the "what" — what are students supposed to know, understand, and be able to do as a result of their education in science. It then discusses "who" should be responsible for various aspects of assessment activities, with a particular focus on students. Finally, it looks at "how"— the formats and procedures of assessment.

WHAT SHOULD BE ASSESSED?

The three learning outcomes of inquiry-based education involve both knowledge and understanding. The *Standards* define these two terms as follows:

> Scientific knowledge refers to facts, concepts, principles, laws, theories, and models. . . . Understanding science requires that an individual integrate a complex structure of many types of knowledge, including the ideas of science, relationships between ideas, reasons for these relationships, ways to use the ideas to explain and predict other natural phenomena, and ways to apply them to many events. Understanding encompasses the ability to use knowledge, and it entails the ability to distinguish between what is and what is not a scientific idea (NRC, 1996, p. 23).

Although understanding has a higher status in science education than knowledge, it is a mistake to think that all instruction or assessments should aim for the higher level of outcome. Indeed, when students fail at complex tasks, one never knows whether they are lacking specific skills or the knowledge needed for success unless one also has examined these requisites. For example, at the beginning of their units on the phases of the moon and static forces, Mr. Gilbert and Mr. Hull probed their students' knowledge of the phenomena being investigated to establish a foundation on which to build more complex ideas.

Some of the abilities of inquiry can be assessed in a relatively straightforward way. For example, teachers can observe and listen to students to determine whether they can "use data to construct a reasonable explanation" (as specified in the K-4 standard), "develop descriptions, explanations, and models using evidence" (5-8), and "formulate and revise scientific explanations and models using logic and evidence" (9-12).

Other inquiry abilities, such as designing and conducting a scientific investigation, are more complex assessment challenges. Champagne, Kouba, and Hurley (in press) have proposed that teachers assess student inquiry by examining four phases of student investigations: precursor, planning, implementation, and closure/extension. For each phase, the teacher should delineate the expected products, abilities, and information. For example, in the planning phase the products include the plan, its rationale, and critiques of peers' plans; abilities include developing a plan, explaining it, and revising it; and the information includes descriptions of characteristics of investigations whose methods are well matched to the question under investigation.

DeJong and Van Joolingen (1998) have summarized a parallel body of research done on inquiry abilities and understandings. Students often are unfamiliar with what a hypothesis should look like (i.e., variables and the relationships between them), are not able to state or adapt hypotheses on the basis of data gathered, and avoid hypotheses that have a high chance of being rejected. In designing experiments, they tend to seek information that confirms a hypothesis, change too many variables at one time, or manipulate variables irrelevant to the hypothesis. Frequent problems in the interpretation of data include confirming the hypothesis regardless of what the data indicate and difficulty in interpreting graphs (Roberts et al., 1997). Teachers benefit from assessing their students' initial ideas about what it means to conduct an investigation and think scientifically and how these ideas and their skills change over time.

It is easy to say that students should not simply learn isolated facts or definitions without understanding. It is harder to say what the understanding of a concept looks like or how students should produce evidence of their understanding. In the New Standards Project, in which several states and urban districts are working together to develop an assessment system based on the *Standards*, conceptual understanding is described as follows:

> The student demonstrates conceptual understanding by using a concept accurately to explain observations and make predictions and by representing a concept in multiple ways (through words, diagrams, graphs, or charts, as appropriate). Both aspects of understanding — explaining and representing — are required to meet this standard (New Standards, 1997, p. 133).

Similarly, the AAAS Assessment Blueprint (AAAS, 1998) suggests posing questions that stress reflective thinking, requiring the integration of information, rather than reflexive thinking, where a memorized response is called for. As the Blueprint puts it, "Students should be asked to address questions such as, 'How do we know this?' and 'What difference does it make?' rather than being asked to reproduce memorized vocabulary items or the like."

Again, many of these strategies were apparent in the vignettes in Chapter 3. For example, when Mrs. Flores wanted to assess her students' understanding of the idea of a fair test, she had them evaluate whether a design they had not previously encountered was fair. Ms. Flores also gave her students rich and open tasks such as designing soda bottle homes for their worms based on their observations of the places where they found worms naturally.

However, many of the assessments in Chapter 3 guided the actual day-to-day evolution of lessons, making those assessments susceptible to general judgments and off-the-top evaluations of competence. For assessments that carry stakes, whether of passing courses or assigning grades, "standardized" ways of evaluating knowledge and abilities are needed, preferably ways that can be systematically and reliably reduced to quantitative form. Knowledge and understanding also need to be probed in multiple ways, thus ensuring that a memorized definition does not mask misinformation or misunderstanding.

WHO SHOULD DO THE ASSESSING?

Assessments originate from different parts of the educational system, including administrators and teachers. But a particularly important form of assessment is students' self-assessment. Engaging students in assessment of their own thinking and performance allows them to be more self-directive in planning, pursuing, monitoring, and correcting the course of their own learning. Self-assessment nurtures discovery, teamwork, communication, and conceptual connections.

In a review of more than 580 articles on formative assessment, Black and Wiliam (1998a) point out that "students should be trained in self-assessment, so that they can understand the main purposes of their learning and thus what they need to achieve." Black and Wiliam also found that improved formative assessment — including self-assessment — was most effective in raising the performance of students at the low end of the performance scale, although students who perform well also benefit from better formative assessment. This approach to assessment therefore narrows the gap in performance between the highest and lowest achievers.

Involving students in assessment both reduces the burden on teachers and lets students know what's expected of them. Unless students can see the criteria by which they will be judged and examples of successful performance, assessment becomes a game of guessing what's in the teacher's head. Students frequently fail to make explicit the connection between what they have just done and the question or problem posed. In this respect, it is not surprising that lower-achieving students benefit the most from learning the criteria for success and being shown examples of how to achieve these criteria.

One way of involving students in assessment is to engage them in devising the scoring guide for a task or project. Their first person statements, "I explain my ideas clearly and in detail," and "I used words, numbers, drawings, tables, diagrams, or graphs to show my ideas," are the students' translations of the performance standards for inquiry abilities. Giving students the rubric before they start does not mean giving them the "correct answer" to their investigation. Rather, it is giving them the criteria by which the quality of their conclusions will be judged.

An example of such criteria can be

seen in the Chapter 3 vignettes in the journals Ms. Idoni has her students keep as they conduct their field work. By having her students organize their journals according to the inquiry abilities described in the *Standards*, Ms. Idoni provides them with a way of monitoring their own progress in achieving the standards. The conceptual organization of the journals also provides a framework that students can use in their final project at the end of the course.

HOW SHOULD STUDENT LEARNING BE ASSESSED?

Educators long have known that an effective teacher learns a great deal about what students know and do not know, and how they think about scientific ideas, simply by listening to them. A number of years ago, Rowe (1974) identified the very effective instructional strategy of "wait time," where teachers' silence allows students to pose and answer more thoughtful questions than they do when teachers quickly break a silence. She suggested thinking in terms of questions that individual students bring with them — for example, questions of values (e.g., "Who cares?"), ways of knowing (e.g., "What is the evidence?"), actions (e.g., "What must I do with what I know?"), and consequences (e.g., "Do I know what would happen?"). In writing about assessment, she noted that, "Learning to have conversations instead of inquisitions is a very powerful way of starting to get data into context" (Rowe, 1991, p. 91).

Gallas (1995) also emphasizes the value of listening to students; she reports gathering her elementary students for open-ended discussions around a particular topic or question

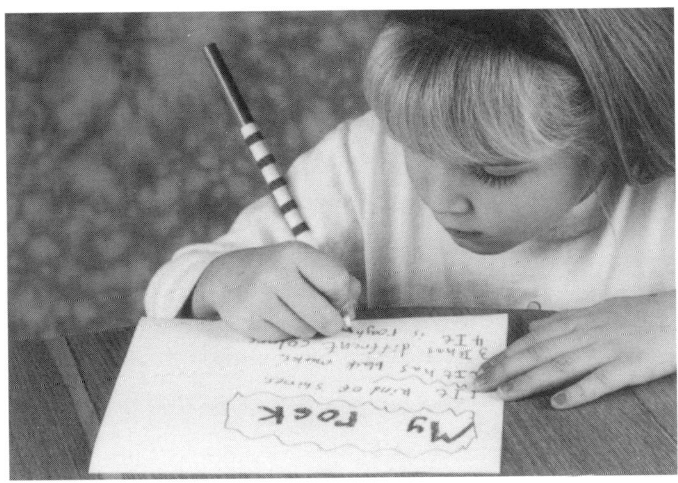

that she calls "Science Talks." She allows her students to explore their own ideas, which may or may not be related to the experiences she has planned for them. "Children know when we are 'taking over' their agenda. They can sense when the 'I wonder' in their questions is absorbed into a teacher's 'let's find out and show' agenda" (Gallas, 1995, p. 71). She always asks students to draw, right after the talk, an idea or ideas that they felt answered the question best, which she uses to follow and document the progress of their learning.

Several important dimensions of the

Table 4-1. Assessment Formats and Procedures

	On demand →			Over time
Formats	multiple choice, true/false, matching	constructed response, essays	investigations, research reports, projects	portfolios, journals, lab notebooks
Amount of time	typically ~1 min 2-3 min with justifications	1-2 min short answers 5-15 min open-ended responses	days, weeks, or months	months or even years
Whose questions? (audience for the answer)	anonymous or the teacher's	anonymous or the teacher's	the teacher's or the student's	the teacher's or the student's
What kind of questions?	posed narrowly	posed narrowly	posed more openly	varies
Source of answer	anonymous or the teacher's	the student's	the student's	the student's
What kind of answers?	right/wrong	extent of correctness	standards or criteria for quality	standards or criteria for quality
Resources available during assessment	usually none	none or some equipment	equipment, references	equipment, references
Opportunity for feedback, revision	none	usually none	usually some from teachers and peers	usually some from teachers and peers

familiar formats of multiple choice, constructed response, projects, and portfolios, are displayed in Table 4-1. The challenge for teachers increases from the left side of the table to the right, as the products of assessment go from being right or wrong to having qualities that must be negotiated with other members of the school community. In other words, what are the teacher's, the school's, or the science community's criteria for an excellent response to a particular question?

Discussions among teachers at a school or district level, calibrated with the participation of outsiders, are a component of most effective assessment systems. As Daro (1996, p. 260) puts it:

> If standards are to have any real consequence, it will have to be

through the engagement of teachers in a professional community holding each other to a mutually accountable standard. They can only hold each other to standards they understand in terms of their own students' work. Thus, deliberating upon their students' work with their colleagues in open but moderated scoring discussions will be needed to make standards a reality for teachers and thereby for students.

In choosing the appropriate format for an assessment, the nature of the standard needs to be examined. Is it something that can and should be assessed "on demand," with little time for reflection or revision? Multiple choice and short-answer responses are convenient for assessing the things that students should know "at the drop of a hat" or "cold." Many of the things valued in the *Standards*, however, require at least the time for reflection (more than a couple of minutes). Consequently, many assessments require formats that take more time.

The vignettes in Chapter 3 emphasize assessments on the right side of Table 4-1, in part to demonstrate the varied uses of assessments. But the full range of assessment formats and procedures could be used in any of the lessons described in Chapter 3. In particular, a combination of evaluative tools likely would be needed to conduct the summative assessments of how much each student had learned from the lessons.

Sometimes teachers, like commercial publishers and district officials, rely on multiple choice formats because they are easy to score accurately, or because teachers are encouraged to prepare students for state or district tests that are in that format. However, it can be difficult to assess understandings, inquiry abilities, or inquiry understandings using just a multiple choice format. One way to make multiple choice questions more meaningful is to ask students to justify their selections, both by saying why they think their choice is best and why the others are not satisfactory.

An additional consideration involves students with limited proficiency in the language of the assessment. Students who are still acquiring basic knowledge of English vocabulary, syntax, and semantics can have problems both understanding and responding to language-based assessment items. It therefore is important to distinguish between what students know in a subject area and how well they can interpret and respond to specific questions.

The State Collaborative on Assessment and Student Standards under the Council of Chief State School Officers (1999) has developed procedures and materials designed to produce more appropriate assessment of English language learning students. These materials point out that assessments can be affected by linguistic issues (such as the omission of certain letters or sounds that are unknown in a native language), cultural influences (different ways of interpreting a question), and the degree of familiarity with English (whether at a social or academic level). Certain patterns of difficulties emerge among students who are learning English, and a knowledge of these patterns can help make assessments more accurate.

The most comprehensive assessment systems include a variety of instruments. For example, the system developed by the New Standards Project has three interrelated components: performance standards, examinations, and portfolios (New Standards, 1997). The performance standards translate the *National Science Education Standards* into statements that indicate the kinds of activities through which students could demonstrate competence in a standard. These standards also include examples of student work with commentary that explains what aspects of the work illustrate the standard and why it is appropriate for that grade level. The examinations use a combination of selected and constructed response items, including hands-on performance tasks, to yield scores in (1) conceptual understanding, (2) scientific thinking: design and acquisition of knowledge, (3) scientific thinking: analysis and evidence, and (4) life, earth, and physical sciences. The portfolio system includes exhibits for conceptual understanding, scientific thinking, tools and communication, and investigation. Having different exhibits highlights the different types of evidence that need to be presented for these qualitatively different types of standards.

The expectation for quality in the portfolio is higher than the expectation on the exam, as adequate time, feedback, and opportunity for revision are in place for the former. Some of the performance standards, such as working productively in a group, can best be assessed by teacher observation, so certification forms for such expectations are included in the portfolio. Successful implementation depends on the development of a cadre of teachers who are experienced in scoring against a standards-based rubric and on an abundance of examples of standards-setting work from a diverse range of students.

A similar system of multiple formats has been employed in California for several years by the Golden State Exam in High School Biology, Chemistry, and Integrated Science. The examination includes multiple choice items, constructed response items, and laboratory performance tasks. The portfolio is optional and thus is used only to improve a student's score, not to lower it.

CONCLUSION

This chapter has demonstrated that assessment for inquiry-based science education differs from more familiar, traditional assessments for a number of reasons: the nature of inquiry, the goals of inquiry-based instruction, the alignment of inquiry with the *Standards*, and the capacity of a particular assessment to measure actual progress toward the *Standards*.

These differences in assessment extend both to formative assessments done to guide learning and to summative assessments designed to measure learning, including large-scale (district-wide, state, national, or international) assessments. Summative assessments also must meet a number of additional criteria: they should be systematic, replicable, reliable, equitable for all students, comparable across classes and schools, and interpretable. By meeting these criteria, summative assessments can provide evidence needed to make fair high-stakes decisions — whether about an individual student's grades or a system's need to redesign professional development approaches for its teachers.

5
Preparing Teachers for Inquiry-Based Teaching

For students to understand inquiry and use it to learn science, their teachers need to be well-versed in inquiry and inquiry-based methods. Yet most teachers have not had opportunities to learn science through inquiry or to conduct scientific inquiries themselves. Nor do many teachers have the understanding and skills they need to use inquiry thoughtfully and appropriately in their classrooms.

What do teachers need to know and be able to do to use inquiry effectively? What kinds of professional development can help prospective and practicing teachers both develop and use inquiry-based strategies?

The *National Science Education Standards* — and particularly the standards for the professional development of science teachers — are a useful organizer for these questions. In the context of inquiry, these professional development standards can be organized into four categories:

- Standard A: Learning Science through Inquiry
- Standard B: Learning to Teach Science through Inquiry
- Standard C: Becoming Lifelong "Inquirers"
- Standard D: Building Professional Development Programs for Inquiry-Based Learning and Teaching

The latter part of this chapter is organized around these four themes. The chapter begins, however, with a broad overview of the role professional development can play in redirecting teaching and learning toward inquiry.

THROUGH A TEACHER'S EYES: A VIEW OF PROFESSIONAL DEVELOPMENT FOR INQUIRY-BASED TEACHING

In the following vignette, Steve, a high school physics teacher, reflects on the three-year professional development program that led to his Master of Arts in Teaching Integrated Sciences. His story raises important issues about teachers' motivations, values, understandings, and experiences as they learn about inquiry and about how to teach science using inquiry.

A Teacher Discusses Professional Development for Inquiry-Based Teaching:
Steve's Story

When I began my three-year masters program, I had several reservations about teaching through inquiry. I thought it would require more time than my typical lecture and laboratory teaching. I also thought it would conflict with the demand for "coverage" of science content. And I didn't want to leave my "comfort zone" where my students and I generally knew what was expected.

At the same time, I felt that I was not exposing my students to enough of the important and interesting ideas of physics. I had known for years, based on the questions I asked on tests and during classes, that my students weren't retaining much of anything I "taught." They seemed to know a lot and understand very little. It was obvious to me that the students were memorizing the terms and equations only long enough to answer questions on a test and then the information vanished.

I gained a number of insights as I tried and refined various methods introduced during my masters program. The program consisted of six-week full-time summer institutes and seminars during the academic year. My first important insight occurred when I was involved in a long-term inquiry at the beginning of the first summer. Being

challenged to ask good questions, to design effective investigations, and to carefully craft our explanations of what we found as we explored the watershed in southern Colorado—these experiences demonstrated the complexity and importance of learning to *do* science as well as learning *about* science. Another important step forward came when I appreciated the significance of focusing on the "big ideas" in physics. For example, I had planned to teach a physics unit on energy, and I decided to look more deeply into the subject. In the course of the reading I did as part of the program, I gained a much deeper understanding of the relationships among the storage, transfer, transformations, and conservation of energy. As I reflected on my past teaching, I realized that I had taught this subject in a piecemeal manner, jumping from one topic to the next. I never gave my students this broad vision of physics because I never had it myself.

My greater understanding of energy became the basis for a unit that was, without question, the most effective I had ever taught up to that time. I sought to have my students use inquiry to understand about energy conservation, different kinds of energy, and energy transformation. For example, I used a relatively open-ended laboratory in which I brought in a large "Rube Goldberg" contraption in which various bells and whistles were activated as balls and other devices were in motion. I asked the students to identify some questions they had about what was going on in the contraption related to energy, thinking about ideas of energy conservation, different kinds of energy, and energy transformation that we had been studying. They also identified how they thought they could answer their questions, what experiments they could design, and data they could collect that would provide sufficient evidence to explain what was happening. It was obvious from the high level of student engagement in their investigations and from their performance and feedback that they were making sense of the physics concepts and building their inquiry skills simultaneously. Teaching to the "big ideas" of physics through inquiry also helped me implement my state's science content standards, which had been developed to be consistent with the *National Science Education Standards*. Furthermore, the assessments I gave students at the end of the unit demonstrated to me that they had learned more about energy than when I had taught it in earlier classes.

One of my previous ideas about inquiry was that it consisted mainly of doing laboratory activities. I discovered that, although labs can aid in the process of sense-making, they often don't because they are either "cookbook" (they don't allow the students to make choices or judgments) or "confirmatory" (they follow lectures or students' reading). What I have realized is that the essence of inquiry does not lie in any elaborate, equipment-intensive laboratory exercise. It lies, rather, in the interactions between the student and the materials, as well as in the teacher-student and student-student interactions that occur dozens of times each and every class period.

One way that we learned about student-teacher interactions in my program was through a series of videotapes of teachers. We also were encouraged to try our hand at such behaviors as listening, clarifying statements, and open-ended questioning. I found myself responding to students with statements like, "Tell me more about Y," "What is the evidence for that conclusion?" and "How did you decide on that explanation over the one you were convinced of yesterday?"

I tried more small-group activities that were structured to encourage the team members to talk, debate, and come up with predictions based on initial observations and with explanations based on evidence. I informally assessed my students' knowledge almost daily. Frequently, I began lessons with activities to set the context for helping students discuss conceptual ideas and make my presentations more meaningful.

Another major step I took in my growth as a teacher was to begin allowing student questions to influence the curriculum. Instead of always framing the questions myself, I encouraged the students to pose questions that arose in their minds. This idea was a revelation! Listening to the students' questions has uncovered countless points of confusion that otherwise would have gone completely unrecognized.

As part of my masters program, I decided to monitor how much I was listening. I recorded the amount of time I was talking and the amount of time my students were talking. At first, the proportion of teacher/student talk time was approximately 80/20. By midway through the first semester, this proportion had been exactly reversed. This small piece of research was a turning point in my appreciating the value of teaching through inquiry.

Our professional development program allowed ample time during each of our classes for us to talk with each other about our recent "experiments" in our classrooms. Although the group was quite diverse in backgrounds and grades taught, those conversations were important to my growth and encouraged me to keep trying inquiry approaches. As I reflect on the three years I spent in the program, I know I gained immensely from the other teachers and from the education faculty and scientists with whom we worked closely.

Steve's account reflects some concerns that are common among teachers early in their exploration of inquiry. Initially he perceived that his teaching was already successful and that an important part of his role as science teacher was to help students become familiar with the myriad facts and concepts of science. Yet he also suspected that his students were not really learning (and retaining) what he wanted them to know. And he knew he was neglecting the need to help his students learn inquiry skills and understand how scientists used those skills to produce knowledge.

Steve came to see that moving toward inquiry-based teaching meant adopting a different role as a teacher. He created more opportunities for his students to explore ideas alone, with materials, and with each other. He listened more so he could learn what they understood and misunderstood, what they were thinking, and what they were learning. And he learned to structure his lessons around "big ideas" rather than around the facts and formulas that he had previously seen as central to the discipline of physics.

Steve's reflections demonstrate many of the changes that can reorient teaching toward inquiry. He is using inquiry in all three of the ways specified by the *Standards* by teaching inquiry abilities, an understanding of inquiry, and science subject matter through inquiry. He is paying more attention to student questions and creating opportunities for them to collect evidence and use it as the basis for explanations, and he is doing this before he presents material to them rather than after.

Steve's reflections also point out some important features of professional development for inquiry-based teaching. One is the need for teachers to *do* inquiry to learn its meaning, its value, and how to use it to help students learn. Another is the importance of a community of teacher-learners that mirrors scientific communities. According to the *Standards*, such communities both challenge and support the development of knowledge by scientists, students, and, in this case, teachers.

Steve's reflections also demonstrate that it can take a significant amount of time to make transformational changes in teaching. Steve's program included six-week-long summer institutes and monthly academic-year seminars. By his own account, Steve was able to make headway on his journey to inquiry-based teaching but by no means reach a final destination. Finally, the professional development in which Steve engaged gave him a wide range of opportunities with inquiry, from field work to inquiries fed by the literature to inquiries into his own classroom behaviors, such as his research on teacher-student talk time.

Steve's experiences provide a basis

from which to explore the four main topics discussed in the professional development standards, beginning with how teachers learn the science they need to know to do inquiry-based teaching.

LEARNING SCIENCE THROUGH INQUIRY

Teachers have very different levels of knowledge and skills in science. Prospective teachers in colleges and universities may have only high school science courses behind them. Experienced teachers who are certified in other fields may find themselves teaching science. Veteran science teachers or scientists who aspire to

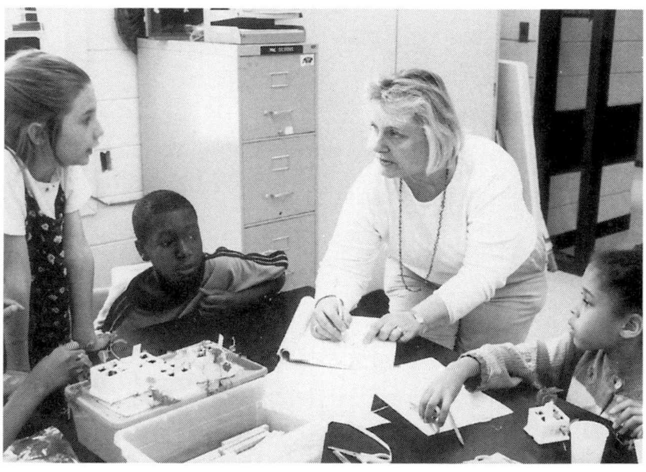

teach may have a strong but traditional science background or may be teaching a science different from their background. All may find themselves challenged by the need to learn more or a different kind of science.

To teach their students science through inquiry, teachers need to understand the important content ideas in science — as outlined, for example, in the *Standards.* They need to know how the facts, principles, laws, and formulas that they have learned in their own science courses are subsumed by and linked to those important ideas. They also need to know the evidence for the content they teach — how we know what we know. In addition, they need to learn the "process" of science: what scientific inquiry is and how to do it.

But *how* can teachers learn the major ideas in the scientific disciplines? There are many possibilities, from formal preservice or in-service classes, to independent programs of study, to serious reflection on their interactions with students in their inquiry-based classrooms. The next three vignettes in this chapter describe a range of science courses and professional development experiences that give teachers an opportunity to learn the major ideas of science disciplines through inquiry. The first vignette tells the story of a university-based physicist who teaches teachers within the structure of a university course. The second describes the experiences of a teacher taking part in that same course. And the third tells of a kindergarten teacher who is immersed in science at a program in a science museum.

Besides changing the traditional lecture approach in a science course, some college professors have developed special science courses for K-12 teachers. The Physics Education Group in the Department of Physics at the University of Washington offers special courses for both preservice and inservice teachers. The curriculum is based on *Physics by Inquiry* (McDermott et al., 1996), a set of laboratory-based modules that have been developed on the basis of research on the learning and teaching of physics. (References to relevant research can be found in McDermott and Redish, 1999.) The courses help teachers develop a functional understanding of important physical concepts. This level of understanding

---

A University-Based Physicist Discusses Concept Formation in the Laboratory:
Lillian's Story

The curriculum used in physics courses for teachers should be in accord with the instructional objectives. If the capacity to teach "hands-on" science is a goal, then teachers need to work through a substantial amount of content in a way that reflects this spirit. However, there is another compelling reason why the choice of curriculum is critical. Teachers often try to implement instructional materials in their classrooms that are very similar to those that they have used in their college courses. Whether intended or not, teaching methods are learned by example. The common tendency to teach physics from the top down, and to teach by telling in lectures, runs counter to the way precollege students (and many university students) learn best. Therefore, courses for precollege teachers should be laboratory-based.

In the curriculum that we have developed and use in our courses for preservice and inservice teachers, all instruction takes place in the laboratory. The students work in small groups with equipment similar to that used in precollege programs. The approach differs from the customary practice of introducing a new topic by stating definitions and assertions. Instead, students are presented with a situation in which the need for a new concept becomes apparent. Starting with their observations, they begin the process of constructing a conceptual model that can account for the phenomenon of interest. Carefully structured questions guide them in formulating operational definitions of important concepts. They begin to think critically about what they observe and learn to ask appropriate questions of their own. As they encounter new situations, the students test their model and find some instances in which their initial model is inadequate and that additional concepts are needed. The students continue testing, extending, and refining the model to the point that they can predict and explain a range of phenomena. This is the heart of the scientific method, a process that must be experienced to be understood.

To illustrate the type of instruction summarized above, here is a specific example based on a topic included in many precollege programs. It describes how we guide students to develop a conceptual model for a simple dc (direct current) circuit. Mathematics is not necessary; qualitative reasoning is sufficient.

The students begin the process of model-building by trying to light a small bulb with a battery and a single wire. They develop an operational definition for the concept of a complete circuit. Exploring the effect of adding additional bulbs and wires to the circuit, they find that their observations are consistent with the following assumptions: a current exists in a complete circuit and the relative brightness of identical bulbs indicates the magnitude of the current. As the students conduct further experiments (some suggested, some of their own devising), they find that the brightness of individual bulbs depends both on how many are in the circuit and on how they are connected to the battery and to one another. The students are led to construct the concept of electrical resistance and find that they can predict the behavior of many, but not all, simple circuits of identical bulbs. They recognize the need to extend their model beyond the concepts of current and resistance to include the concept of voltage (which will later be refined to potential difference). As bulbs of different resistance and additional batteries are added, the students find that they need additional concepts to account for the behavior of more complicated circuits. They are guided in developing more complex concepts, such as electrical power and energy. Proceeding step-by-step through deductive and inductive reasoning, the students construct a conceptual model that they can apply to predict relative brightness in any circuit consisting of batteries and bulbs.

We have used this guided-inquiry approach with teachers at all educational levels, from elementary through high school. Having become aware of the intellectual demands through their own experience, the teachers recognize that developmental level will determine the amount of model-building that is appropriate for their students. For the teachers, however, the sense of empowerment that results from in-depth understanding generates confidence that they can deal with unexpected classroom situations.

connotes the ability to do the reasoning necessary to apply the concepts to new situations. Lillian's story tells how the program is structured.

In Lillian's story, we see the instructors' decision to *guide* the learning process so that the college students are forced to confront difficult conceptual ideas and to go through the reasoning necessary to reach their own understanding. Generalizations and elucidation of general principles come after experience and in iterative fashion. They are not presented first as a base for students' investigative work. The guided activities are purposely selected by the instructors based on years of prior experience with college students (including teachers) and extensive knowledge of students' typical thinking about key ideas in physics. Carefully chosen questions are designed to elicit debates and hard thinking about these ideas based on guided investigations, related readings, and small group and individual work. Specific laboratory investigations have been selected by the staff — activities they know will cause the students to confront their existing beliefs about physics. This guided inquiry is essential at the introductory level so that the students can later use their developing knowledge and conceptual understanding to dig more deeply into the key ideas of physical science. The University of Washington program is based on the belief that both lecturing on basic principles and providing unstructured lab time are less effective strategies for bringing about student growth in conceptual understanding and reasoning skills.

Below, in Lezlie's Story, we see the impact of this type of instruction on an elementary school teacher. Lezlie was at the beginning of her career when she first participated in the NSF Summer Institute for Inservice Teachers at the University of Washington. Today, more than 25 years later, she reflects on how her experience in the program has affected her professional development as a teacher.

An Elementary School Teacher Reflects on her Learning and Teaching Through Inquiry:
Lezlie's Story

In late spring of my first year of teaching, I was informed that a drop in enrollment would result in the elimination of the 2nd grade position that I held. The good news, however, was that I was welcome to take a newly-created position as the science specialist for grades K-4. Not wanting to relocate and not stopping to consider that my major in French might not have appropriately prepared me for this new position, I quickly agreed to take it for the following year. The district science supervisor suggested that we start with a couple of Elementary Science Study units, *Clay Boats* and *Primary Balancing*. The unit guides and equipment were ordered. I was all set to begin my new teaching role.

Never having had a science lesson in elementary school, I was not predisposed, as I had been with the other subjects, to teach it as I had been taught. In fact, without any real textbook to guide the students, I was left with the materials and a few general instructions in the teacher's guide. And so it was that my students and I became "explorers of materials." We had a great time. The students were engaged. They talked a lot about what they were doing and we all asked a lot of questions. But I wanted to do more than just explore and ask questions. I wanted to learn some basic principles and have a clear vision of where we were going. I wanted to lead my students to discover and understand something. But what was it that we should understand? I hadn't a clue. This is when I first came to recognize that if I were to become a truly effective teacher, I would need scientific skills and understandings that I had not been required to develop during my undergraduate years.

Not long after this recognition of my deficiencies, I happened to glance through the school district's newsletter, and came across a notice for a Summer Institute in Physics and Physical Science for Elementary Teachers. I applied and was accepted.

The professional development provided by that first summer's intense coursework was the first meaningful education I had experienced since high school. Nothing I had been exposed to in college had really addressed what I needed to know to guide my students to develop the conceptual understanding and thinking and reasoning skills needed to make sense of the world around them.

I walked away from that summer feeling that my brain had been to boot camp. No course of study, no one teacher had ever demanded so much of me. I had never before been asked to explain my reasoning. A simple answer was no longer sufficient. I had been expected to think about how I came to that answer and what that answer meant. It had been excruciating at times, extricating the complicated and detailed thought processes that brought me to a conclusion, but I found it became easier to do as the summer progressed. I also began to realize that just as important as what I came to understand, was how I came to understand it. Through the process of inquiry, I had come to an understanding of content that I had always felt was beyond me. I wanted to be able to ask the questions that would lead my students to the same kind of understanding. The key to the questions was first understanding the content.

The content had been the focus of the summer institute and as a result I had developed a conceptual understanding of several basic science concepts including balance, mass, and volume. Along with these concepts I had discovered an appreciation for the need to control variables in an experiment. I was now better equipped to take a more critical look at the science units I had used the previous year. I recognized that *Clay Boats* had probably not been the best choice for a teacher with only a budding understanding of sinking and floating, but *Primary Balance* seemed to be an appropriate choice since I had explored very similar materials and had some ideas of how I could lead students to discover, through experiments in which they would come to understand the need to control variables, which factors seem to influence balance and which do not.

Now, after many years of professional development in the UW summer institutes, both as a participant and as an instructor, I feel comfortable teaching most, if not all, of the science concepts covered in elementary and middle school. It is an understanding of the content that allows me to teach with confidence units such as electric circuits, magnetism, heat and temperature, and sinking and floating. And although this content knowledge was essential, simply understanding the content did not assure that I could bring my students to an understanding appropriate for them.

How does one begin to develop some expertise in these strategies we call *inquiry?* For me, I can only suppose that it began by reflecting upon my personal experiences. I don't believe that this was ever a deliberate exercise on my part until recently. However, in subtle ways, over a period of many years, I began to teach in the way in which I had been taught in the summer institutes.

I know that early on I began to pay attention to the questions that I asked, for the questions stood out in my mind as the tools that, when deftly wielded, resulted in the desired state of understanding in me. I knew, too, that questions would help me to discover the intellectual status of my students. In other words, where they were. Armed with the necessary conceptual understanding, aware of several "pitfalls" (misconceptions) that I had personally encountered, I was prepared to think about questions that would help me find out where I needed to start. I envisioned the terrain between the students and their conceptual understanding. I liken the terrain to an aerial photograph that clearly details all the various roads that lead to the designated destination. It also indicates the "dead ends" and the hazards from which I want to steer my students clear. I am well acquainted with this terrain, because I have traversed it on more than one occasion myself, and have conversed with others who have, perhaps, taken a different path to the same destination. It is in this way that I can offer guidance to my students, so that they may not wander too far from a fruitful path. I want them to encounter some difficulties and to resolve conflicts and inconsistencies, and to grow intellectually from these experiences. But I do not want them to wander aimlessly or to plunge headlong over a cliff. I want them to arrive at the destination relatively unscathed. For this reason it is crucial, that like a vigilant parent, I continue to offer support in their intellectual insecurity. I question and listen carefully. I scan the territory to find where the explanations and responses to my questions place them, and then plan my next strategy to keep them moving ahead. I recall from my own experience as a learner that sometimes this next strategy is a question such as, *"What would you need to do to find out?"* Sometimes it is a suggestion of some experiment to try. And sometimes it is a comment such as, *"Why don't you think about that for a bit."* It has only been through many years of trying these strategies out that I have learned to gauge which tactic is appropriate at what time and with which student.

There are, of course, other considerations in the teaching of inquiry-based science to elementary students. Engagement has never been a problem for the students with whom I have worked. Science is naturally engaging. Developmental appropriateness is another matter. I have come to a much clearer recognition of what will "fly" and what will not as a result of the research-based curriculum I worked through in the summer institutes. These materials were carefully designed to build conceptual understanding in logical, sequential steps. You do not, for instance, begin to think about why things sink or float without first developing an understanding of what we mean by mass, and what we mean by volume, in terms of concrete operational definitions. Only then can one begin to think about how these two variables may influence sinking and floating.

In summary, the most important step for me in becoming a more effective teacher of science was gaining a sound understanding of the subject matter content. It was equally important that this content was learned in an environment of inquiry-based instruction. It was then necessary to reflect on my experience as a learner so that I could put into practice what had been modeled for me. Finally, I must add that it is essential to take a critical look at what we are doing and to evaluate what is working and what is not. If what we are doing does not result in a better understanding of the content by our students, it could be that the problem lies with us and not with them.

This description illustrates a change in college science coursework toward a more inquiry-based format and its impact on a teacher's knowledge and skills. University coursework, which traditionally has been didactic with hands-on activity relegated to labs that confirm the lectures or reading, has been a source of concern to many involved in K-12 teaching and learning. Numerous reports emphasize the necessity of changing the way science courses are taught to teachers (AAAS, 1990; Project Kaleidoscope, 1991; NRC, 1996). Some provide examples of inquiry-based teaching at the university level and strategies for doing so (NRC, 1997). Still others strongly recommend that every undergraduate preparing to teach have as part of their coursework the experience of engaging in original research under the supervision of a research scientist (NRC, 1990).

The above description also illustrates a change in college science coursework toward an instructional sequence that is inquiry-based. It demonstrates the important features of beginning with exploration of a phenomenon, delaying the teaching of terms and principles until they are needed, emphasizing the formation of concepts, and applying newly learned concepts to other situations. The result is mastery of subject matter

---

A Kindergarten Teacher Learns Inquiry at a Science Museum:
Joanna's Story

How do I design a classroom environment that facilitates children's efforts to conduct investigations? How do I behave to promote, support, and observe inquiry?

I had been teaching kindergarten for many years before coming to a two-week workshop on light and color at a prominent science museum. I was ready to learn a new way to teach science. I was convinced that traditional approaches were not giving my students a sense of the skills they would need to succeed in later science courses and in a technologically advanced world.

But instead of learning about teaching, we began as learners of science. First the instructors set the stage for a long-term inquiry. We played with different ways to mix colored pigments and colored light. I had always believed in hands-on activities for my students, but I had never had the opportunity to engage in a long term investigation of my own — I had only taken high school laboratory classes where you filled in the blanks on worksheets. What a surprise doing an inquiry turned out to be! I thought I knew about hands-on science, but I discovered that there is big difference between inquiry and hands-on.

From the starting points provided to us by the staff, we came up with a series of questions that would guide our investigations. The staff told us that, like scientists, we might take some twists and turns, but that the time spent on our investigation would

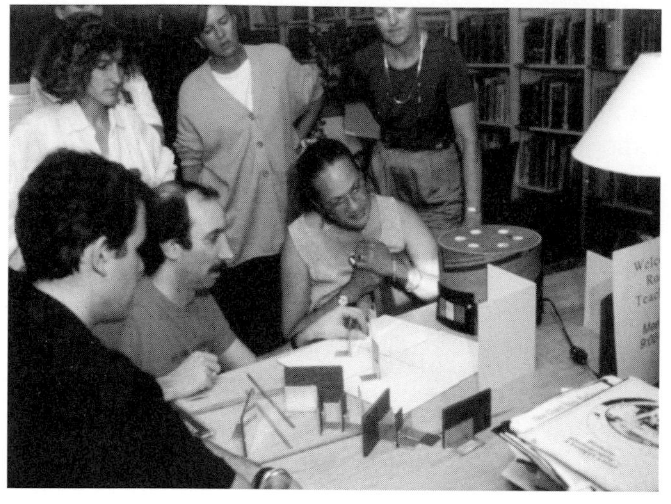

lead us to new understandings about light and color and also about the process of inquiry.

In partnership with two other teachers from my district, we choose our own question to investigate. We all had been intrigued with an exhibit called colored shadows; it didn't make sense to us that colored lights (red, blue, green, etc.) could cast different colored shadows (yellow, magenta, cyan, etc.). We figured that if we could explain it to ourselves, then we could explain it to others and really understand the phenomenon.

At first we re-created all the colors of the light spectrum and then determined what shadows each created. As predicted, our investigation took many twists and turns, but each gave us a new piece of the puzzle. For example, with staff assistance, we made visits to other exhibits, one of which was color removal, a demonstration of how removing colors (by putting colored filters in front of a light source) changed the light that reached our eye. We also read about the frequencies of visible light and about how the eye perceives those frequencies. If we had more time we could have gone in many more directions. As it was, we felt we had learned a tremendous amount of science content and also how to go about answering our own questions.

As we worked, we talked with other investigators, shared ideas, and began to understand how important it is to collaborate. When the time came to share our inquiries, we were amazed to see how far our group had come in a few short days and how well our investigation meshed with the other inquiries into light and color.

As elementary school teachers, most of us had never undertaken independent investigations in any of the sciences. We felt proud of our ability to pick a question and pursue it to some conclusions. In addition, by experiencing inquiry firsthand we came to appreciate some of its critical pieces, such as the power of questioning at every stage. Establishing a question to pursue at first was important, but so were other questions, such as, how can you explain what you observe? What evidence do you have that your explanation is a good one? Is there an alternative explanation you can think of and why is your other one more credible? We were given models, materials, and subtle guidance for how to inquire. We learned important scientific content by experimenting, interacting with scientists, and consulting a variety of resources, including the exhibits at the museum. We gained an understanding about the complex interplay of color addition (light) and color subtraction (pigment) and about what causes the colors that we see. We tasted firsthand the sense of competence and confidence that comes with being a self-reliant learner.

with deep understanding *through* inquiry. This form of teaching also enhances students' understanding of the process of scientific inquiry itself.

Joanna's experiences illustrate the explicit teaching of inquiry to teachers as learners. As she and other participants explored light and color, they came to understand inquiry as a long-term and often unpredictable process. They learned how to learn with and from others pursuing similar scientific questions, the importance of models and materials, and how to communicate their findings to others. The workshop gave them an opportunity to "immerse" themselves in the essential features of classroom inquiry and to learn many important scientific concepts related to light.

As illustrated by the three vignettes in this section, learning science through inquiry gives teachers opportunities to learn firsthand several essential aspects of inquiry-based teaching:

- How both science subject matter and inquiry outcomes can be built into learning experiences.
- How a deeper understanding of scientific concepts can promote discussion and the formulation of productive questions.
- How the essential features of classroom inquiry can be woven into a learning experience.
- What it feels like to learn this way, complete with frustrations and struggles.
- What roles and behaviors instructors can use that promote and support learning.

LEARNING TO TEACH SCIENCE THROUGH INQUIRY

As important as it is for teachers to understand inquiry, develop their skills of inquiry, and learn science concepts through inquiry, teachers also need to learn how to teach this way. This can be done through professional development that extends their own inquiries to the implications for their teaching. Or it can be done through professional development designed especially to help teachers teach through inquiry. The following vignette illustrates the former through the continuation of Joanna's story: how this kindergarten teacher carried her learnings back into her classroom.

A Kindergarten Teacher Applies What She Learned Through Inquiry:

Joanna's Story Continues

After my investigation into colored light at the science museum, I began to consider seriously how I might begin to create a classroom environment focused on inquiry for my kindergarten class. I began to understand that inquiry has a structure that I could use to enable my students to ask and answer their own questions about light and color. That was four years ago, and each year I get a little better at understanding how kindergartners do inquiry.

I now have several light sources and lenses that can be tinted different colors as regular learning stations. Students investigate light and color all year long, with many opportunities to revisit their work. Some years the students call themselves the "Rain-

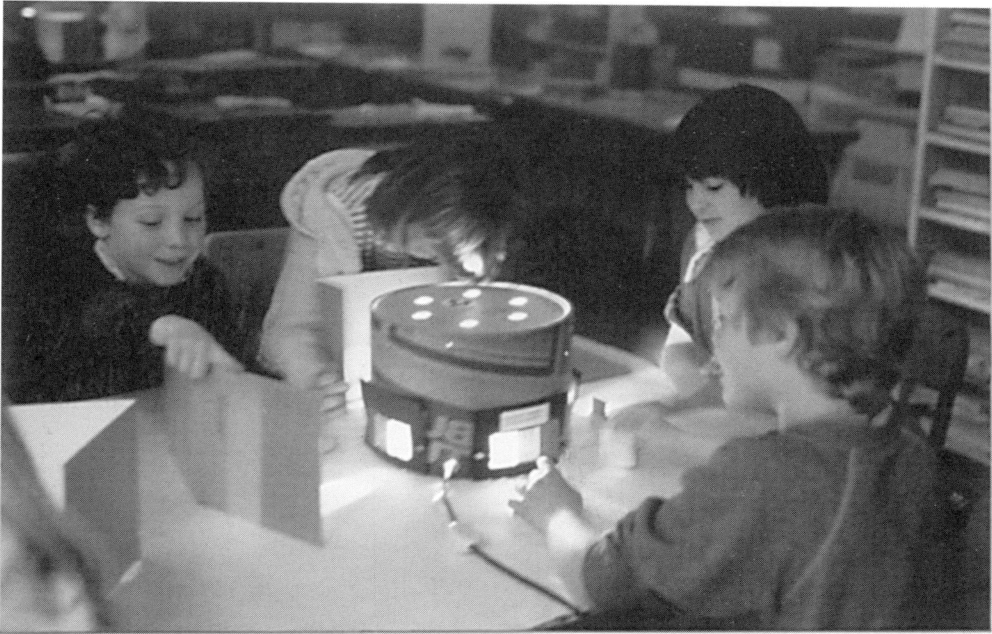

bow Kids" because we typically start our work with light using prisms. The *National Science Education Standards* call for young children to gain an understanding of the properties of objects and materials as well as of light. We pursue these understandings in part through our mixing of different colored paints and then the mixing of colored lights. Each year the students make books of their experiences.

One of my particular interests in the past four years has been to encourage my students to develop their language skills using science as the subject of talk. At the workshop I learned the importance of learning how to ask questions, work with materi-als, and listen. I begin each year by modeling these skills. For example, I show them how to ask questions using prisms and shadows as a starting point.

I have noticed that many kindergartners do not have the language skills to express their questions, but that they often ask questions with their bodies by moving objects around. I help this ability along. I model the beginning of questions by saying: "I'm going to think out loud now — I'm wondering how I can find out if this prism will work if I move it to this side of the window — that's asking a question." As students are working with the mirrors and light, I model how to ask their questions. For example, I'll say: "I see by the way you are moving that mirror that you are wondering, 'Can I bend the light?'" I copy down students' questions and post them for all to see.

I allow time for free exploration with materials in a safe environment, so that mirrors and prisms are as much regular parts of the classroom as are paints and sand. Now that I have learned how to set up the classroom environment, I am trying harder to listen to their questions, watch their actions, and gently guide small groups into planning and conducting longer investigations.

Looking back, I can see how my own experience with inquiry has shaped how I work with my students. I want them to experience the curiosity, success, and perseverance that I felt. I know that they can accomplish much with the right kind of teaching and that their feelings of competence grow with each step along the way. I feel that I am helping students to learn for themselves to become independent thinkers, a skill that will serve them well in their future schooling. And they will never look at light, shadow, and color the same way again.

Joanna's story demonstrates her continuing development of "pedagogical content knowledge," a term coined by Lee Shulman (1986) to represent a third component of teaching expertise that is unique to teachers. Pedagogical content knowledge is the integration or synthesis of teacher' pedagogical knowledge (what they know about teaching) and their subject matter knowledge (what they know about what they teach) (Cochran, 1992). As Shulman (1986) notes, pedagogical content knowledge

> . . . embodies the aspects of content most germane to its teachability. Within the category of pedagogical content knowledge I include, for the most regularly taught topics in one's subject area, the most useful forms of representation of those ideas, the most powerful analogies, illustrations, examples, explanations, and demonstrations — in a word, the ways of representing and formulating the subject that make it comprehensible to others. . . [It] also includes an understanding of what makes the learning of specific concepts easy or difficult: the conceptions and preconceptions that students of different ages and backgrounds bring with them to the learning (p. 9).

As an example, experienced biology teachers planning a unit on photosynthesis draw on their pedagogical content knowledge when they know the specific ideas students are likely to bring to the classroom (such as the idea that plants get their food from the soil), the ideas most likely to be difficult (such as how ATP-ADP transformations occur), and how to best deal with these difficult concepts using examples, analogies, models, and demonstrations (Hashweh, 1987). In Joanna's case, her experiences with inquiry learning and teaching are building her pedagogical content knowledge. Her understanding and abilities of inquiry were sharpened in the museum program where she learned to ask good questions and design investigations to gather evidence she could use to explain

the observations that piqued her interest. As she engages her own students in inquiry, she has become conscious of how they learn to ask questions about scientific phenomena and how she can help them do so. She observes how they combine their developing language skills with use of their bodies. She is learning what materials stimulate her children and help them develop explanations of light and color. She has arranged the learning environment to reflect all of the essential features of classroom inquiry.

Joanna's professional development program emphasized her experiences with inquiry and focused less on how she could bring these into her classroom. Other kinds of professional development programs focus more directly on inquiry-based teaching. They help teachers think in new ways about what they want their students to learn, how they can help them learn it, and how they will know whether and what students have learned. They focus more directly on strengthening teachers' pedagogical content knowledge in science.

Preservice or graduate courses and in-service workshops are still the most prevalent formats for teachers to develop and improve their inquiry teaching. But many other strategies also are being used throughout the country to help both prospective and practicing teachers learn more about teaching science through inquiry. Loucks-Horsley et al. (1998) have identified 15 different strategies for professional development, including case discussions, examining student work, action research, study groups, technology-based learning, curriculum implementation, coaching and mentoring, and immersion in scientific inquiry (the approach taken in Joanna's workshop). Their research suggests that strategies in which teachers study their own or others' practice are especially powerful in building their knowledge of how students learn most effectively. Some examples of this kind of professional development are the study of videos of classroom teaching; discussion of written cases of teaching dilemmas; and study of curriculum materials and related student work (assignments, lab reports, assessments, etc.).

Written teaching cases and videotapes of teaching are especially useful in allowing teachers to examine many aspects of inquiry-based teaching and learning. Student thinking can be analyzed as students respond to problems or questions posed by the teacher or to those that they themselves have posed. Teachers can study the responses given by the teacher in the video or case study and the effect of those responses on the students. They also can consider the teaching decisions that were or could be made to help the students learn.

Looking at student work, such as the write-up of an inquiry or the results of a performance assessment, can be a valuable process for teachers. A number of questions can be asked and discussed about the student's inquiry abilities. Has the student asked a question that can be addressed? Does the design of the investigation demonstrate that the student understands how to control variables? How elaborate is this student's explanation? Is it based on evidence? Has the student applied his or her new knowledge appropriately to this new situation?

Working with curriculum materials can take many forms. Teachers can work through lessons to learn inquiry and science subject matter as well as to analyze what students will learn, where they might have trouble, and how teachers might help at those points. Teachers can try out a "replacement unit," substituting an inquiry-oriented unit for one in their current curriculum. Or teachers can analyze how students are learning a particular set of outcomes from a unit that the teachers are all teaching at the same time.

The following vignette illustrates several of the ways teachers can learn and practice their teaching of inquiry using a new set of curriculum materials.

A Fifth-Grade Teacher Learns to Teach Through Inquiry as She Works with New Curriculum Materials: Sandy's Story

I used to lack confidence about teaching science, largely because my own science background was limited. I tended to put my efforts into teaching literacy and numeracy. So when our school decided to adopt a new "hands-on inquiry" science program, I was anxious.

All teachers, plus the principal and librarian, were expected to participate in four professional development sessions: two days at the beginning and midway through term one, and a half day at the beginnings of terms two and three. Between sessions, we would teach one assigned unit (there were three per grade level) with the support of colleagues in the building.

Jenny, the district professional developer, had organized my school and three other schools to do the course together. She began the first session with an overview of the course and the curriculum materials. For each grade level there was a teacher's book (and a student book) that focused a series of units, each on a major concept and a major skill. We participated in a number of activities that helped us see what was in the materials and experience some of the active investigations on which they were based.

In the afternoon, all of the fifth-grade teachers met together. We reviewed the first lesson for the unit on animal behavior that we would be teaching that term, viewed and discussed a video of a few minutes of teacher-student interactions during the lesson, and looked at some student papers in which they responded to the question about the topic of the unit, which focused on the behavior of mealworms: "What do you know and what questions do you have about mealworms?" We had a wonderful discussion about what the unit was designed to teach students and how the combination of materials, student activities, and teacher-student interactions could best help them achieve the goals. Then we were each asked to choose a lesson that interested us from early in the unit and come prepared after teaching it to lead an in-depth discussion among the teachers at our next session three weeks later. We were to bring some "artifact" to focus discussion — for example, some student work, a video or audiotape of a teaching episode, or some student assessments. For example, I chose the lesson on how mealworms behave toward light — whether they move toward it, away from it, or are neutral to it. I brought in an audiotape of a small group discussion in which the students were puzzling over the mealworms' behavior when they were placed different distances from a bright lamp. The students' data indicated that the mealworms closest to the lamp moved away from it, but those within about a meter moved towards it. One student noted that it may be the heat that was influencing the mealworms' behavior, not the light: another student said that they had too many things in the experiment that were varying and asked how they could determine the influence of light only, if lights were always hot. Another student looked around the room and located a relatively cool light and so they together devised a way to distinguish between the influences of light and heat on the mealworm behavior. It was a remarkable example

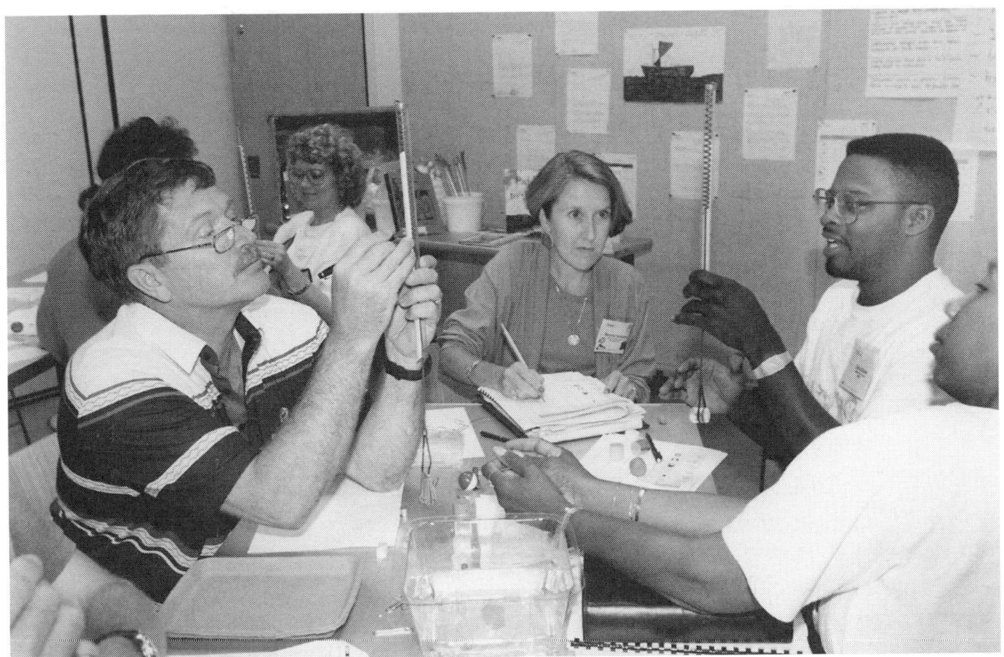

of students solving a problem and in the process learning not only about the behavior of mealworms but also developing an appreciation for controlling variables in an investigation. We teachers talked about whether I could have done anything differently in both setting up the activity for the students or in my questioning of them during their investigation. It was very stimulating to be able to "stop action" on a lesson, to clarify learning goals, and to examine the different possible consequences of different teaching behaviors.

We learned a lot from the experience of sharing our work with students. Working together, we figured out how to use the set of lessons to stimulate, respond to, and draw out the students' thinking. By the end of the session, we had a good idea about how to complete the unit in the next few weeks, how to teach the full unit next time, and also how to teach the other two units.

While we were teaching, we had support from our school's science coordinator, who had taken an in-depth one-week summer session on the curriculum and participated in monthly follow-up seminars with the other coordinators. Jenny had a strong science background and had previously pilot tested the curriculum materials we were learning to use. She had release time to help with the equipment or any problems we were having.

When we met at the beginning of term two, we again had much to share. Although each of us had some problems, we all were fortified by the positive way our students had responded to the activities. I know that I learned even more science that term than my students. I also adapted cooperative learning to use in my mathematics program, with much success.

In the third professional development session that preceded our second unit, we divided responsibility for studying and presenting to other teachers one lesson from the new unit that we would teach that term. The unit was about density and focused on sinking and floating objects. As we shared our thinking about each of the lessons and developed our plans, we realized how much more careful we were being to identify the outcomes we wanted for our students. In some cases, we needed to problem-solve with Jenny about how to be certain that our students had learned these outcomes. The materials addressed both inquiry outcomes as well as science subject matter, so we paid attention to both.

For the final session of the year, Jenny brought in a videotape of part of her lesson on sinking and floating. The students were investigating which objects sank and which floated, and they were developing their explanations of why. They seemed to have concluded that when air is inside an object (e.g., a boat or holes in a log) it would float and when there's no air (e.g., a penny, a chunk of clay), it wouldn't. Jenny was stuck. She didn't know what to do next. She wondered how she could help her students get to the "right" explanation when their explanations were all over the map.

We had a long and thoughtful discussion of this problem. We needed to consult our teacher's guide to understand density better. We also needed to determine what the students' observations and explanations told us about what they knew and where they needed to go. We asked, Are these students old enough to explain something they can't really see? Are they really basing their explanations on the evidence they have? Have they considered enough of the explanations being posed by others? Have they listened and tried to understand how those explanations differ from their own? Can they explain in turn why they weren't swayed to other explanations? At what point should I as the teacher come in and tell them which is the scientifically correct explanation, and what might be the consequences of doing so?

It was a terrific discussion and emphasized for us how important it is to consider our students' thinking, our role as teachers in building on their ideas and helping them to learn, and how important it is to increase their inquiry abilities so they can investigate more carefully and discover important science ideas from the *National Science Education Standards.*

Sandy's story illustrates how the use of a new curriculum can provide a vehicle for students to learn, at the same time as it helps teachers learn. Study and use of strong, inquiry-based curriculum materials can sharpen a teacher's understanding of inquiry and the science students are learning through inquiry. It can create situations that stretch the teacher's knowledge, stimulate focused discussions with colleagues, and motivate the teacher to seek more knowledge about science content and teaching approaches.

Sandy's story is likely to continue as she and her colleagues repeat the same units with new students the next year. As they increase their comfort with the materials, they will be able to focus on student thinking and learning and adjust their questioning, probing, and elaborating to deepen students' understanding. Ongoing collaboration with other teachers, and with others with more expertise in science and student learning, helps teachers such as Sandy continue to learn science concepts, inquiry abilities, and how scientific knowledge advances.

Professional development that focuses on improving teaching through inquiry achieves several simultaneous objectives:

- It provides teachers with learning experiences different from the more traditional college course or in-service workshop to include one-on-one experiences such as coaching, collaborative work such as study groups, and "job-embedded" learning such as action research.
- It focuses on important aspects of teachers' practice, including the organization and presentation of curriculum, student work, and teaching dilemmas.
- It helps teachers think carefully about how their students come to understand important science concepts through inquiry, what help their students need in developing the specific abilities of inquiry, and what learning experiences can make the work of scientists "real" to their students.

BECOMING LIFE-LONG "INQUIRERS"

This chapter uses the term "professional development" to refer to opportunities that teachers have to learn at all stages of their careers. It thus encompasses learning experiences for prospective, beginning, and experienced teachers through preservice, induction, and in-service programs, respectively. This chapter also emphasizes the importance of thinking about professional development as a continuum. Teachers at any level may know an enormous amount about some things but not others, and the stage of their careers should not dictate what they will learn and in what depth they will learn it.

The *Standards* emphasize the importance of lifelong learning by making it one of four professional development standards. Professional development must satisfy the ongoing need of all prospective and practicing teachers to continue to grow, to increase their knowledge and skills, and to improve their value to their students. A commitment to inquiry — as something that all humans must do to improve their lives and those of others — is an important theme for professional development, in addition to its other goals.

The most effective professional development not only stimulates the need to continue to learn. It also provides knowledge about where to look for information, it provides opportunities to improve teaching and learning, and it introduces teachers to tools for continuous improvement. These tools include strategies to analyze classroom experiences; to observe and provide useful feedback to others; to record and document observations and important information from other sources; and to search databases for useful guidance and material.

The vignettes in this chapter show several of these tools in action. Several of these stories were drawn from the journals of teachers. Some journal writing was required by the teacher's professional development experience. Other teachers simply keep journals as a tool for self-reflection and as a way to take time to understand their activities and experiments.

Several of the vignettes also illustrate ongoing learning through inquiry. Steve describes a component of his program in which he was asked to define a research question about his teaching, design and use a data collection and analysis scheme to address the question, and then report the results to his colleagues. Such action research projects are important sources of information for teachers. They organize what might otherwise be random impressions, unsystematic observations, and unconscious behaviors into a frame that can inform teachers' practice. They give teachers a tool that they can use to pursue questions about teaching throughout their careers.

In Joanna's case, a teacher who had not previously experienced inquiry had her eyes opened to its possibilities as a source of ongoing learning. Through professional development, she acquired the confidence to continue to inquire into science concepts. Joanna's motivation to think deeply about how her students were learning and what abilities they needed to keep learning produced continual refinements in her teaching and the learning environment she established for her students.

The following vignette demonstrates many of these aspects of becoming a life-long inquirer.

A Ninth-Grade Teacher Learns Geology in the Field: Gabe's Story

Last summer I had my first experience in doing real scientific inquiry. I signed up for a three-week institute sponsored by a nearby federal energy laboratory because I had been assigned to teach environmental science and had never done so before. It gave me the opportunity to learn more science as well as how to teach science.

Over the three-week period, we were immersed in four "scenarios"— problems that required us to use a wide variety of investigative skills and integrate knowledge from a number of scientific disciplines. I'll describe just one of those scenarios here: the environmental geology scenario. The program staff loaded us into two field vehicles, with one geologist per vehicle, and we drove to a ravine where a farmer had dumped many kinds of waste, from diapers to leftover herbicide. The question posed to us was: what is the impact of this kind of dumping? A geologist asked: "What do you think you would need to know to address the question?" We suggested many questions about the soil, water, the underlying rock, the nature of the waste material, and so on. We then got back into the vehicles to do a thorough tour of the land.

We began 38 miles from the dump site and learned — through several stops and through reading materials provided to us — about the economy of the area, the rock deposits, and the water diverted for agriculture from the Grand Coulee Dam. We stopped near a roadcut and were given a handout with a cross-section of the area. A geologist asked: "Why is water seeping out between the two formations that we can observe in this roadcut?" We discussed possible explanations, and then the geologist talked about the difference in "hydraulic conductivity" between the two formations. We went on to another roadcut through the same formation and the geologist asked us to predict how water applied at the surface might move through the deposits. We came up with a couple of explanations and argued about the nature of evidence for each. We decided not to try to resolve our differences until we had more data.

After several more stops, we began to observe differences in the soils around the formations. We decided to take soil samples that we could analyze back in the laboratory. When we reached the dump site again, the geologists asked us to describe the general topography of the land and compare it to the contour lines on a topographic map. We investigated vegetation changes, what these changes suggest about water movement in the area, and the kinds of sediment predicted to occur in this location. We then scattered around the dump site and took both soil and water samples, marking clearly on the map where they were taken from.

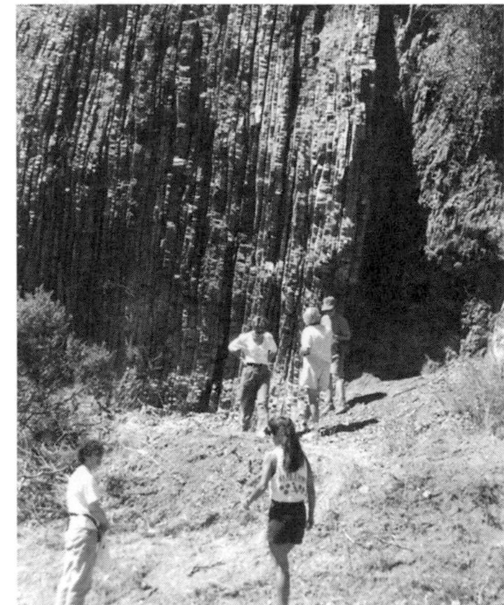

We spent the next day in the laboratory testing water and soil samples and working with our descriptions, maps, and calculations to address the primary question (as well as many other questions that arose over the course of the day in the field). With input from the geologists and a laboratory chemist, we formulated answers to the question about the impact of dumping. We made predictions about where runoff from the site would go, how fast it would move, and how we could test our predictions. In this way, I feel that we developed a keen understanding of the scientific ideas behind our observations, analyses, and conclusions.

Gabe was introduced to a nearby resource, a federal energy research laboratory, where scientists cared about education and made it possible for teachers (and, in other programs, students) to participate in the actual research being conducted. The professional development gave him an opportunity to actually "do" science, which neither his preservice program nor previous inservice programs had given him. In this situation, he was introduced to his local environment in a way that he had not known it before. It also taught him a variety of ways to inquire about this environment. In sum, it equipped him to think about how the inquiry process and inquiry abilities could interweave with science subject matter and how he could use the local environment as a primary locale for his students' learning.

PROFESSIONAL DEVELOPMENT PROGRAMS FOR INQUIRY-BASED TEACHING

Professional development often suffers from being piecemeal and fragmented. Preservice programs are often simply a collection of courses. Great rifts exist between science courses and education courses and between courses within both science and education. New teachers are often placed in the least desirable teaching positions, with full teaching loads, many preparations, difficult-to-teach students, and little or no support to ease the challenging transition from student to full-time professional. Similarly, professional development for in-service teachers is generally fragmented, consisting primarily of short workshops that are neither connected to each other nor to the teachers' classroom work (National Commission for Teaching & America's Future, 1996).

Professional development that is supposed to improve inquiry-based teaching can have all these ills, and in addition, it often does not explicitly help teachers learn inquiry abilities and understandings. Programs are needed that explicitly attend to inquiry — both as a learning outcome for teachers and as a way for teachers to learn science subject matter. Furthermore, these programs need to help teachers learn how to teach through inquiry.

The vignettes in this chapter

describe very different professional development programs, from Lillian's university courses for prospective teachers, to immersion in inquiry in a science museum, to a three-year masters program. Yet all share some attributes of effective professional development programs.

First, they offer coherent opportunities for teachers to learn over time. Three-year masters programs and long-term curriculum implementation help teachers to gain new knowledge and apply it to their teaching with support by colleagues, their schools, and districts. Second, many of these professional development programs were the product of a collaboration of many people and organizations. Partnerships between educators, universities, and research institutions involved scientists in creating opportunities for teachers to conduct scientific research — an activity so critical to their teaching that it merits inclusion in both preservice and inservice programs. Finally, all of the programs illustrated here had a clear commitment to the vision of the *National Science Education Standards*, which call for giving teachers the knowledge and abilities they need to address the science literacy needs of all their students. All of the programs viewed inquiry as a set of abilities and understandings that teachers themselves needed to have, and their students needed to learn — as well as being a vehicle through which subject matter could be learned, and learned well. This lies at the heart of the *Standards'* view of inquiry. All of the programs helped teachers learn science subject matter, develop inquiry abilities, and do so through their own opportunities to inquire.

Professional development for inquiry-based teaching and learning is critical to the future of science education as envisioned in the *Standards,* which note:

> The current reform effort requires a substantive change in how science is taught; an equally substantive change is needed in professional development practices (National Research Council, 1996, p. 56).

Long-term, comprehensive, inquiry-based professional development is an absolute requirement for the success of standards-based reform.

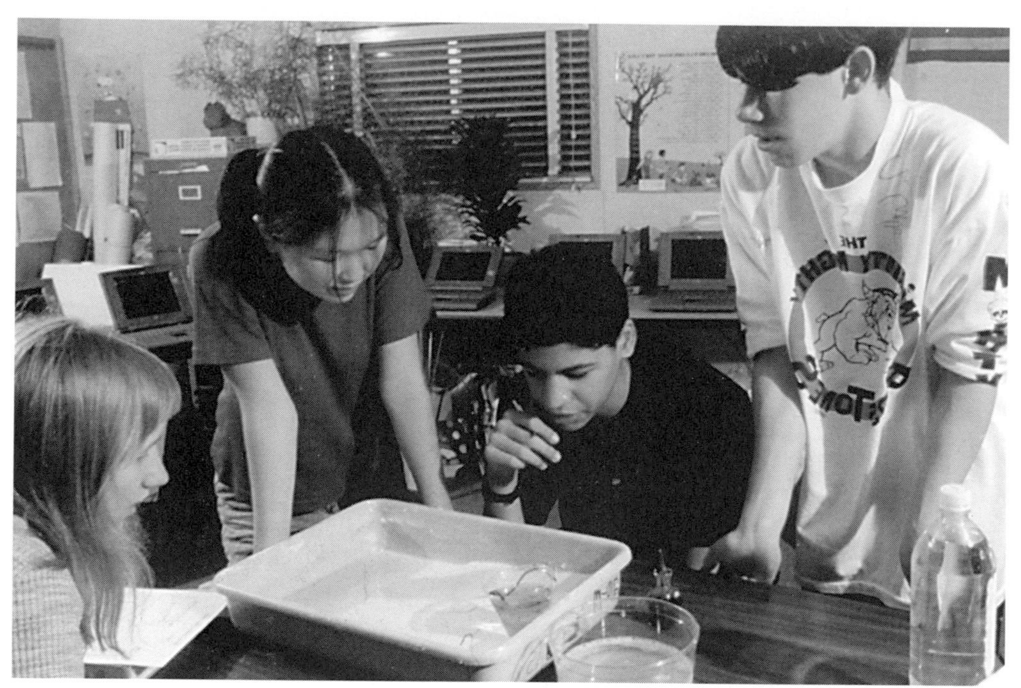

6

Making the Case for Inquiry

Educators need evidence drawn from research to help them implement and justify inquiry-based approaches to teaching and learning science. Many science teachers, for example, question why they should reorient their teaching toward inquiry-based methods. School boards may want to know why they should support inquiry-based curricula and professional development. Preservice teachers may question the need for an inquiry approach in their courses. Parents may want to know why their sons and daughters need to learn so differently from the way they did. Indeed, everyone should want to know the basis for choices about teaching and learning.

Chapter 2 defined inquiry-based teaching as experiences that help students acquire concepts of science, skills and abilities of scientific inquiry, and understandings about scientific inquiry. That chapter also pointed out, as does the *National Science Education Standards*, that effective science teachers use many teaching strategies. For example, there are times when explicit or direct instruction is a more appropriate choice and will complement inquiry-based teaching, especially when students have already had a great deal of direct experience with a particular phenomenon.

This chapter closely examines the research base for inquiry-based teaching. It begins by looking at the research on learning and the kinds of learning environments that promote learning. This research is of particular interest because of the strong parallels between how research says students learn important science concepts and the processes of scientific inquiry that are used in inquiry-based teaching. The chapter then addresses research that is specifically focused on inquiry-based science teaching. Throughout, connections are made with the images and ideas discussed in previous chapters. Finally, the chapter describes the limitations of educational research in general.

Taken together, the research findings presented in this chapter build a powerful argument for inquiry-based teaching and learning of science.

HOW STUDENTS LEARN SCIENCE

A recent report of the National Research Council entitled *How People Learn* (Bransford et al., 1999) demonstrates a broad consensus about how learning occurs. The report synthesized research from a variety of fields, including cognition, child development, and brain functioning. It also drew from research across content areas, with important contributions from the research on science learning.

Several general findings from the study are presented below, with illustrations drawn from research on science learning. These findings are in turn connected to the definition of inquiry introduced in Chapter 2 and used throughout this volume.

Research Finding 1: Understanding science is more than knowing facts. The emphasis of recent research has been on learning for understanding, which means gaining knowledge that can be used and applied to novel situations. Research on people who have expertise in a field demonstrates that they (a) have a deep foundation of factual knowledge, (b) understand facts and ideas in the context of a conceptual framework, and (c) organize knowledge in ways that allow for retrieval and application (Donovan et al., 1999). They also have inquiry procedures available that help them solve new problems efficiently and effectively. Their extensive and well-organized bodies of knowledge affect what they notice and how they organize, represent, and interpret the information in their environments. In turn, this interaction with their environments affects their abilities to remember, reason, and solve problems. For their knowledge to be usable in these ways, it must be connected and organized through important concepts. Experts must know the contexts in which knowledge is applicable and must be able to transfer that knowledge from one

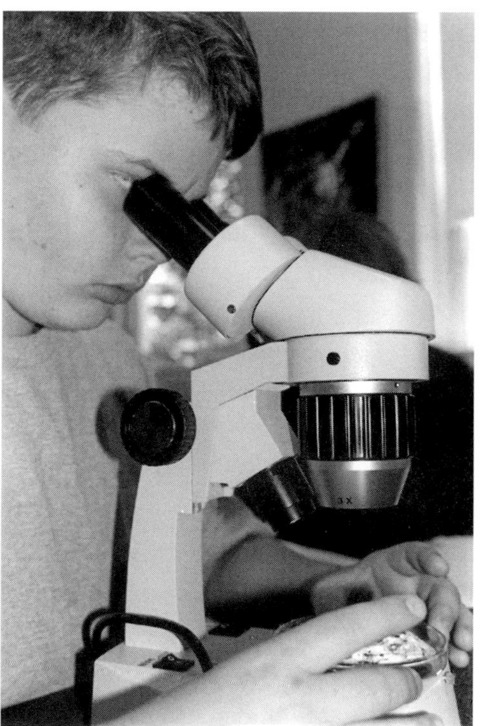

context to another. What this means for science teaching is that for students to be able to use what they learn, they must understand the major concepts, build a strong base of supporting factual information, and know how to apply their knowledge effectively (Bransford et al., 1999).

Knowing science, however, is not only knowing scientific concepts and information. The research on learning indicates that students need to develop abilities to inquire similar to those in the *Standards* (and discussed in Chapter 2). All students need to learn strategies for scientific thinking (Linn et al., 1989). They should be able to describe a problem in detail before attempting a solution, determine what relevant information should enter the analysis of a problem, and decide which procedures can be used to generate descriptions and analyses of the problem (Glaser, 1992). Through scientific inquiry, students can gain new data to change their ideas or deepen their understanding of important scientific principles. They also develop important abilities such as reasoning, careful observing, and logical analysis (Minstrell, 1989; Rosebery et al., 1992). Thus the research on expertise confirms the importance of helping students understand major scientific concepts and related factual information, and develop a variety of inquiry abilities.

Research Finding 2: Students build new knowledge and understanding on what they already know and believe. Students have conceptions about natural phenomena, and those conceptions influence their learning. When consistent with ideas accepted by the scientific community, this "prior" or "informal" knowledge forms a strong base on which to build deeper understandings. Many learners' preconceptions, however, are inconsistent with accepted, extant science knowledge. These preconceptions are generally ideas that are reasonable and appropriate in a limited context, but students inappropriately apply them to situations where they do not work (Anderson and Smith, 1987; Driver et al., 1985; 1994). Students often hold tenaciously to these ideas, and their preconceptions can be resistant to change, particularly using conventional teaching strategies (Wandersee et al., 1994). For example, many students continue to believe that the earth is hotter in the summer because it is closer to the sun, even after being "taught" the correct reason. In Chapter 3, Mr. Gilbert uncovered and worked with his students' preconceived ideas about the moon's phases as did Mr. Hull with his students' conceptions of forces on stationary objects. In Chapter 5, Lezlie comments about recognizing her own "misconceptions" about physics, which made her pay more attention to those of her students. The research on students' conceptions of science principles is substantial, addressing a wide range of scientific areas (Driver et al., 1985; 1994; Minstrell, 1989; 1992; Novak, 1987).

Research Finding 3: Students formulate new knowledge by modifying and refining their current concepts and by adding new concepts to what they already know (Driver et al., 1985; 1994). The research on conceptual change indicates that students change their ideas when they find these ideas to be unsatisfactory, that is, when their present ideas do not sufficiently describe or explain an event or observation. Further, they change their ideas when they discover alternatives that seem plausible and appear to be more useful (Hewson and Thorley, 1989). This is what happened with students in Ms. Flores's elementary classroom as they considered why the trees grow differently, illustrated in Chapter 3, and Lillian's college students, whose understanding of electrical circuits grew substantially as they were challenged with more complex phenomena, described in Chapter 5. Other research suggests that whether and how learners change their ideas depends on what they view as evidence for or against a competing idea (Duschl and Gitomer, 1991). This relates to students' views of science and scientific explanations. Students often think of science as a collection of facts to be memorized and explanations as reports of isolated events. When this is true, there is less likelihood that students will actively

seek evidence for different explanations, think about why one set of evidence is stronger than another, and make good decisions about which explanation has the most support. Their ideas about natural phenomena are unlikely to change on the basis of sound scientific reasoning (Songer and Linn, 1991).

Research Finding 4: Learning is mediated by the social environment in which learners interact

with others. Saying that learners construct their own knowledge does not imply that they do so alone. Research indicates that learners benefit from opportunities to articulate their ideas to others, challenge each others' ideas, and, in doing so, reconstruct their ideas (Rosebery et al., 1992). Students in every vignette in Chapter 3 had all these opportunities as they developed explanations for basic observations like dying trees, moon phases, and murkiness of lake water. Teachers in Chapter 5 similarly experienced and then recognized the benefits of collaboration to their learning of both science and pedagogy.

Research Finding 5: Effective learning requires that students take control of their own learning. Students need to learn to recognize when they understand and when they need more information. They need to be able and know when to ask: What kinds of evidence do I need in order to believe particular claims? How can I build my own theories of phenomena and test them effectively (White and Frederiksen, in press)? Good learners articulate their own ideas, compare and contrast them with those of others, and provide reasons why they accept one point of view rather than another. They are "metacognitive," that is, they are aware and capable of monitoring and regulating their thoughts and their knowledge (American Psychological Association, 1993). Students in all four Chapter 3 vignettes worked hard to devise clear arguments for their conclusions; Mr. Gilbert's students went further by reflecting on how good the models were that they used to explain moon phases and how they needed to account for the models' deficiencies. In Chapter 5, Sandy and her teacher colleagues shared student work and videos of their teaching to reflect on how what they were doing did or did not help their students learn. Research underscores the value of student self-assessment in developing their understanding of science concepts, as well as their abilities to reason and think critically (Black and Wiliam, 1998b; Duschl and Gitomer, 1997). As Black and Wiliam (1998b) note, it is only when students are trained in and given opportunities for self-assessment that "they can understand the main purposes of their learning and thereby grasp what they need to do to achieve." (p. 143)

Research Finding 6: The ability to apply knowledge to novel situations, that is, transfer of learning, is affected by the degree to which students learn with understanding. In order to use what they learn, learners must achieve an initial threshold of knowledge, practice using the knowledge in a variety of contexts, and then get feedback on how well they did. To be able to use their learning in the future, people need time during their learning to grapple with specific information, explore underlying concepts, and make connections to what they already know. They need tasks that are challenging but not frustrating and social opportunities to see the usefulness of what they are learning and to see its impact on others. Finally, they are more apt to apply what they know to novel situations if they have learned to extract the underlying themes and principles from their learning experiences (Bransford et al., 1999; Bruer, 1993; Byrnes, 1996). Students in Ms. Idoni's class, for example, were called on to apply their learning to a hypothetical situation of a fish kill, which was quite different from what they had observed in the lake. They needed to apply their understanding of the nature and consequences of pollution to this new challenge. Several teachers in Chapter 5, for example, Steve in his physics teaching and Lezlie with her kindergarten classes, took the ideas they learned through professional development directly into their classrooms.

These findings from research into learning connect in important ways with the definition of inquiry presented earlier. The *Standards* stress understanding major science concepts and building abilities to "do" science. These are the capacities recognized in experts, who have a well-structured understanding of the major ideas in their field and inquiry abilities that help them solve new problems efficiently and effectively (Finding 1). The research suggests that to develop expertise requires achieving both kinds of outcomes specified in the *Standards*: learning subject matter as well as the thinking strategies needed to use and inquire more deeply into those concepts.

Inquiry focuses on a scientifically-oriented question, problem, or phenomenon, beginning with what the learner knows and actively engaging him or her in the search for answers and explanations (Findings 2, 3). This search involves gathering and analyzing information; making inferences and predictions; and actively creating, modifying, and discarding some explanations (Finding 3). As students work together to discuss the evidence, compare results, and, with teacher guidance, connect their results with scientific knowledge, their understanding broadens (Findings 3, 4). As they develop their abilities to question, reason, and think critically about scientific phenomena, they take increasing control of their own learning (Finding 5). They can use their broadened science knowledge and inquiry abilities to address other questions and problems and to develop or test explanations for other phenomena of interest (Finding 6). In this way, effective learning involves the reorganization of the deep structure of one's thought processes. The learner comes to own a new idea or new way of thinking. Without this, school learning becomes a transitory experience with little application to future thought and action.

EFFECTIVE LEARNING ENVIRONMENTS AND EXPERIENCES

Research on student learning leads to a question of great practical importance: What kinds of learning experiences and learning environments promote science learning? The research synthesized in *How People Learn* (Bransford et al., 1999) suggests that effective teachers employ strategies that attend to four elements: learners, knowledge, assessment, and community.

Learner-centered environments pay careful attention to the knowledge, skills, attitudes, and beliefs that learners bring to the educational setting. Accomplished teachers respect and understand their students' prior experiences and understandings and use these as a foundation on which to build new understandings (Duckworth, 1987; American Psychological Association, 1993). For example, in Chapter 3, Ms. Flores and Mr. Gilbert both elicited students' knowledge before launching into their new topics and used what they learned to focus student inquiries. In Chapter 5, Joanna and her teacher colleagues at the science museum were carefully supported to begin with what they knew and pursue questions of interest in order to deepen and broaden their understandings.

Research on students who are learning English as a second language points clearly to the need for teachers' attention to what these students bring to the science classroom (Fradd and Lee, 1999; Rosebery et al., 1992).

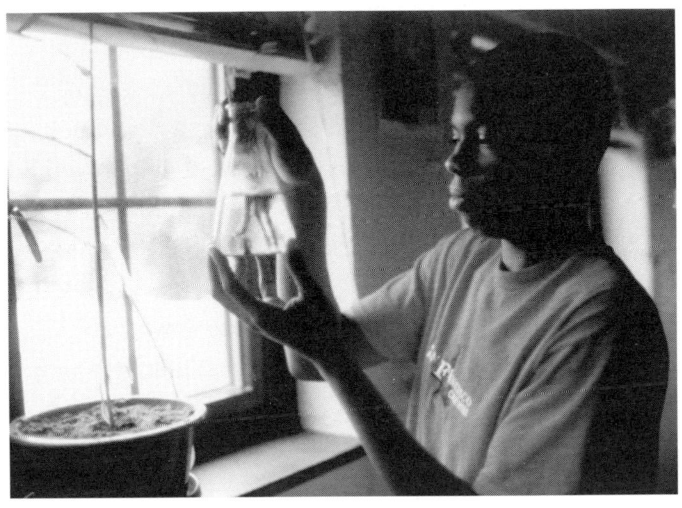

Students from diverse language backgrounds vary greatly in their abilities to express, communicate, discuss, and demonstrate their understandings of science and of scientific concepts by virtue of their developing language abilities (CCSSO, 1999). Further, like all students, they vary in what they understand of science; this is complicated by the fact that their home cultures may not have exposed them to science as generally taught in schools. As Fradd and Lee (1999) note, "the norms and values of science are more familiar to students from the mainstream middle-class than to students from diverse languages and cultures (p. 15)." Therefore, learner-centered environments in which teachers build new learning on the knowledge, skills, attitudes, and beliefs that students bring to the classroom, are critical to science learning of English language learners.

Knowledge-centered environments help students develop well-organized bodies of knowledge and organize that knowledge so that it supports planning and strategic thinking. In these kinds of environments, students "learn their way around" a discipline. Like experts, they are able to make connections among ideas. In these kinds of learning environments, teachers help students think about the general principles or "big" ideas in a subject. When they learn new knowledge, students also learn where it applies and how. They have opportunities to practice using it in novel situations. Their learning environments promote the sort of problem-solving behavior observed in experts (Bransford et al., 1999). All of the Chapter 3 vignettes showed students attacking problems using their firsthand observations and science knowledge from other sources to build new general ideas. In Chapter 5, Gabe's and Steve's field experiences, Joanna's experience in the science museum, and Lezlie's experience in the physics laboratory created opportunities to learn science through firsthand observations gained from "doing" science.

Assessment-centered environments help students learn to monitor and regulate their own learning. They learn to question why they believe what they believe and whether there is sufficient evidence for their beliefs (White and Frederiksen, in press). These environments provide students with opportunities for feedback and revision. Assessment-centered environments also help teachers shape classroom activities, diagnose students' ideas and products, and guide teachers' decisions (Duschl and Gitomer, 1997; Gitomer and Duschl, 1995). As Black and Wiliam (1998b) note from their extensive review of the research on classroom assessment, "there is a body of firm evidence that formative assessment is an essential component of classroom work, and that its development can raise standards of achievement." (p. 148) Assessment plays a major role in the classrooms depicted in Chapter 3, as elaborated in Chapter 4.

Community-centered environments require students to articulate their ideas, challenge those of others, and negotiate deeper meaning along with other learners. Such environments encourage people to learn from one another. They value the search for understanding and acknowledge that mistakes are a necessary ingredient if learning is to occur. Studies of effective environments for learning science "emphasize the importance of class discussions for developing a language for talking about scientific ideas, for making students' thinking explicit to the teacher and the rest of the class, and for learning to develop a line of argumentation that uses what one has learned to solve problems and explain phenomena and observations." (Bransford et al., 1999, p. 171) Further, such environments are open to new ideas and ways of thinking, as the community members are both encouraged and expected to provide each other with feedback and work to incorporate new ideas into their thinking. The development of community and use of community as both stimulus and context for learning is well illustrated in the Chapter 3 vignettes and in the teachers' stories of their own collaborative learning in Chapter 5.

A number of studies have examined learning environments that incorporate all four of these elements. In their studies of high school physics teaching and learning, Minstrell (1982, 1989, 1992) assessed the following research-based instructional techniques: making students' thinking visible; bridging from students' preconceptions to scientifically-based conceptions; and facilitating students' ability to restructure their own knowledge. The approach depicts the teacher's role as coach in developing student understanding of major ideas in physics such as force and motion, rather than as a dispenser of facts.

In their studies of young Haitian students' development of scientific ideas, Rosebery et al. (1992) describe classrooms in which students explore their own questions, design studies, collect information, analyze data and

construct evidence, consult experts and literature to help them interpret their test results, and debate the conclusions they derive. The teacher's role is to guide and support them as they explore problems, define questions, and build and argue about theories. The learning environment these researchers describe incorporates all the features discussed above.

Many research studies of environments in which students learn for understanding use standardized measures of student achievement, although these measures do not emphasize the kinds of deep understanding on which the research is focused. According to the National

Research Council (Bransford et al., 1999), "in some cases there is evidence that teaching for understanding can increase scores on standardized measures (e.g., Resnick et al., 1991); in other cases, scores on standardized tests are unaffected, but the students show sizable advantages on assessments that are sensitive to their comprehension and understanding rather than reflecting sheer memorization (e.g., Carpenter et al., 1996; Secules et al., 1997)" (p. 177).

Research on effective learning and learning environments has interesting parallels to the process of scientific inquiry itself (Duschl, 1992). Both learner and scientist actively construct knowledge through confrontation with a new question, problem, or phenomenon, gathering information, and creating explanations. Throughout the process of inquiry, both constantly evaluate and reevaluate the nature and strength of evidence and share and then critique their explanations and those of others. A classroom in which students use scientific inquiry to learn is one that resembles those that research has found the most effective for learning for understanding. This consequence strengthens the argument for inquiry-based teaching.

RESEARCH ON INQUIRY-BASED SCIENCE TEACHING

The final line of research supporting the use of inquiry in teaching and learning involves the study of specific science programs. In the 1960s and 1970s, a number of curriculum projects, including the Biological Sciences Curriculum Study (BSCS) programs in biology, the Physical Sciences Study Committee (PSSC) materials in physics, and the Science Curriculum Improvement Study (SCIS) and Elementary Science Study (ESS) units for elementary school science, incorporated approaches to teaching and learning that today would fall, at least in part, under the heading of inquiry. The term "inquiry" was used explicitly in studies of various NSF-funded curriculum projects (Shymansky et al., 1983). These studies examined teaching techniques such as "inquiry-discovery" (Wise and Okey, 1983), project-based science instruction (Blumenfeld, 1994; Krajcik et al., 1994; Ladewski et al., 1994; Marx et al., 1994), and newer technology-enhanced curriculum (White and Frederiksen, in press). Although this research suffers from the lack of a shared, precise definition of inquiry, it is possible to look for patterns that show up across studies.

In the 1980s, several meta-analyses were done of the original research projects, in which the individual projects are re-analyzed as a whole to yield broader results than any one study alone can produce. In general, these meta-analyses show that inquiry-based teaching produces positive, although in some cases modest, results across a variety of indicators. For example, studies of inquiry-oriented curriculum programs (Shymansky et al., 1983; Shymansky et al., 1990; Mechling and Oliver, 1983) demonstrated significant positive effects on various quantitative measures, including cognitive achievement, process skills, and attitudes toward science. (However, there was essentially no correlation between positive results and expert ratings of the degree of inquiry in the materials.) Wise and Okey (1983) showed a positive effect for what they called inquiry-discovery teaching for cognitive outcomes. Although Lott (1983) found only small differences between inductive and deductive approaches, the differences were in favor of the inductive approach, which incorporates elements of inquiry teaching and learning. Other meta-analyses conducted independently at approximately the same time, such as those by Weinstein et al. (1982) and Bredderman (1982), produced similar positive results. Studies in particular subject areas, such as biology (Hurd, 1998), also generally favored inquiry-based approaches.

Other studies have demonstrated a range of other specific outcomes from inquiry-based teaching, including vocabulary knowledge and conceptual understanding (Lloyd, 1988), critical thinking (Narode, 1987), inquiry abilities and physics understanding (White and Frederiksen, in press), and positive attitudes toward science (Shymansky et al., 1983). In studies of underrepresented and underserved populations, inquiry-oriented strategies enhanced scientific ways of thinking, talking, and writing for language learners and helped them to acquire English and reasoning skills (Rosebery et al., 1992).

David Haury (1993) has provided a brief, but thorough, summary of the above research. His review concludes that inquiry-oriented teaching can result in outcomes that include scientific literacy, familiarity with science processes, vocabulary knowledge,

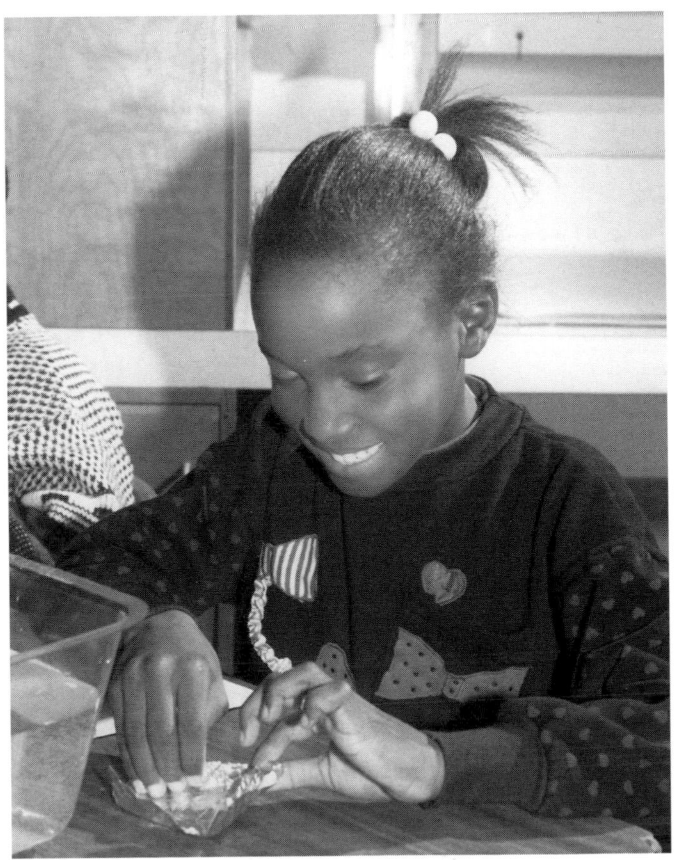

conceptual understanding, critical thinking, and positive attitudes toward science. Another review from Flick (1995) addresses research on explicit instruction as well as inquiry-oriented instruction. He notes that explicit teaching can produce major gains in student achievement on selected kinds of instructional objectives, but goes on to point out that "The high levels of teacher supervision implied by explicit teaching models may not foster the kinds of thinking required for instruction with complex and more ill-structured tasks" (p. 17).

In the final analysis, review of the research on the effectiveness of inquiry-based teaching and learning leads to a discussion of one's objectives for science education. If one accepts the full sweep of content in the *National Science Education Standards*, including conceptual understanding of science principles, comprehension of the nature of scientific inquiry, development of the abilities for inquiry, and a grasp of applications of science knowledge to societal and personal issues, this body of research clearly suggests that teaching through inquiry is effective.

Research on inquiry is continuing. Some studies are directed at special student populations. For example, research on teachers' roles in promoting science inquiry with students from diverse language backgrounds, although in its infancy, has pointed to the need to consider carefully how best to design and structure inquiries for these students (Fradd and Lee, 1999). Research by Delpit (1995) suggests the importance of students receiving explicit instruction in the skills they need to engage in science inquiry and learn from inquiry experiences. Other research by Rosebery et al. (1992), as noted earlier, indicates that students learning English can successfully engage in science inquiry and learn science concepts as well as the language in culture of science. In their research on students with learning disabilities, Scruggs et al. (1993) found significantly higher learning with an inquiry-oriented approach. Studies continue in other countries as well. A study in university-level biochemistry in Turkey (Basaga et al., 1994) found higher achievement for students using an inquiry-oriented approach than those in a traditional approach. Another university-level study in Ireland (Heywood and Heywood, 1992) found similar results on pupil tests for students in discovery and expository approaches, but greater student motivation with discovery approaches. A pattern of general support for inquiry-based teaching continues to emerge from the research.

THE LIMITATIONS AND CONTRIBUTIONS OF EDUCATIONAL RESEARCH REGARDING DECISIONS ABOUT POLICY

In addition to examining the research base for inquiry, it is important to understand what research can and cannot provide. As Hiebert (1999) points out in his discussions of the research support for the national mathematics standards, the question about the strength of that research is fair, even though it does not have a simple answer. Simple answers, in fact, do not provide the credibility necessary to support a substantially different approach to teaching and learning.

Research has several limitations. First, research cannot determine goals or standards, which are primarily a reflection of values (Hiebert, 1999). The standards being written by some states and districts are largely lists of factual information to be memorized. These reflect a different set of values than those behind the *National Science Education Standards*, which focus on major concepts in science and on learning for understanding. The methods of teaching most appropriate for these different kinds of standards vary as well. Inquiry-based teaching that encourages questioning, developing alternative explanations, challenging each others' ideas, and conducting open-ended, long-term projects may not be most appropriate if the goal is for students to memorize information.

Second, research alone cannot establish what is best. Education is a very complicated enterprise, and most outcomes are influenced by more factors than can be identified, let alone controlled.

Third, research cannot prescribe a curriculum or pedagogical approach for all students and for all times. Such decisions must always be made within a given context, and the level of confidence with which they are made changes with new information and new conditions.

This said, there are several things that research can do (Hiebert, 1999). It can be used to make decisions that are based on probabilities that a certain outcome will ensue. Thus, research can inform decisions but not guarantee that they are right for all circumstances. By reviewing many studies done under a variety of conditions and looking for patterns in the results, decision-makers can increase the possibility of success. Indeed, looking at a variety of studies can sensitize decision-makers to the complexities involved in a decision and to the crucial issues involved.

Research also can help prevent mistakes. It can show that some goals, however lofty, are unattainable. And it can probe below the surface to indicate why certain results occur: why certain programs do not work as expected or certain goals are not achieved. Of particular interest when student learning is being assessed is the nature of the opportunities students had to learn and achieve the outcomes.

Research can also show what is possible and what looks promising. It can illuminate what students are capable of, what improvements are feasible, and what parts of reform visions are reasonable. In this respect, research can suggest what is not known and could benefit from some additional examination. For example, given the importance of formative assessment established in Chapter 4, research has begun to focus on listening and feedback in science classrooms.

THE CASE FOR STANDARDS-BASED INQUIRY

The research on inquiry-based teaching and learning comes from a number of sources. The research base on learning and on effective learning environments makes a strong case for inquiry-based approaches. Research on programs and materials that incorporate inquiry also shows positive influences on many critical dimensions of student learning. Although the research demands a clearer definition of terms and falls short of illuminating all the complexities of teaching for understanding, the evidence from several streams of research is both positive and promising.

Effective science teachers take a number of approaches to teaching. However, as this chapter has argued, their use of inquiry can have a powerful influence on their students' science learning.

How People Learn
Brain,
Mind,
Experience,
and
School
NATIONAL RESEARCH COUNCIL
Resources for Teaching
MIDDLE SCHOOL
Science
National
Science
Resources
Center
Smithsonian Institution
National Academy of Sciences
National Academy of Engineering
Institute of Medicine

Resources for Teaching
ELEMENTARY SCHOOL
Science
NATIONAL SCIENCE RESOURCES CENTER
NATIONAL ACADEMY OF SCIENCES • SMITHSONIAN INSTITUTION

explore
Selecting
Instructional Materials
learn
A Guide for
K-12 Science
understand
NATIONAL RESEARCH COUNCIL

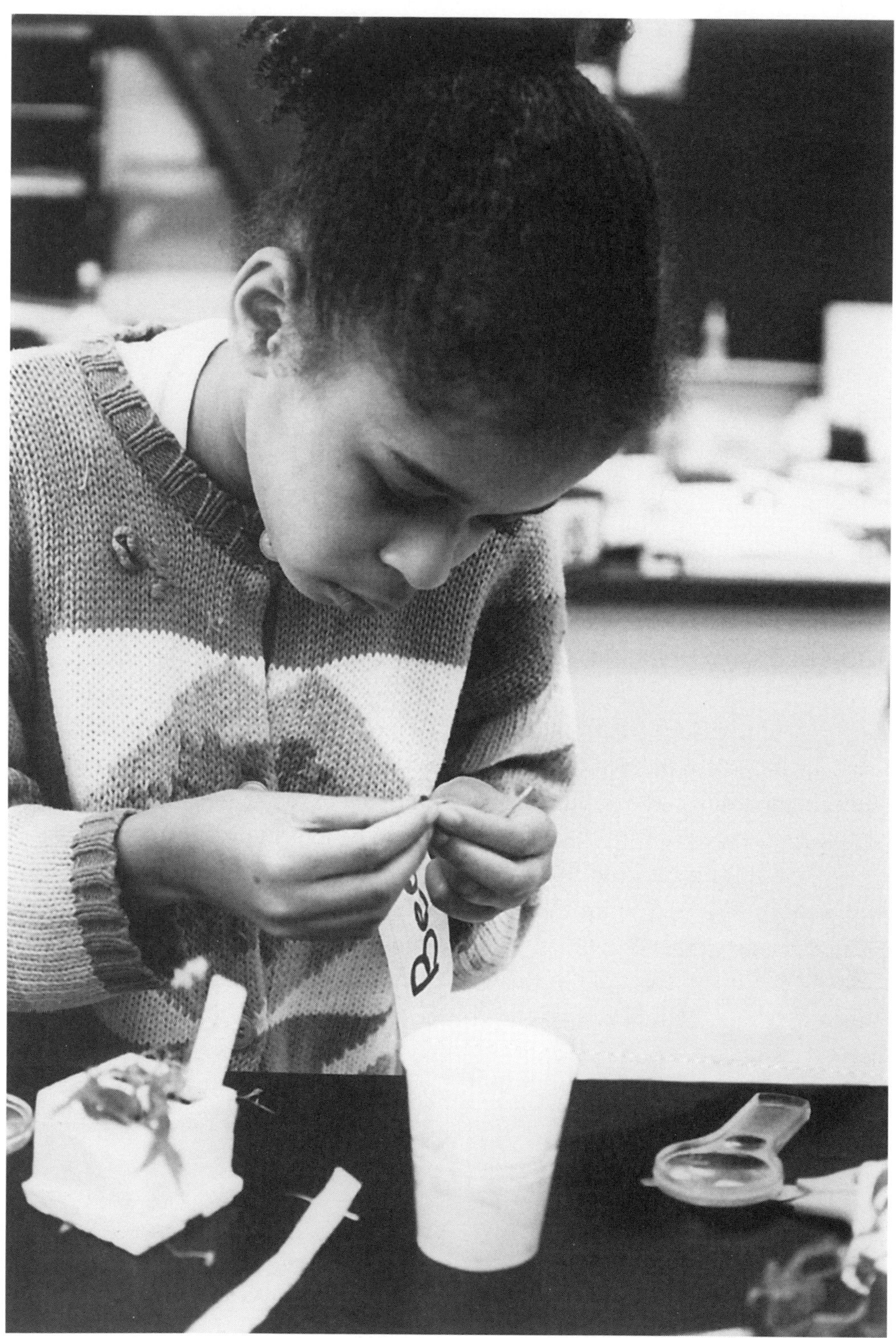

7
Frequently Asked Questions About Inquiry

Science teachers, administrators, and teacher educators (both preservice and inservice) often face difficult questions about inquiry-based teaching and learning. Many of these questions they raise themselves. Others come from teachers, administrators, preservice teachers, students, and parents who are unfamiliar with this perspective on learning and teaching science. This chapter presents answers to some of the most commonly asked questions. Other chapters respond to additional questions that may be asked.

In inquiry-based teaching, is it ever okay to tell students the answers to their questions?

Yes. Understanding requires knowledge, and not all the knowledge that is needed can be acquired by inquiry. Decisions about how to respond to students' questions depend on the teacher's goals and the context of the discussion. For example, a student may pose the question "What is the boiling point of water at sea level?" One way to respond to that question would be to set up a simple investigation to find out. The investigation could set the stage for more complex inquiries. If learning to use reference material is important, a teacher might have the student look up the information. Or, if there is a higher priority for how the student spends his or her time, the teacher could simply provide the answer.

The important point is that investigations lead to deeper understanding and greater transfer of knowledge. Decisions about responding to students' questions should reflect that fact.

Q

Should a teacher ever say "no" to an investigation that students propose themselves?

A

Yes. As noted in the previous answer, a teacher's response should depend on his or her goals for the students. What might they learn if they conducted the inquiry? Are there cost or safety concerns that might weigh against doing a particular investigation? What topics and approaches are most feasible in light of the school science curriculum and guiding standards? Would it be best for students to design their own investigations or conduct investigations proposed either by the teacher or provided by the instructional materials?

A large number of learning outcomes, particularly inquiry abilities, are best learned through investigations, and those motivated by students' own questions can be invaluable learning opportunities. Students also learn the characteristics of questions that can be properly investigated if they have opportunities to pose and investigate questions. One approach might be for teachers to ask students (or help them determine) what learning goals they will achieve by pursuing their questions and which goals they will not achieve.

The fact that students are motivated to ask questions and inquire into them is an indication that the teacher is making science relevant and exciting. But not all investigations that students propose will be worth pursuing.

Q

Is it more important for students to learn the abilities of scientific inquiry or scientific concepts and principles?

A

They need to learn both. Furthermore, as the *National Science Education Standards* make clear, these are equally important learning outcomes that support each other.

In many teaching and learning sequences, students employ inquiry abilities to develop understanding of scientific concepts. Sometimes teachers assume that students develop inquiry abilities just because they use them. However, there is no guarantee of this. Instead, teachers have to work to ensure a proper balance between learning scientific concepts and inquiry abilities.

The development of inquiry abilities should be an explicit student learning outcome. Teachers can select specific abilities on which to focus and develop strategies to achieve those outcomes.

The vignettes in Chapter 3 demonstrate how the learning of science content and improving inquiry abilities can be symbiotic. Scientific concepts and inquiry abilities switch from primary to secondary focus and back again as needed to promote the effective integration of both. Also, as pointed out in Chapter 6, research describes expertise as knowing both the subject matter content (the "big ideas" of the disciplines) and the ways of inquiring into new questions — and it makes the case for teaching both.

How can students do a science investigation before they have learned the vocabulary words with which to describe the results?

A

Scientific investigations, whether conducted by students or scientists, begin with observations of something interesting or perplexing, which lead to scientific questions, and then to reflections on what the person already knows about the question. It may seem that students need some concepts and vocabulary to begin, but investigations can be designed and carried out without knowing all the specific terms and definitions involved. In fact, the observations, data collection, and analysis involved in an investigation generally provide the context for developing operational definitions, science concepts, inquiry abilities, and an understanding of scientific inquiry, which can later be associated with names or "vocabulary." This is well illustrated in the vignettes in earlier chapters, and is advocated in the Foreword.

Knowing vocabulary does not necessarily help students develop or understand explanations. Rather, once students begin to build and understand explanations for their observations, the proper names and definitions associated with those events become useful and meaningful. In essence, words become symbols for their understanding of the phenomena. As a result, definitions based on direct experience more often result in understanding than just memorizing words.

The issue of vocabulary development is particularly relevant to working with students who are English-language learners. As noted in

Chapters 4 and 6, teachers of these students need to pay special attention to whether assessment of students' science knowledge is confounded by their use of the language, and to how student learning is supported when their language skills are just developing. As noted in research synthesized by Fradd and Lee (1999), when formulating their teaching strategies, teachers need to consider how stu-

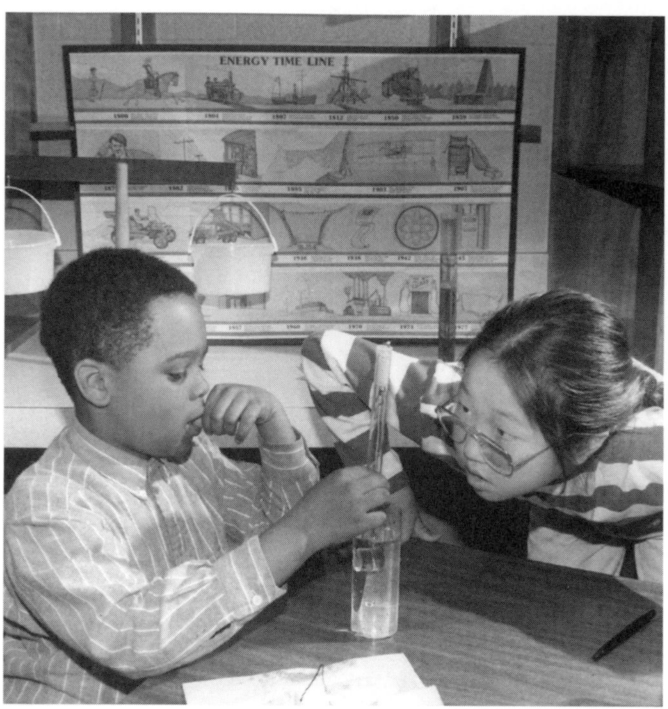

dents of diverse cultures and languages think about science, the experiences they have had in learning science, and, ultimately, how to structure new science learning experiences to optimize students' opportunities to learn important science concepts and inquiry abilities. The degree of structure given to lessons and the amount of direct "teaching" of inquiry skills need to depend on teachers' keen assessment of students' language development, current science knowledge, skills, and beliefs, and cultural orientations (Fradd and Lee, 1999).

Why did the Standards *choose to leave out the science process skills such as observing, classifying, predicting, and hypothesizing?*

The "process skills" emphasized in earlier science education reforms may appear to be missing from the *Standards*, but they are not. Rather, they are integrated into the broader abilities of scientific inquiry. As the *Standards* point out, "The standards on inquiry highlight the abilities of inquiry and the development of an understanding about scientific inquiry. Students at all grade levels and in every domain of science should have the opportunity to use scientific inquiry and develop the ability to think and act in ways associated with inquiry, including asking questions, planning and conducting investigations, using appropriate tools and techniques to gather data, thinking critically and logically about relationships between evidence and explanations, constructing and analyzing alternative explanations, and communicating scientific arguments" (National Research Council, 1996, p. 105). The *Standards* thus include the "processes of science" and require that students combine those processes and scientific knowledge to develop their understanding of science.

Do the Standards *imply that teachers should use inquiry in every lesson?*

No. In fact, the *Standards* emphasize that many teaching approaches can serve the goal of learning science:

"Although the *Standards* emphasize inquiry, this should not be interpreted as recommending a single approach to science teaching. Teachers should use different strategies to develop the knowledge, understandings, and abilities described in the content standards. Conducting hands-on science activities does not guarantee inquiry, nor is reading about science incompatible with inquiry" (National Research Council, 1996, p. 23).

Everyone knows that investigations often take longer than other ways of learning, and there are simply not enough hours or days in the school year to learn everything through inquiry. The challenge to the teacher is to make the most judicious choices about which learning goals can be best reached through inquiry (remembering that deep understanding is most likely to result from inquiry), and what the nature of that inquiry should be (see Chapter 2 for some variations). Other teaching strategies can come into play for other learning goals.

Q *How can teachers cover everything in the curriculum if they use inquiry-oriented materials and teaching methods?*

A As noted above, the *Standards* do not suggest that all science should be learned through inquiry. However, investigations are important ways to promote deep understanding of science content and the only way to help students practice inquiry abilities. So there is still the issue of coverage vs. learning strategy to address.

Analysis of data collected in the Third International Mathematics and Science Study (TIMSS) reveals that the typical U.S. eighth-grade science textbook includes about 65 topics. A similarly large number of science topics appears yearly in state and local science standards and curriculum guides. Teachers, understandably, feel obligated to teach all of the topics called for in their local science curriculum. The result can be the "mile wide and an inch deep" curriculum often decried in U.S. education. Furthermore, research shows that this "cover everything" approach provides few opportunities for students to acquire anything but surface knowledge on any topic (Schmidt et al., 1997).

There are several steps that teachers and administrators can take to deal with this problem. They can renegotiate the expectations embodied in the curriculum. They can carefully select a few areas to emphasize, spending more time teaching those areas though inquiry. They can carefully analyze the curriculum expectations and combine several learning outcomes in lessons and units. They can work with other grade-level teachers to eliminate the redundancies that often exist in a curriculum, but rarely deepen understanding. If they teach subjects other than science, they can integrate science outcomes into other subject areas (for example, presenting the findings of an investigation in a language arts lesson).

Teachers and administrators can be helped by district and state decision-makers who can reduce the number of topics that teachers are required to teach.

Q *How much structure and how much freedom should teachers provide in inquiry-oriented science lessons?*

A The type and amount of structure can vary depending on what is needed to keep students productively engaged in pursuit of a learning outcome. Students with little experience in conducting scientific inquiries will probably require more structure. For example, a teacher might want to select the question driving an investigation. She or he also might decide to provide a series of steps and procedures for the students guided by specific questions and group discussion. The instructional materials themselves often provide questions, suggestions, procedures, and data tables to guide student inquiry.

As students mature and gain experience with inquiry, they will become adept at clarifying good questions, designing investigations to test ideas, interpreting data, and forming explanations based on data. With such students, the teacher still should monitor by observation, ask questions for clarification, and make suggestions when needed. Often, teachers begin the school year providing considerable structure and then gradually provide more opportunities for student-centered investigations.

Many teachers in the primary grades have considerable success with whole class projects. An example is a class experiment to answer the question: "What is the 'black stuff' on the bottom of the aquarium?" Guided by the teacher, the students can focus and clarify the question. They can ponder where the "black stuff" came from based on their prior knowledge of goldfish, snails, and plants. Using their prior knowledge, the students then can propose explanations and decide what they need to set up a fair test. How many aquariums will they need? What

will be in each aquarium? What are they looking for? How will they know when they have answered the question? After a number of well-structured whole-class inquiries with ample time to discuss procedures and process as well as conclusions and explanations, students are more prepared to design and conduct their own inquires such as the "tree problem" conducted by Mrs. Graham's fifth-grade class described in Chapter 1.

How can teachers use inquiry and maintain control of their students?

To have productive experiences, inquiry requires considerable planning and organization on the part of both teachers and students. Teachers need to create systems for organization and management of materials and guidelines for student use of materials and conversation. Students need to learn how to work with materials in an organized fashion, communicate their ideas with one another, listen to each other's ideas with respect, and accept responsibility for their own learning. In addition, it always is helpful when students know what is expected of them in terms of behavior and performance. As students become collaborators, they recognize the conditions for progress themselves and need less external control, as noted in Chapter 4.

How much do teachers need to know about inquiry and about science subject matter to teach science through inquiry?

The more teachers know about inquiry and about science subject matter, and the more they themselves are effective inquirers, the better equipped they are to engage their students in inquiries that will help them understand scientific concepts and inquiry. It generally does not work for teachers to stay one step ahead of the students when using an inquiry-oriented program.

However, to a certain extent, teachers can develop their own understanding through inquiry as they investigate with their students and participate in professional development programs. Teachers also can consult with other teachers to learn more about a topic, refer to science background material printed in teachers guides, participate in professional development, and invite into the classroom parents, scientists, and others who have expertise to help in learning about the topic. Like their students, teachers should view themselves as learners, being eager to try new ways of teaching and extend and sharpen their subject matter knowledge. And they should use their own teaching to inquire about how to improve it, so that their ability to teach through inquiry increases in each successive year.

Q

What can teachers do who are provided only traditional instructional materials?

A

Teachers who want their students to learn to inquire and to learn through inquiry are hampered if their materials are text-based and focus students on memorizing scientific laws and terminology. However, a teacher's curriculum is not defined by the materials alone, but more broadly by what students focus their attention on, how they learn, and how and on what they are assessed. Teachers can use the *Standards* to determine goals for their students and decide which pieces of their materials they can use to help students reach those goals. They can consider decreasing the "cookbook" nature of whatever "labs" or hands-on activities are included with their materials and resequencing them to come *before* the readings or lectures so students can explore in a concrete may before learning the concepts and terms. Teachers can emphasize learning the major concepts and downplay the vocabulary. They can reconstruct test items to assess major science concepts, inquiry abilities, and understandings about inquiry; they can create one full and open inquiry for students to conduct for several weeks of class. And they can supplement the materials they are given with other materials they receive in professional development or from colleagues, or locate on the Web. The important thing is to determine a set of learning goals for students that reflect the *Standards* and let those guide how and what students learn. The next question provides ideas about non-text materials.

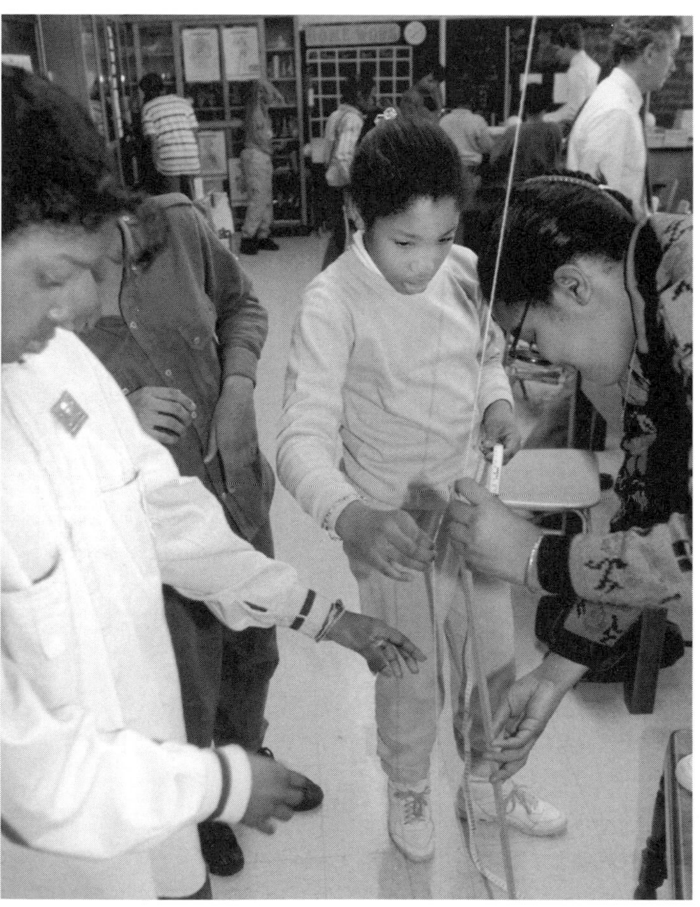

Q

Where can teachers get the equipment, materials, and supplies they need to teach through inquiry?

A

The National Science Foundation (NSF) has supported the development and field testing of a number of inquiry-oriented science curriculum programs (see Appendix C). These science programs, complete with student and teacher guides and materials for student activities or laboratories, are now available through commercial publishers. [See Appendix B for guide to materials selection or *Selecting Instructional Materials: A Guide for K-12 Science* (NRC, 1999b).] Many districts that have adopted these programs operate a centralized district materials center and loan the materials to teachers. Some districts supply a certain number of kits per grade level that are housed at school sites, with consumable supplies being replenished as needed by the district. Where districts have not adopted such programs, individual teachers and schools have developed a variety of mechanisms to provide needed materials and supplies. Some teachers develop a list of common household materials and supplies and have students collect them from home and bring them to school. Often, a group of teachers at a school will collaborate on a project so they can share materials.

If inquiry is to be the norm rather than an exception, schools must realize that materials are an essential element of teaching and should devote adequate resources and organizational structures to purchase and support use of appropriate materials. Teachers should not be expected to supply the essential supplies of teaching. Chapter 8 discusses strategies for supporting an inquiry-oriented program in more detail.

Q

Where can teacher educators obtain inquiry-oriented programs to use in preparing teachers?

A

Many teacher educators use curriculum materials developed for use in K-12 classrooms to help prospective students experience and learn to use inquiry-based materials. In addition, there are materials that can be used by teacher educators, at both the preservice and inservice levels, that are designed to use for teacher learning. Appendix C contains lists of inquiry-based materials for K-12 students and for use with teachers, both prospective and practicing.

What barriers are encountered when implementing inquiry-oriented approaches?

A

In addition to the external barriers teachers face, their beliefs and values about students, teaching, and the purposes of education can impose obstacles to inquiry-oriented approaches. Research demonstrates many of the predicaments that teachers face when considering new approaches. In a cross-site analysis of schools that had successfully initiated new approaches to science and mathematics instruction, three kinds of problems were noted: technical, political, and cultural (Anderson, 1996). Technical problems included limited teaching abilities, prior commitments (for example, to a textbook), the challenges of assessment, difficulties of group work, the challenges of new teacher roles, the challenges of new student roles, and inadequate in-service education. Political problems included limited in-service education (i.e., not sustained for a sufficient number of years), parental resistance, resistance from principals and superintendents, unresolved conflicts among teachers, lack of resources, and differing judgments about justice and fairness. Cultural problems — possibly the most important because beliefs and values are central to them — included the textbook issue, views of assessment, and the "preparation ethic" (i.e., an overriding commitment to "coverage" because of a perceived need to prepare students for the next level of schooling). In addition to this study's findings, barriers experienced currently include the widespread attitude that science is not a "basic" and the lack of appropriate instructional materials, both print and hands-on.

How can teachers improve their use of inquiry in science teaching?

A

Research indicates that teachers have a fairly pragmatic approach to teaching. They tend to focus on what works to involve students or manage their classrooms, rather than on melding theory and practice (Blumenfeld, 1994). Teachers anchor their understanding in classroom events and base their actions on stories and narratives more than on theories and propositional knowledge (Krajcik et al., 1994). Thus, theory, beliefs, values, and understandings are important as teachers acquire an inquiry approach, but teachers should not be expected to address such mental constructs in isolation from their teaching context.

Collaboration can be an important catalyst of change. New understandings develop and new classroom practices emerge when teachers collaborate with peers and experts. Collaboration addresses not only the technical problems of reform but cultural issues as well. As Anderson (1996) says, "Collaborative working relationships among teachers provide a very important context for the re-assessment of educational values and beliefs. In this context — where the focus is the actual work of each teachers' own students — one's values and beliefs are encountered at every turn. It is a powerful influence. The reforming teachers in our cases did not do their work in isolation; they worked together with fellow teachers in their team or department. Crucial reform work takes place in this context." Collaboration stimulates the reflection that is fundamental to changing beliefs, values, and understandings.

The appropriate professional development is a powerful way for teachers to improve their use of inquiry, as long as it is viewed as support for ongoing learning that is apt to take many years to change teaching practice significantly. Teachers can become wise consumers of professional development as they broaden their images and sources of learning, as well illustrated in Chapter 5.

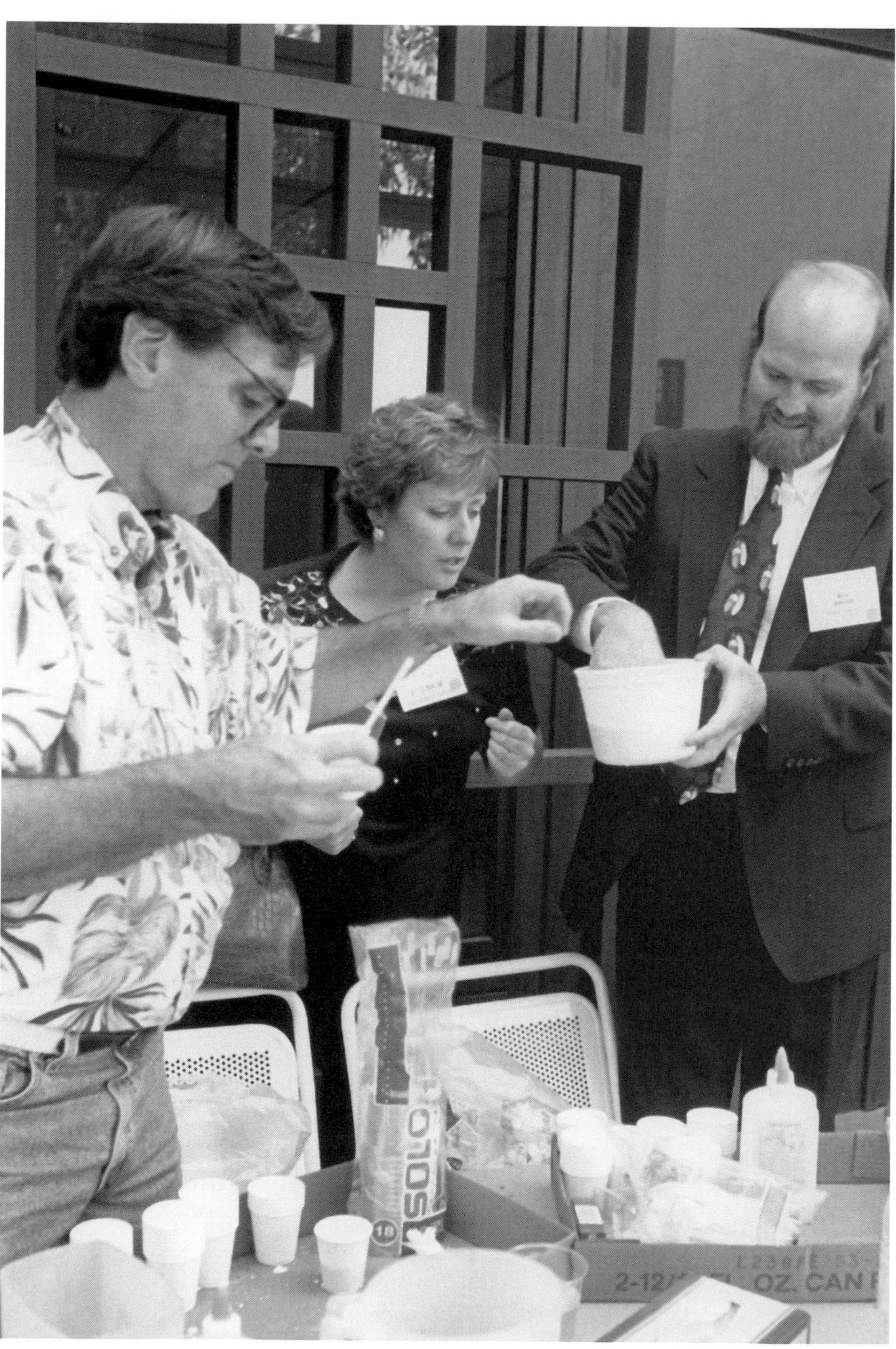
SOLO
OZ. CAN

8
Supporting Inquiry-Based Teaching and Learning

School principals, district administrators, and teacher leaders (including department chairs) are essential links in the adoption of inquiry as a way of teaching and learning. Extensive research evidence gathered over many years points to the importance of leadership from principals and other building level administrators in improving the quality of teaching and learning in their schools (Fullan, 1991; Prather, 1996). Support, guidance, and leadership are vital if teachers are to make major shifts from a traditional didactic style of teaching to one that emphasizes inquiry.

This support needs to have many dimensions, be on-going, and be tailored to meet the changing needs of the science staff as their teaching changes. Furthermore, it won't be just the science teachers who will be changing; if inquiry-based teaching is to succeed, students, parents, administrators, and teachers of other subjects will be changing as well.

Support for inquiry-based teaching and learning must encompass several different elements:

- Understanding what is meant by inquiry-based teaching and learning and knowing the advantages documented for inquiry by research;
- Understanding the change process that occurs when teachers are learning to teach through inquiry and students are learning to learn through inquiry so that all of their concerns can be anticipated and support can be tailored to meet their evolving needs; and
- Providing a coordinated support system that maximizes the staff's opportunity to grow and succeed in teaching through inquiry.

The coordinated support system likewise has a number of dimensions:

- Professional development
- Administrative assistance and support

- Providing instructional materials, kits, and equipment
- Communication with parents and the public
- Student assessment procedures aligned with the outcomes of inquiry
- Promoting inquiry and problem solving in other subject areas
- Teacher evaluation consistent with inquiry teaching

There is no magic formula or recipe to follow in incorporating inquiry into classrooms and schools. Success requires creativity and sensitivity to a particular context and set of goals.

UNDERSTANDING INQUIRY

Providing leadership and support for inquiry-based teaching and learning requires a working knowledge of the topic. It will be necessary to interpret and, at times, defend the practice with other administrators, parents, and staff members not engaged in inquiry-based teaching. Comparisons of inquiry as it is carried out by scientist and by students — such as the comparison in Chapter 1 — can begin to build a case for teaching and learning through inquiry.

The short history of inquiry presented in Chapter 2 underscores that it is not a new idea or fad. It is a powerful way to engage with the content of many disciples, not just science. In addition, the research evidence described in Chapter 6 documents some of the benefits students will gain from the experience. Not only will they learn the science they need in a deeper way, but the process of developing the abilities of inquiry will help them "learn how to learn," a valuable tool for all students.

UNDERSTANDING THE CHANGE PROCESS

Teaching and learning through inquiry is a new experience for most faculty members, administrators, parents, and students. It therefore requires a significant change in attitude and behavior on the part of all groups. As indicated in the previous section, inquiry has been a part of education for many years but in a form somewhat different than the specific outcomes described in the *Standards*. For example, inquiry-based teaching is not the same as teaching the processes of science or the "discovery learning" of 25 years ago because it places more emphasis on helping students develop the cognitive abilities scientists use to build scientific knowledge. Even for many teachers who are using kits or programs that claim to be inquiry-based, the approach to inquiry described in this report and in the *Standards*, if taken seriously, will be a significant change.

Fortunately, an extensive body of knowledge is available about how change can occur effectively in educational settings (Fullan, 1991, 1993).

Much of the recent literature on change recognizes that it is both an individual and an organizational phenomenon. Change affects every educator, administrator, and parent as well as the school or school system of which they are a part. This research also observes that change has a number of inherent features:

- Change is a process that takes time and persistence. Early in a change, people often feel awkward, frustrated, and clumsy as they try to use new behaviors and coordinate new materials, activities, and relationships. A significant change in teaching often takes several years to master.
- As individuals progress through a change process, their needs for support and assistance change.
- Change efforts are effective when the change to be made is clearly defined, assistance and opportunities to collaborate are available, and administrators and policies support the change.
- Most systems and institutions resist change.
- Organizations that are continuously improving have ongoing mechanisms for setting goals, taking actions, assessing the results of their actions, and making adjustments.
- Change is complex because it requires people to communicate with one another about complex topics in organizations that are, for the most part, large and structured (Loucks-Horsley et al., 1998).

Teaching through inquiry requires teachers to think and act in new ways, which takes the form of new skills, behaviors, instructional activities, assessment procedures, and so on. The conventional wisdom has been that changing teachers' thinking or beliefs will produce new behaviors. Research on teacher change, however, indicates that the process often works the other way around: changes in attitudes or belief patterns often result when teachers use a new practice and see their students benefiting from it (Guskey, 1986). Thus, changes in teaching often result in new attitudes and commitment to the new approach.

In addition, how teachers think and feel about change appears to be developmental. Many studies of individuals who have changed their practice over time — both on their own initiative and when decisions to do so were made by others — have revealed that individuals go through stages in how they feel about the change (Fullan, 1991; Hall and Hord, 1987; Huberman and Miles, 1984). Many educators find the progression of stages of concern a valuable lens for facilitating change in schools (Lieberman and Miller, 1991; Joyce, 1990). Table 8-1 outlines the stages of concern about the use of a teaching practice such as inquiry that calls for a significant change in behavior (Hord et al., 1987).

By being aware of these stages in teachers and others involved in change, administrators and teacher

Table 8-1. Typical Expressions of Concern About an Innovation

Stage of Concern	Expression of Concern
6. Refocusing	I have some ideas about something that would work even better.
5. Collaboration	How can I relate what I am doing to what others are doing?
4. Consequence	How is my use affecting learners? How can I refine it to have more impact?
3. Management	I seem to be spending all my time getting materials ready.
2. Personal	How will using it affect me?
1. Informational	I would like to know more about it.
0. Awareness	I am not concerned about it.

Adapted from Hord et al., 1987. *Taking Charge of Change.* Alexandria, VA: ASCD.

leaders can effectively select the types of support that will be the most useful to teachers as they experience this process. It is not a coincidence that this bears some resemblance to the inquiry process itself.

PROVIDING A VARIETY OF SUPPORT FOR STAFF

Changes implemented by individual teachers can succeed and endure only with simultaneous changes in the district, school, or department in which the teacher is working. Research has demonstrated that the ability of individuals in a system to change their teaching behavior is dictated to a large degree by the underlying structures in the organization such as rewards, policies, and the overall culture of the organization (O'Day and Smith, 1993). Effective change thus requires that a school adopt new approaches to support individual teachers. The remainder of this chapter discusses a number of these strategies.

Professional development. As described in Chapter 5, professional development comes in many forms (Loucks-Horsley et al., 1998). If teachers do not have access to such opportunities, administrators can help teachers find them or can create them in the school or in cooperation with other schools. Many of the rich variety of potential learning experiences for teachers will not occur in an organized, formal class.

Every school has a measure of expertise and experience that can be tapped. Even if formal arrangements for assistance include outside help, administrators or teacher leaders can facilitate internal support mechanisms such as the study groups described in

the next section. Fostering "communities of learners" within schools will create a norm of experimentation and evaluation that will apply to many other innovations. (See Teaching Standard F on page 51 and Program Standard E on page 222 of the *National Science Education Standards*.)

Administrative assistance and support. As teachers pass through the stages of concern described in Table 8-1, administrators need to provide them with professional development experiences appropriate to their progress in constructing a new view of teaching and creating the new behaviors required to practice it. For example, at an early stage of concern, teachers who are beginning to practice new inquiry behaviors will want information about inquiry and its place in the curriculum. Administrators can provide them with reference materials and with access to other teachers, university professors, or scientists who can answer their questions.

When the need for information is coupled with personal concerns (at stage of concern number 4, for example), teachers often express worries about whether the new teaching strategies will be acceptable to the principal, other teachers, and parents. These worries need to be listened to and addressed, understanding that they are a natural part of the change process. One way to address this concern is to encourage small groups

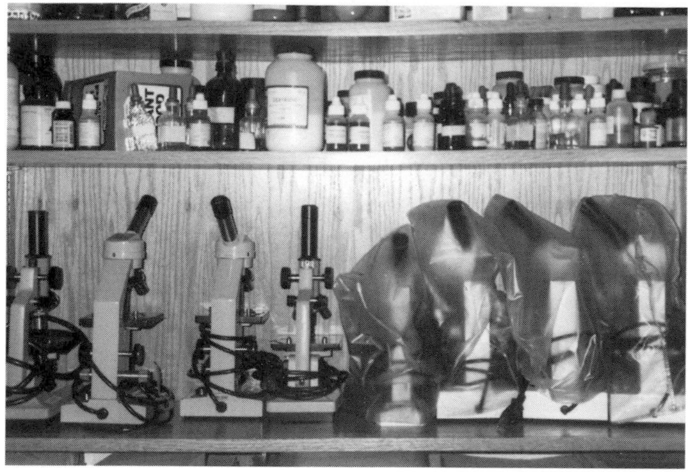

of teachers to form study and support groups that meet on a regular basis (during the school day if at all possible). Small study groups not only provide information; they also provide the mutual support that teachers need as they progress through their concerns. The collegiality provided by this community of learners can also enhance teachers' growth in learning to use inquiry far more rapidly and deeply than if each teacher were doing it alone.

As the new teaching practices begin, teachers will have many concerns about their effectiveness, the amount of work required, and their acceptance by others. Administrators need to assure teachers that they know and support what the teachers are doing. Other teachers also need to hear that administrators are behind the inquiry-based approach. Public expressions of support can reiterate the importance of inquiry in the context of many competing demands for time and attention.

Availability of instructional materials, kits, and equipment. As personal concerns are resolved, many teachers have concerns about making things work (stage of concern number 3). At this point, teachers have many "how to" questions about finding the time for inquiry activities, covering the content, keeping the students on task, having enough equipment, and so on. For example, is the schedule conducive for inquiry-based teaching? Are the periods or teaching blocks long enough to complete most activities in one day? Do instructional units or courses of study incorporate inquiry as the main teaching and learning strategy?

Traditional textbooks and units are often not conducive to inquiry-based teaching. Success is much more likely when the teachers are using materials that have inquiry "built in." Administrators need to make an effort to see that teachers have such materials. See Chapter 7 for ways to adapt traditional materials to support inquiry-based learning, should this be impossible. Does the school or district emphasize inquiry-oriented materials when approving textbooks and instructional materials? Are the criteria for selection based on standards (national or state) that have a strong inquiry component? Administrators have an opportunity, an obligation, and often the authority to influence the procedures and criteria used. Two recent resources from the Center for Science, Mathematics, and Engineering Education will be of help in this matter (NRC, 1999a; NRC, 1999b), as will Appendix B.

Nothing interferes with inquiry-based teaching more than lacking an adequate supply of instructional materials. Administrators need to ensure that teachers have appropriate kits, equipment, and supplies, and that consumable supplies are replaced regularly. Is the storage space adequate and secure? Experienced teachers can help find the answers to some of these questions, as can administrators who pay attention to the problems teachers are having.

Only by working through management questions can a teacher construct an image and an understanding of how inquiry-based teaching will benefit his or her students (stage of concern number five). Teachers at this stage will ask hard questions about the effectiveness of their teaching. They often will seek answers from the research and from careful student assessments to assure themselves that they and the approach they are using are effective. Study groups can seek help from local university researchers or district level science education specialists in addressing these concerns. Small action research projects (Miller and Pine, 1990; Holly, 1991; Calhoun, 1994) and examination of student work (Loucks-Horsley et al., 1998) by members of the group could be both motivating and helpful.

Interpreting inquiry-based teaching and learning for parents and other members of the public. Many administrators have learned the hard way that it is much better to be proactive with the community than reactive. Administrators cannot wait until the letters and phone calls start coming in from parents and other members of the public. They need to introduce and explain inquiry to parents whose students are involved. Newsletters, parent meetings, open houses, phone trees, and special invitations to "science nights" are all ways to inform parents that inquiry-based teaching and learning is being used in their child's class. Administrators need to know and share the advantages of teaching and learning this way and, at the same time, be open about the pitfalls or adjustments that some students will have to make to succeed. Teachers also can be asked to describe what they will do to help.

Building support with the public cannot stop with parents. Local businesses, government agencies and laboratories, museums, professional societies, and so on will be interested in supporting standards-based reform efforts and often can provide resources of materials, kits, scientists as consultants, or access to laboratories for field trips. The local media may be interested in a story that features a local innovation consistent with national improvement efforts. By stressing the acquisition of fundamental science knowledge through inquiry, administrators can avoid creating the image that inquiry is about exploring any interesting idea or simply the latest fad on the educational scene.

Student assessment procedures aligned with the outcomes of inquiry. Students and parents quickly judge what is valued by the tests and grading system the teachers and the schools use, and they adjust their behavior accordingly. If the inquiry activities and investigations are simply interludes between memorizing material from the text and other sources, the motivation to acquire inquiry-based abilities will be limited. If a teacher's tests and those required by the school do not assess the abilities and understanding of inquiry or, for that matter, the deep understanding of science concepts, students and parents may wonder why time is being spent on inquiry.

To avoid these pitfalls, administrators can encourage teachers to communicate clearly to students and parents what they expect students in their classes to know and be able to do and how they will assess and grade them. Teachers should be encouraged to use the kinds of classroom assessments described in Chapter 4, to embed their assessments in instruction, to consider how students' language development influences assessment results if they teach English language-learners, and to use assessments to inform both their immediate responses to students and their ongoing designs for instruction. Administrators can review the quality of the inquiry used in a class as well as students' mastery of subject matter. Do teachers include questions on their quizzes (in the grades and courses where this is appropriate) and use hands-on assessment tasks to measure inquiry abilities? Assessments of inquiry are a very useful topic for teacher study groups and for action research projects.

If tests are mandated by the district or state, what is their impact on teachers? If the tests do not measure inquiry, how can the requirement or the nature of the tests be modified? Changing the policies involved is a tall order but well worth the effort. Many administrators and teachers are ready and willing to join in this task.

Until such changes can be made, administrators need to be open about the fact that the tests only measure a portion of the science objectives or standards. And students who achieve a deep understanding of science content through inquiry usually do well on conventional tests (Bransford et al., 1999).

Promoting inquiry and problem solving in other subject areas. Inquiry is not exclusive to science or science teaching. Teachers in other departments at the secondary level and teachers teaching other subject areas at the elementary level can and often do use inquiry-like strategies. Teachers want and need the moral and collegial support of working with other teachers on innovative and, what they consider, risky projects. They also need the sense that they are not out on an "intellectual limb"; that inquiry has its counterparts in other disciplines in addition to science.

Mathematics educators have long advocated problem solving as an overarching process for teaching mathematics. The TIMSS eighth grade video study of mathematics instruction (Stigler et al., 1999) highlighted the value of individuals or small groups of students working through a complex problem independent of the teacher before the teacher, with the help of several students, displays one or more acceptable solution strategies. Innovative social studies instructional materials have incorporated inquiry strategies by providing original source materials for students to use in their investigations and an inductive approach to reaching the big ideas and principles. When the majority of teachers in a school are working on a common goal, the level and amount of professional talk in the building goes up (Little, 1993) and teachers begin to support each other in a common effort to change the way they teach and their students learn.

Appropriate teacher evaluation procedures. Problems are sure to arise if the formal and informal evaluation of teachers is inconsistent with the essential elements of inquiry. Teachers need to be assured that the innovative strategies they are using are understood, objectively evaluated, and rewarded when executed well. The evaluator must understand inquiry to know what to observe in the classroom. For example, evaluation of inquiry-based teaching requires more than one class period visit. What one day looks like confusion, and maybe even chaos, might be the exploration phase of instruction that will be followed the next day when experiments and ideas come together for most of the students.

Evaluators also need to look for how the teacher uses curriculum materials, interacts with students to increase their understanding, and assesses student work and thinking in ways that influence teaching plans. Teachers can be asked to explain how student work demonstrates growth in student understanding. Talking to students can reveal their understanding of the content and the methods of inquiry they are using. Lesson plans and the instructional model being used can indicate whether students are actively engaged in inquiry.

CONCLUSION

Teaching science through inquiry requires a new way of engaging students in learning. It therefore requires that all educators take on the role of change agents. To foster the changes in teaching required by inquiry-based approaches, administrators and other leaders need to provide a wide array of support — from opportunities to learn, to materials and equipment, to moral support, encouragement, and "running interference." Without such support, inquiry-based science programs are unlikely to succeed and even less likely to be sustained. With it, all students are much more likely to understand, appreciate, and actively participate in the scientific world.

References

American Association for the Advancement of Science. (1998). *Blueprints for Science Literacy.* New York: Oxford University Press.

American Association for the Advancement of Science. (1989). *Science for All Americans.* Washington, DC: American Association for the Advancement of Science.

American Association for the Advancement of Science. (1990). *This Year in School Science 1990: Assessment in the Service of Instruction.* Washington, DC: American Association for the Advancement of Science.

American Psychological Association and Mid-Continent Regional Educational Laboratory. (1993). *Learner-Centered Psychological Principles: Guidelines for School Redesign and Reform.* Denver: Mid-Continent Regional Educational Laboratory.

Anderson, C. W., & Smith, E. L. (1987). Teaching Science. In Koehler-Richardson (Ed), *Educators' Handbook: A Research Perspective* (pp. 84-111). White Plains, NY: Longman.

Anderson, R. D. (1996). *Study of Curriculum Reform.* Washington DC: U.S. Government Printing Office.

Atkin, J. M., & Karplus, R. (1962). Discovery or Invention. *The Science Teacher, 29*(2), 121-143.

Atwater, B. F. (1987). Evidence for Great Holocene Earthquakes Along the Outer Coast of Washington State. *Science, 236,* 942-944.

Baron, J. B. (1990). Performance Assessment: Blurring the Edges among Assessment, Curriculum, and Instruction. In A. B. Champagne, B. E. Lovitts, & B. J. Calinger (Eds), *Assessment in the Service of Instruction: This Year in School Science 1990.* Washington, DC: AAAS.

Basaga, H., Geban, O., & Tekkaya, C. (1994). The Effect of the Inquiry Teaching Method on Biochemistry and Science Process Skill Achievements. *Biochemical Education, 22*(1), 29-32.

Black, P., & Wiliam, D. (1998a). Assessment and Classroom Learning. *Assessment in Education, 5*(1), 7-74.

Black, P., & Wiliam, D. (1998b). Inside the Black Box: Raising Standards through Classroom Assessment. *Phi Delta Kappan, 80*(2), 139-148.

Blank, R. (Chair, CCSSO/SCASS Science Team for Measures of the Enacted Curriculum). (1997). *How is Science Taught in Schools?* Washington, DC: CCSSO.

Blumenfeld, P. C. (1994). Lessons Learned: How Collaboration Helped Middle Grade Science Teachers Learn Project-based Instruction. *The Elementary School Journal, 94*(5), 539-551.

Bransford, J. D., Brown, A. L., & Cocking, R., (Eds). (1999). *How People Learn: Brain, Mind, Experience, and School.* Washington, DC: National Academy Press.

Bredderman, T. (1982). *Elementary School Science Process Programs: A Meta-analysis of Evaluation Studies.* (Final Report of NSF-RISE Grant SED 18717).

Bruer, J. T. (1993). *Schools for Thought.* Cambridge, MA: MIT Press.

Bybee, R. W. (1997). *Achieving Scientific Literary: From Purposes to Practices.* Portsmouth, NH: Heinemann.

Bybee, R. W., & DeBoer, G. (1993). Goals for the Science Curriculum. In *Handbook of Research on Science Teaching and Learning.* Washington, DC: National Science Teachers Association.

Byrnes, J. P. (1996). *Cognitive Development and Learning in Instructional Contexts.* Boston: Allyn and Bacon.

Calhoun, E. F. (1994). *How to Use Action Research in the Self-Renewing School.* Alexandria, VA: Association for Supervision and Curriculum Development.

Carpenter, T., Fennema, E., & Franke, M. (1996). Cognitively Guided Instruction: A Knowledge Base for Reform in Primary Mathematics Instruction. *Elementary School Journal, 97*(1), 3-20.

Champagne, A. B., Kouba, V. L., & Hurley, M. (In press). *Assessing Inquiry.* Albany, NY: State University of New York.

Cochran, K. F. (1992) Pedagogical content knowledge: Teachers' Transformations of Subject Matter. In F. Lawrenz, K. Cochran, J. Krajcik, & P. Simpson (Eds), *Research Matters...To the Science Teacher.* Monograph Number Five of the National Association of Research in Science Teaching.

Council of Chief State School Officers. (1999). *Guide to Scoring LEP Student Responses to Open-Ended Science Items.* Washington, DC: SCASS LEP Consortium Project, CCSSO.

Daro, P. (1996). Standards and Portfolio Assessment. In J. B. Baron & D. P. Wolf (Eds), *Performance-Based Student Assessment: Challenges and Possibilities* (pp. 239-260). Chicago, IL: University of Chicago Press.

De Jong, T., & Van Joolingen, W. R. (1998). Scientific Discovery Learning with Computer Simulations of Conceptual Domains. *Review of Educational Research, 68*(2), 179-201.

DeBoer, G. E. (1991). *A History of Ideas in Science Education: Implications for Practice.* New York: Teachers College Press, Columbia University.

Delpit, L. (1995). *Other People's Children: Cultural Conflict in the Classroom.* New York: W.W. Norton.

Dewey, J. [1933 (1910)]. *How We Think.* Lexington, MA: D.C. Heath.

Donovan, M. S., Bransford, J. D., & Pellegrino, J. W. (Eds). (1999). *How People Learn: Bridging Research and Practice.* Washington, DC: National Academy Press.

Driver, R., Guesni, E., & Tiberghiem, A. (1985). *Children's Ideas in Science.* Philadelphia: Open University Press.

Driver, R., Squires, A., Duck, P., & Wood-Robinson, V. (1994). *Making Sense of Secondary Sciences: Research into Children's Ideas.* London: Routledge.

Duckworth, E. (1987). *The Having of Wonderful Ideas and Other Essays on Teaching and Learning.* New York: Teachers College Press, Columbia University.

Duschl, R. A. (1992). Teaching of Theory: A Guiding Concept in Science Education. Chapter IX in *Teaching About the History and Nature of Science and Technology: Background Papers.* Colorado Springs: Biological Sciences Curriculum Study (BSCS).

Duschl, R. A., & Gitomer, D. H. (1991). Epistemological Perspectives on Conceptual Change: Implications for Educational Practice. *Journal of Research in Science Teaching, 28*(9), 839-858.

Duschl, R. A., & Gitomer, D. H. (1997). Strategies and Challenges to Changing the Focus of Assessment and Instruction in Science Classrooms. *Educational Assessment, 4*(1), 37-73.

Flick, L. B. (1995). *Complex Classrooms: A Synthesis of Research on Inquiry Teaching Methods and Explicit Teaching Strategies.* Paper presented at the annual meeting of the National Association of Research in Science Teaching, San Francisco (ED 383 563).

Fradd, S. H., & Lee, O. (1999). Teachers' Roles in Promoting Science Inquiry with Students from Diverse Language Backgrounds. *Educational Researcher, 28*(6), 14-42.

Fullan, M. G. (1993). *Change Forces: Probing the Depths of Education Reform.* New York: The Falmer Press.

Fullan, M. G. (1991). *The New Meaning of Educational Change*. New York: Teachers College Press.

Gallas, K. (1995). *Talking Their Way Into Science: Hearing Children's Questions and Theories, Responding with Curricula*. New York: Teachers College Press.

Gitomer, D. H., & Duschl, R. A. (1995). Moving Toward a Portfolio Culture in Science Education. In M. S. Glynn & R. Duit (Eds), *Learning Science in the Schools: Research Reforming Practice* (pp. 299-325). Mahwah, NJ: Lawrence Erlbaum.

Glaser, R. (1992). Expert Knowledge and Process of Thinking. In D. F. Halpern (Ed), *Enhancing Thinking Skills in Science and Mathematics* (pp. 63-75). Hillsdale, NJ: Erlbaum.

Guskey, T. R. (1986). Staff Development and the Process of Teacher Change. *Educational Researcher, 15*(5), 5-12.

Hall, G. E., & Hord, S. M. (1987). *Change in Schools: Facilitating the Process*. Albany: State University of New York Press.

Harms, N., & Kahl, S. (1980). *Project Synthesis: Final Report to The National Science Foundation*. Boulder, CO: University of Colorado.

Harms, N., & Yager, R. E. (1981). *What Research Says to the Science Teacher, Vol. 3*. Washington, DC: National Science Teachers Association.

Hashweh, M. Z. (1987) Effects of Subject Matter Knowledge in the Teaching of Biology and Physics. *Teaching and Teacher Education, 3*, 109-120.

Haury, D. L. (1993). Teaching Science Through Inquiry. *ERIC CSMEE Digest* (March Ed 359 048).

Herbart, J. (1901). *Outlines of Education Doctrine*, C. DeGarmo (Trans); A. Lange (Ed). New York: Macmillan.

Hewson, P. W., & Thorley, N. R. (1989). The Conditions of Conceptual Change in the Classroom. *International Journal of Science Education, 11*(5), 541-553.

Heywood, J., & Heywood, S. (1992). The Training of Student-Teachers in Discovery Methods of Instruction and Learning. (No. 1/92) ED 358 034 . Dublin, Ireland: Department of Teacher Education, The University of Dublin.

Hiebert, J. (1999). Relationship Between Research and the NCTM Standards. *Journal for Research in Mathematics Education, 30*(1), 3-19.

Holly, P. (1991). Action Research: The Missing Link in the Creation of Schools as Centers of Inquiry. In A. Lieberman & L. Miller (Eds), *Staff Development for Education in the '90s: New Demands, New Realities, New Perspectives* (pp. 133-157). New York: Teachers College Press.

Hord, S. M., Rutherford, W. L., Huling-Austin, L., & Hall, G. E. (1987). *Taking Charge of Change*. Alexandria, VA: Association for Supervision and Curriculum Development.

Huberman, A. M. & Miles, M. B. (1984). *Innovation Up Close: How School Improvement Works*. New York: Plenum.

Hurd, P. D. (1998). Scientific Literacy: New Minds for a Changing World. *Science Education, 82*, 407-416.

Joyce, B. (Ed). (1990). *Changing School Culture Through Staff Development, 1990 Yearbook*. Alexandria, VA: Association for Supervision and Curriculum Development.

Krajcik, J. S., Blumenfeld, P. C., Marx, R. W., & Soloway, E. (1994). A Collaborative Model for Helping Middle Grade Science Teachers Learn Project-based Instruction. *The Elementary School Journal, 94*(5), 483-497.

Ladewski, B. J., Krajcik, J. S., & Harvey, C. L. (1994). A Middle Grade Science Teacher's Emerging Understanding of Project-based Instruction. *The Elementary School Journal, 94*(5), 499-515.

Layman, J. W., Ochoa, G., & Heikkinen, H. (1996). *Inquiry and Learning: Realizing Science Standards in the Classroom*. New York: College Entrance Examination Board.

Lieberman, A., & Miller, L. (Eds). (1991). *Staff Development for Education in the '90s: New Demands, New Realities, New Perspectives* (2nd ed.). New York: Teachers College Press.

Linn, M. C., Clement, C., Pulos, S., & Sullivan, P. (1989). Scientific Reasoning in Adolescence: The Influence of Instruction in Science Knowledge and Reasoning Strategies. *Journal of Research in Science Teaching, 26*(2), 171-187.

Little, J. W. (1993). Teachers' Professional Development in a Climate of Educational Reform. *Educational Evaluation and Policy Analysis, 15*, 129-151.

Lloyd, C. V. (1988). *The Relationship Between Scientific Literacy and High School Biology Textbooks.* Paper presented at the annual meeting of the National Reading Conference, Austin, TX.

Lott, G. W. (1983). The Effect of Inquiry Teaching and Advance Organizers upon Student Outcomes in Science Education. *Journal of Research in Science Teaching, 20*(5), 437-451.

Loucks-Horsley, S., Hewson, P. W., Love, N., & Stiles, K. E. (1998). *Designing Professional Development for Teachers of Science and Mathematics.* Thousand Oaks, CA: Corwin Press, Inc.

Malley, M. (1992). The Nature and History of Science. Chapter V in *Teaching About the History and Nature of Science and Technology: Background Papers* (pp. 67-80). Colorado Springs: Biological Sciences Curriculum Study (BSCS).

Marx, R. W., Blumenfeld, P. C., Krajcik, J. S., Blunk, M., Crawford, B. Kelley, B., & Meyer, K. M. (1994). Enacting Project-Based Science: Experiences of Four Middle Grade Teachers. *The Elementary School Journal, 94*(5), 517-538.

Mayer, W. (1978). *Biology Teacher's Handbook* (3rd ed.). Colorado Springs: Biological Sciences Curriculum Study (BSCS).

McDermott, L. C., & the Physics Education Group at the University of Washington. (1996). *Physics by Inquiry* (Volumes I & II). New York: John Wiley.

McDermott, L. C., & Rcdish, E. F. (1999). Resource Letter: PER-1: Physics Education Research. *American Journal of Physics 67*(10), 755-767.

Mechling, K. R., & Oliver, D. L. (1983). *Promoting Science Among Elementary School Principals.* Washington, DC: National Science Teachers Association.

Millar, R., & Driver, R. (1987). Beyond Process. *Studies in Science Education, 14*, 33-62.

Miller, D. M., & Pine, G. J. (1990). Advancing Professional Inquiry for Educational Improvement Through Action Research. *Journal of Staff Development, 11*(3), 56-61.

Minstrell, J. (1982). Explaining the At-Rest Condition of an Object. *The Physics Teacher, 20*, 10.

Minstrell, J. (1989). Teaching Science for Understanding. In L. B. Resnick & L. E. Klopfer (Eds), *Toward the Thinking Curriculum: Current Cognitive Research* (pp. 129-149). Alexandria, VA: Association for Supervision and Curriculum Development.

Minstrell, J. (1992). Facets of Students' Knowledge and Relevant Instruction. In R. Duit, F. Goldberg, & H. Niedderer (Eds), *Proceedings of the International Workshop on Research in Physics Education: Theoretical Issues and Empirical Studies* (pp. 110-128). Kiel, Germany: Instituit fur die Padagogik de Naturiwissenshaften.

Narode, R. (1987). *Teaching Thinking Skills.* NEA Professional Library. Washington, DC: National Education Association.

National Commission for Teaching & America's Future. (1996). *What Matters Most: Teaching for America's Future.* New York: Author.

National Research Council. (1990). *Fulfilling the Promise: Biology Education in the Nation's Schools.* Washington, DC: National Academy Press.

National Research Council. (1996). *The National Science Education Standards.* Washington DC: National Academy Press.

National Research Council. (1997). *Science Teaching Reconsidered. A Handbook.* Washington, DC: National Academy Press.

National Research Council. (1999a). *Designing Mathematics and Science Curriculum Programs: A Guide for Using Mathematics and Science Education Standards.* Washington, DC: National Academy Press.

National Research Council. (1999b). *Selecting Instructional Materials: A Guide for K-12 Science.* Washington, DC: National Academy Press.

Neill, D. M., & Medina, N. J. (1989). Standardized Testing: Harmful to Educational Health. *Phi Delta Kappan 70*(9), 688-697.

Nelson, A. R., Atwater, B. F., Bobrowsky, P. T., Bradley, L. A., Clague, J. J., Carver, G. A., Darienzo, M. E., Grant, W. C., Krueger, H. W., Sparks, R., Stafford, T. W., & Stuiver,

M. (1995). Radiocarbon Evidence for Extensive Plate-boundary Rupture about 300 Years Ago at the Cascadia Subduction Zone. *Nature, 378*, 371-374.

New Standards Project. (1997). *New Standards Performance Standards.* Washington, DC: National Center on Education and the Economy.

Novak, J. D. (1987). *Proceedings of the Second International Seminar: Misconceptions and Educational Strategies in Science and Mathematics* (Volumes I-III) . Ithaca, NY: Cornell University.

O'Day, J., & Smith, M. (1993). Systemic Reform and Educational Opportunity. In S. H. Fuhrman (Ed), *Designing Coherent Education Policy: Improving the System* (pp. 312-322). San Francisco: Jossey-Bass.

Piaget, J. (1975). *The Development of Thought.* New York: Viking Press.

Piaget, J., & Inhelder, B. (1969). *The Psychology of the Child.* New York: Basic Books.

Prather, J. P. (1996). The Role of the School Principal in Science Education Reform. In J. Rhoton & P. Bowers (Eds), *Issues in Science Education.* Arlington, VA: National Science Teachers Association and National Science Education Leadership Association.

Project Kaleidoscope. (1991). *What Works: Building National Science Communities, Strengthening Undergraduate Science and Mathematics.* Washington, DC: Author.

Raizen, S. A., & Kaser, J. S. (1989). Assessing Science Learning in Elementary School: Why, What, and How? *Phi Delta Kappan, 70*(9), 718-722.

Resnick, L. B., Bill, V. L., Lesgold, S. B., & Leer, M. N. (1991). Thinking in Arithmetic Class. In B. Means, C. Chelemer, & M. S. Knapp (Eds), *Teaching Advanced Skills to At Risk Students* (pp. 27-53). San Francisco: Jossey-Bass.

Roberts, L., Wilson, M., & Draney, K. (1997). *The SEPUP Assessment System: An Overview.* Berkeley, CA: Berkeley Evaluation and Assessment Research Center.

Rosebery, A. S., Warren, B., & Conant, F. R. (1992). Appropriating Scientific Discourse: Findings from Language Minority Classrooms. *The Journal of the Learning Sciences, 2*(1), 61-94.

Rowe, M. B. (1991). Implications of the New Science Curricula. In S. M. Malcom & G. Kulum (Eds), *Science Assessment in the Service of Reform.* Washington, DC: American Association for the Advancement of Science (now published by Lawrence Erlbaum).

Rowe, M. B. (1974). Wait Time and Rewards as Instructional Variables, Their Influence on Language, Logic, and Fate Control: Part One - Wait Time. *Journal of Research in Science Teaching, 11*, 81-94.

Satake, K., Shimazaki, K., Tsuji, Y., & Ueda, K. (1996). Time and Size of a Giant Earthquake in Cascadia Inferred from Japanese Tsunami Record of January 1700. *Nature, 379*, 246-249.

Schmidt, W. H., McKnight, C. C., & Raizen, S. A. (1997). *Splintered Vision: An Investigation of U.S. Science and Mathematics Education.* Boston: Kluwer Academic Publishers.

Schwab, J. (1960). What Do Scientists Do? *Behavioral Science, 5*(1).

Schwab, J. (1966). *The Teaching of Science.* Cambridge, MA: Harvard University Press.

Scruggs, T. E., Mastropieri, M.A., Bakken, J. P., & Brigham, F. J. (1993). Reading Versus Doing: The Relative Effects of Textbook-based and Inquiry-oriented Approaches to Science Learning in Special Education Classrooms. *The Journal of Special Education, 27*(1), 1-15.

Secules, T., Cottom, C. D., Bray, M. H., Miller, L. D., & The Cognition and Technology Group at Vanderbilt. (1997). Schools for Thought: Creating Learning Communities. *Educational Leadership, 54*(6), 56-60.

Shulman, L. S. (1986). Those Who Understand: Knowledge Growth in Teaching. *Educational Researcher, 15*(2), 4-14.

Shymansky, J. A., Hedges, L. V., & Woodworth, G. (1990). A Reassessment of the Effects of Inquiry-based Science Curriculum of the '60s on Student Performance. *Journal of Research in Science Teaching, 27*, 127-144.

Shymansky, J. A., Kyle, W. C., & Alport, J. M. (1983). The Effects of New Science Curricula on Student Performance. *Journal of Research in Science Teaching, 20*(5), 387-404.

Songer, N. B., & Linn, M. C. (1991). How Do Students' Views of Science Influence Knowledge Integration? *Journal of Research in Science Teaching, 28*(9), 761-784.

Stake, R. E., & Easley, J. A. (1978). *Case Studies in Science Education.* Urbana, IL: Center for Institutional Research and Curriculum Evaluation, University of Illinois.

Stigler, J. W., Gonzales, P., Kawanaka, T., Knoll, S., & Serrano, A. (1999). *The TIMSS Videotape Classroom Study. Methods and Findings from an Exploratory Research Project on Eighth-Grade Mathematics Instruction in Germany, Japan, and the United States.* Washington, DC: U.S. Government Printing Office.

Wandersee, J. H., Mintzes, J. J., & Novak, J. D. (1994). Research on Alternative Conceptions in Science. In D. L. Gabel (Ed), *Handbook of Research on Science Teaching and Learning* (pp. 177-210). New York: Macmillan.

Weinstein, T., Boulanger, F. D., & Walberg, H. J. (1982). Science Curriculum Effects in High School: A Quantitative Synthesis. *Journal of Research in Science Teaching, 19*(6), 511-522.

Weiss, I. R. (1978). *Report of the 1977 National Survey of Science, Mathematics, and Social Studies Education.* Washington, DC: U.S. Government Printing Office.

Weiss, I. R. (1987). *Report of the 1985-1986 National Survey of Science and Mathematics Education.* Research Triangle Park, NC: Research Triangle Institute.

White, B. Y., & Frederiksen, J. R. (1998). Inquiry, Modeling and Metacognition: Making Science Accessible to All Students. *Cognition and Instruction, 16*(1), 3-118.

White, B. Y., & Frederiksen, J. R. (In press). Metacognitive Facilitation: An Approach to Making Scientific Inquiry Accessible to All. In J. Minstrell & E. Van Zee (Eds), *Teaching in the Inquiry-Based Science Classroom.* Washington, DC: American Association for the Advancement of Science.

Wise, K. C., & Okey, J. R. (1983). A Meta-analysis of the Effects of Various Science Teaching Strategies on Achievement. *Journal of Research in Science Teaching, 20*(5), 419-435.

Appendixes

Appendix A
Excerpts from the *National Science Education Standards*

APPENDIX A-1
FUNDAMENTAL ABILITIES OF INQUIRY: GRADES K-4

Ability	Elaboration
• Ask a question about objects, organisms, and events in the environment.	This aspect of the standard emphasizes students asking questions that they can answer with scientific knowledge, combined with their own observations. Students should answer their questions by seeking information from reliable sources of scientific information and from their own observations and investigations.
• Plan and conduct a simple investigation.	In the earliest years, investigations are largely based on systematic observations. As students develop, they may design and conduct simple experiments to answer questions. The idea of a fair test is possible for many students to consider by fourth grade.

Ability	Elaboration
• Employ simple equipment and tools to gather data and extend to the senses.	In early years, students develop simple skills, such as how to observe, measure, cut, connect, switch, turn on and off, pour, hold, tie, and hook. Beginning with simple instruments, students can use rulers to measure the length, height, and depth of objects and materials; thermometers to measure temperature; watches to measure time; beam balances and spring scales to measure weight and force; magnifiers to observe objects and organisms; and microscopes to observe the finer details of plants, animals, rocks, and other materials. Children also develop skills in the use of computers and calculators for conducting investigations.
• Use data to construct a reasonable explanation.	This aspect of the standard emphasizes the students' thinking as they use data to formulate explanations. Even at the earliest grade levels, students should learn what constitutes evidence and judge the merits or strength of the data and information that will be used to make explanations. After students propose an explanation, they will appeal to the knowledge and evidence they obtained to support their explanations. Students should check their explanations against scientific knowledge, experiences, and observations of others.
• Communicate investigations and explanations.	Students should begin developing the abilities to communicate, critique, and analyze their work and the work of other students. This communication might be spoken or drawn as well as written.

FUNDAMENTAL ABILITIES OF INQUIRY: GRADES 5-8

Ability	Elaboration
• Identify questions that can be answered through scientific investigations.	Students should develop the ability to refine and refocus broad and ill-defined questions. An important aspect of this ability consists of students' ability to clarify questions and inquiries and direct them toward objects and phenomena that can be described, explained, or predicted by scientific investigations. Students should develop the ability to identify their questions with scientific ideas, concepts, and quantitative relationships that guide investigation.
• Design and conduct a scientific investigation.	Students should develop general abilities, such as systematic observation, making accurate measurements, and identifying and controlling variables. They should also develop the ability to clarify their ideas that are influencing and guiding the inquiry, and to understand how those ideas compare with current scientific knowledge. Students can learn to formulate questions, design investigations, execute investigations, interpret data, use evidence to generate explanations, propose alternative explanations, and critique explanations and procedures.

Ability	Elaboration
• Use appropriate tools and techniques to gather, analyze, and interpret data.	The use of tools and techniques, including mathematics, will be guided by the question asked and the investigations students design. The use of computers for the collection, summary, and display of evidence is part of this standard. Students should be able to access, gather, store, retrieve, and organize data, using hardware and software designed for these purposes.
• Develop descriptions, explanations, predictions, and models using evidence.	Students should base their explanation on what they observed, and as they develop cognitive skills, they should be able to differentiate explanation from description — providing causes for effects and establishing relationships based on evidence and logical argument. This standard requires a subject matter knowledge base so the students can effectively conduct investigations, because developing explanations establishes connections between the content of science and the contexts within which students develop new knowledge.
• Think critically and logically to make the relationships between evidence and explanations.	Thinking critically about evidence includes deciding what evidence should be used and accounting for anomalous data. Specifically, students should be able to review data from a simple experiment, summarize the data, and form a logical argument about the cause-and-effect relationships in the experiment. Students should begin to state some explanations in terms of the relationship between two or more variables.

Ability	Elaboration
• Recognize and analyze alternative explanations and predictions.	Students should develop the ability to listen to and respect the explanations proposed by other students. They should remain open to and acknowledge different ideas and explanations, be able to accept the skepticism of others, and consider alternative explanations.
• Communicate scientific procedures and explanations.	With practice, students should become competent at communicating experimental methods, following instructions, describing observations, summarizing the results of other groups, and telling other students about investigations and explanations.
• Use mathematics in all aspects of scientific inquiry.	Mathematics is essential to asking and answering questions about the natural world. Mathematics can be used to ask questions; to gather, organize, and present data; and to structure convincing explanations.

FUNDAMENTAL ABILITIES OF INQUIRY: GRADES 9-12

Ability	Elaboration
• Identify questions and concepts that guide scientific investigations.	Students should formulate a testable hypothesis and demonstrate the logical connections between the scientific concepts guiding a hypothesis and the design of an experiment. They should demonstrate appropriate procedures, a knowledge base, and conceptual understanding of scientific investigations.

Ability	Elaboration
• Design and conduct scientific investigations.	Designing and conducting a scientific investigation requires introduction to the major concepts in the area being investigated, proper equipment, safety precautions, assistance with methodological problems, recommendations for use of technologies, clarification of ideas that guide the inquiry, and scientific knowledge obtained from sources other than the actual investigation. The investigation may also require student clarification of the question, method, controls, and variables; student organization and display of data; student revision of methods and explanations; and a public presentation of the results with a critical response from peers. Regardless of the scientific investigation performed, students must use evidence, apply logic, and construct an argument for their proposed explanations.
• Use technology and mathematics to improve investigations and communications.	A variety of technologies, such as hand tools, measuring instruments, and calculators, should be an integral component of scientific investigations. The use of computers for the collection, analysis, and display of data is also a part of this standard. Mathematics plays an essential role in all aspects of an inquiry. For example, measurement is used for posing questions, formulas are used for developing explanations, and charts and graphs are used for communicating results.

Ability	Elaboration
• Formulate and revise scientific explanations and models using logic and evidence.	Student inquiries should culminate in formulating an explanation or model. Models should be physical, conceptual, and mathematical. In the process of answering the questions, the students should engage in discussions and arguments that result in the revision of their explanations. These discussions should be based on scientific knowledge, the use of logic, and evidence from their investigation.
• Recognize and analyze alternative explanations and models.	This aspect of the standard emphasizes the critical abilities of analyzing an argument by reviewing current scientific understanding, weighing the evidence, and examining the logic so as to decide which explanations and models are best. In other words, although there may be several plausible explanations, they do not all have equal weight. Students should be able to use scientific criteria to find the preferred explanations.
• Communicate and defend a scientific argument.	Students in school science programs should develop the abilities associated with accurate and effective communication. These include writing and following procedures, expressing concepts, reviewing information, summarizing data, using language appropriately, developing diagrams and charts, explaining statistical analysis, speaking clearly and logically, constructing a reasoned argument, and responding appropriately to critical comments.

APPENDIX A-2
FUNDAMENTAL UNDERSTANDINGS OF INQUIRY
GRADES K-4

Understanding	Elaboration
• Scientific investigations involve asking and answering a question and comparing the answer with what scientists already know about the world.	
• Scientists use different kinds of investigations depending on the questions they are trying to answer.	Types of investigations include describing objects, events, and organisms; classifying them; and doing a fair test (experimenting).
• Simple instruments, such as magnifiers, thermometers, and rulers, provide more information than scientists obtain using only their senses.	
• Scientists develop explanations using observations (evidence) and what they already know about the world (scientific knowledge).	Good explanations are based on evidence from investigations.
• Scientists make the results of their investigations public; they describe the investigations in ways that enable others to repeat the investigations.	
• Scientists review and ask questions about the results of other scientists' work.	

FUNDAMENTAL UNDERSTANDINGS OF INQUIRY: GRADES 5-8

Understanding	Elaboration
• Different kinds of questions suggest different kinds of scientific investigations.	Some investigations involve observing and describing objects, organisms, or events; some involve collecting specimens; some involve experiments; some involve seeking more information; some involve discovery of new objects and phenomena; and some involve making models.
• Current scientific knowledge and understanding guide scientific investigations.	Different scientific domains employ different methods, core theories, and standards to advance scientific knowledge and understanding.
• Mathematics is important in all aspects of scientific inquiry.	
• Technology used to gather data enhances accuracy and allows scientists to analyze and quantify results of investigations.	
• Scientific explanations emphasize evidence, have logically consistent arguments, and use scientific principles, models, and theories.	The scientific community accepts and uses such explanations until displaced by better scientific ones. When such displacement occurs, science advances.

Understanding	Elaboration
• Science advances through legitimate skepticism.	Asking questions and querying other scientists' explanations is part of scientific inquiry. Scientists evaluate the explanations proposed by other scientists by examining evidence, comparing evidence, identifying faulty reasoning, pointing out statements that go beyond the evidence, and suggesting alternative explanations for the same observations.
• Scientific investigations sometimes result in new ideas and phenomena for study, generate new methods or procedures for an investigation, or develop new technologies to improve the collection of data.	All of these results can lead to new investigations.

FUNDAMENTAL UNDERSTANDINGS OF INQUIRY: GRADES 9-12

Understanding	Elaboration
• Scientists usually inquire about how physical, living, or designed systems function.	Conceptual principles and knowledge guide scientific inquiries. Historical and current scientific knowledge influence the design and interpretation of investigations and the evaluation of proposed explanations made by other scientists.
• Scientists conduct investigations for a wide variety of reasons.	For example, they may wish to discover new aspects of the natural world, explain recently observed phenomena, or test the conclusions of prior investigations or the predictions of current theories.

Understanding	Elaboration
• Scientists rely on technology to enhance the gathering and manipulation of data.	New techniques and tools provide new evidence to guide inquiry and new methods to gather data, thereby contributing to the advance of science. The accuracy and precision of the data, and therefore the quality of the exploration, depends on the technology used.
• Mathematics is essential in scientific inquiry.	Mathematical tools and models guide and improve the posing of questions, gathering data, constructing explanations, and communicating results.
• Scientific explanations must adhere to criteria such as: a proposed explanation must be logically consistent; it must abide by the rules of evidence; it must be open to questions and possible modification; and it must be based on historical and current scientific knowledge.	
• Results of scientific inquiry — new knowledge and methods — emerge from different types of investigations and public communication among scientists.	In communicating and defending the results of scientific inquiry, arguments must be logical and demonstrate connections between natural phenomena, investigations, and the historical body of scientific knowledge. In addition, the methods and procedures that scientists used to obtain evidence must be clearly reported to enhance opportunities for further investigation.

Appendix B
Selecting Instructional Materials

Science teachers often ask about instructional materials that will help them implement inquiry-based instructional strategies and provide students with opportunities to develop the abilities and understandings of scientific inquiry. This appendix is intended to help identify and select such instructional materials. It begins with a brief summary of the different uses of the term "inquiry" presented early in this document, so that this section can stand alone and be shared with those responsible for selecting instructional materials.

INQUIRY IN THE *NATIONAL SCIENCE EDUCATION STANDARDS*

Inquiry is used several ways in the *Standards.*

1. *Scientific Inquiry.* According to the *National Science Education Standards*, "Scientific inquiry refers to the diverse ways in which scientists study the natural world and propose explanations based on the evidence derived from their work" (p. 23). The *Standards* call for students to develop the abilities and understandings that will enable them to engage in this kind of activity. A key question when selecting instructional materials is the extent to which they support teachers in helping students achieve these goals.

2. *Inquiry-Based Teaching.* The *Standards* state that "inquiry into authentic questions generated from student experiences is the central strategy for teaching science." However, the importance of inquiry "does not imply that all teachers should pursue a single approach to teaching science." Inquiry is a characteristic of both a desired form of teaching and particular kinds of classroom activities. It can be used to teach (1) subject matter of physical, life, earth and space sciences, (2) the nature of the scientific enterprise (i.e., about scientific inquiry), and (3) the abilities

required to conduct scientific inquiry. Inquiry-based teaching is a means, not an end.

3. *Inquiry-Based Learning*. In the *Standards*, inquiry also refers to learning processes. It is an active learning process — "something that students do, not something that is done to them" (p. 2). The *Standards* tie inquiry-based learning both to scientific inquiry and to studies of human learning.

Clearly there are connections among these uses of inquiry in the *Standards*. The task of selecting instructional materials requires consideration of all these ways of thinking about inquiry.

The selection of instructional materials can be helped by standards-based thinking. Instead of asking, "what standards will a particular set of materials meet?" it is better to ask, "if I want to accomplish a certain outcome, what materials do I need?"

ANALYZING INSTRUCTIONAL MATERIALS

The process of analyzing and selecting quality instructional materials includes determining the degree to which they are consistent with the goals, principles, and criteria developed in the *National Science Education Standards*. Well-defined selection criteria help ensure a thoughtful and effective process. To be both usable and defensible, the selection criteria must be few in number and embody the critical tenets of accurate science content, effective teaching strategies, and appropriate assessment techniques.

The process described in the following pages can help teachers, curriculum designers, or other personnel complete a thorough and accurate evaluation of instructional materials. To help make this examination both thorough and usable, references to specific sections of the *National Science Education Standards* are provided, as are worksheets to keep track of the information needed to analyze and select the best instructional materials.

Selection of instructional materials parallels a guided inquiry in many respects. First, questions need to be identified that will guide the analysis and eventually the selection. Such questions include:

- Is "science as inquiry" evident as content in the materials?
- Is the presentation of inquiry as content accurate?
- Is inquiry-based teaching evident in the materials?
- Is there adequate time and opportunity for students to develop the abilities and understandings of scientific inquiry and an understanding of science subject matter concepts?

Second, an investigation of the materials needs to be designed and conducted. The investigation requires systematic observations, accurate and consistent records, and clarification of the questions that guide the process. Are the observations consistent between different sets of materials? Were variables controlled, such as design and layout versus accurate portrayal of inquiry? Were similar techniques used to review all materials? Are the same kinds of data collected for all materials?

Third, recorded observations need to be used to develop summaries of the respective materials. These summaries should be based on what was observed and should differentiate among the materials.

Fourth, rational arguments need to be developed for the selection of materials. The arguments should be based on observations and address alternatives and options.

Finally, the process and final recommendation should be fully documented. This will be helpful for final review by such decision-makers as administrators and school boards.

ANALYSIS PROCEDURES

The procedures outlined in this section include:

- Overview of instructional materials
- Analysis of science as inquiry
- Analysis of inquiry-based teaching
- Analysis of assessment process
- Evaluation of teacher's guide
- Analysis of materials use and management

In this appendix, criteria for analysis of instructional materials focus on their usefulness for classroom teachers and their degree of alignment with the *Standards*. A thorough analysis of instructional materials requires considerable time, collaboration, and attention to detail. Good working notes are helpful in this process. For that purpose, analysis worksheets are included at the end of this section.

OVERVIEW OF THE INSTRUCTIONAL MATERIALS (SEE WORKSHEET 1)

A quick overview of the materials precedes a more detailed examination. The first consideration is whether the materials emphasize the key ideas and abilities from the "Science as Inquiry" standard. To help make this determination, look at the table of contents, index, and glossary. Worksheet 1 contains terms related to science as inquiry taken from the *Standards*. These terms will give a preliminary indication of coverage of these fundamental topics.

Look through both student and teacher materials.

- Are student outcomes listed?
- Are some of these inquiry outcomes?

Look for student investigations or activities.

- Where are they located? Note that in some materials, student investigations are integrated within the reading material. In others, they are located in a separate section — sometimes at the back of a chapter or book or in a separate laboratory manual.
- Do they come after teacher explanations or lectures, or after students have read in their books? Or are they used to engage students in exploring new ideas before explanations are suggested?

Read several relevant paragraphs of student text material.

- What is your judgment about the presentation of scientific inquiry?
- Are the concepts in the students' text consistent with the fundamental concepts and abilities in the *Standards*?
- Does the text include more, fewer, or different concepts?
- Do the photographs and illustrations provide further understanding of science as inquiry?

ANALYSIS OF INSTRUCTIONAL MATERIALS FOR INQUIRY AS CONTENT (SEE WORKSHEET 2)

Look for evidence in discussions in the text and in the student investigations of whether and how the fundamental abilities and understanding are addressed. (See Chapter 2 and Appendix A in this book, refer to a print copy of the *National Science Education Standards*, or access the *Standards* through the World Wide Web at www.nap.edu/readingroom/books/nses.) Examine several lessons in the student and teacher materials. To what degree do the lessons provide students the opportunity to develop the abilities and understandings of scientific inquiry?

Read through the text narrative, looking for student investigations and examining any suggestions for activities outside of class time. Consider:

- Are opportunities provided for students to develop abilities of scientific inquiry such as posing their own questions, designing their own investigations, using appropriate tools and techniques to gather data, using evidence to communicate defensible explanations of cause and effect relationships, or using scientific criteria to analyze alternative explanations to determine a preferred explanation?

• What opportunities are provided for students to develop a fundamental understanding of scientific inquiry?

In addition to the language of the text, examine the teacher's guide for ways to discuss the role and limitations of scientific skills such as making observations, organizing and interpreting data, and constructing defensible explanation based on evidence.

• Is there a discussion of how science advances through legitimate skepticism?
• Is there a discussion of how scientists evaluate explanations of others by examining and comparing evidence, identifying reasoning that goes beyond the evidence, and suggesting alternative explanations for the same evidence?
• Are there opportunities for students to demonstrate these same understandings as a part of their investigations?

ANALYSIS OF PEDAGOGY (SEE WORKSHEET 3)

What students learn about inquiry and the abilities they develop depends on many things, including the accuracy and developmental appropriateness of content and its congruence with the full intent of the content standards. Opportunities to learn should be consistent with contemporary models of learning. The criteria in this section are based on characteristics of effective teaching proposed in Teaching Standards A, B, and E:

• Teaching Standard A — Teachers of science plan an inquiry-based science program for their students.
• Teaching Standard B — Teachers of science guide and facilitate learning.
• Teaching Standard E — Teachers of science develop communities of science learners that reflect the intellectual rigor of scientific inquiry and the attitudes and social values conducive to science learning.

Using the following sequence of questions, examine several lessons in the student materials and the teacher's guide.

• Do the materials identify specific learning goals and outcomes for students that focus on one or more of the fundamental abilities and understandings of Science As Inquiry?
• Study the opening pages of a relevant chapter or section. Does the material on these pages engage and focus student thinking on interesting questions, problems, or relevant issues?
• Does the material provide a sequence of learning activities connected in such a way as to help students build abilities of inquiry and

fundamental understandings about inquiry or a subject matter concept?

• Do the activities incorporate all five essential features of classroom inquiry described in Chapter 2? Are suggestions provided to help the teacher keep students focused on the purpose of the lesson?

• Does the teacher's guide present common student difficulties in developing inquiry abilities and understandings? Does it suggest possible alternative conceptions or misconceptions students may have and how to address them? Are suggestions provided for teachers to find out what their student already know and can do? Are there learning activities designed to help students identify what they know and build new concepts and abilities?

ANALYSIS OF ASSESSMENT PROCESS (SEE WORKSHEET 4)

Assessment criteria in this section are grounded in the Assessment Standards A to E. Examine several lessons in the student and teacher materials for evidence to answer the following questions:

• Is there consistency between learning goals and assessment? For example, if instruction focuses on building and understanding fundamental concepts, do assessments focus on explanations and not on vocabulary?

• Do assessments stress application of abilities and concepts to new or different situations? For example, are the students asked to explain new situations with concepts they have learned? Are they asked to design investigations into questions they have not yet addressed?

• Are assessment tasks fair for all students? For example, does success on assessment tasks depend too heavily on the student's ability to read complex items or write explanations, as opposed to understanding the fundamental concepts or being able to think scientifically?

• Are suggestions for scoring criteria or rubrics provided for the teacher?

EVALUATING THE TEACHER'S GUIDE (SEE WORKSHEET 5)

Examine several lessons in the teacher's guide to help answer the following questions:

• Does the teacher's guide present appropriate and sufficient background in science?

• Are the suggested teaching strategies usable by most teachers?

• Are suggestions provided for pre- and post-investigation discussions focusing on subject matter concept development, inquiry abilities, and inquiry understandings?

• Does the teacher's guide recommend additional professional development?

• Does the teacher's guide indicate

the types of support teachers will need for the instructional materials?

ANALYSIS OF MATERIALS USE AND MANAGEMENT (SEE WORKSHEET 6)

A high degree of alignment of the content, pedagogy, and assessment criteria described in the *Standards* does not necessarily guarantee that instructional materials will be easy to manage. The *Standards* address the importance of professional development, and some aspects of the program standards apply as well. It is useful to ask:

- How many different types of materials must be managed and orchestrated during a typical chapter, unit, or teaching sequence (e.g., student text, teacher's guide, transparencies, handouts, videos, and software)?
- Does the teacher's guide contain suggestions for effectively managing materials?
- Do the instructional materials call for equipment, supplies, and technology that teachers may not have?
- Do the instructional materials identify safety issues and provide adequate precautions?
- Is the cost for the materials and replacements reasonable? Are there special requirements?

WORKSHEET 1: OVERVIEW OF THE INSTRUCTIONAL MATERIALS

1. Terms	Location(s)	Page(s)
scientific questions	________	______
investigation	________	______
variables	________	______
communication	________	______
observation	________	______
critical thinking	________	______
logic	________	______
reasoning	________	______
experiments	________	______
evidence	________	______
explanations	________	______
models	________	______
theory	________	______
skepticism	________	______

Comments on breadth and depth of coverage:

2. Statements of expected student outcomes or inquiry abilities and understandings

Examples:	Location	Page(s)
a. ______________________________	________	______
b. ______________________________	________	______

WORKSHEET 1 (CONTINUED)

3. Student investigations/activities	Location	Page(s)
Titles of example investigations/activities:		
a. ________________	________	______
b. ________________	________	______
c. ________________	________	______

Comments:

4. Presentation of concepts and abilities	Location	Page(s)
Paragraph 1	________	______

Comments:

Paragraph 2	________	______

Comments:

Overall impression from the overview of the materials:

WORKSHEET 2: ANALYSIS OF INQUIRY AS CONTENT

1. What opportunities are provided for students to develop *abilities* of scientific inquiry?

Cite specific examples:	Page(s)
a. Pose relevant questions	______
b. Plan and conduct investigations	______
c. Use appropriate tools and techniques to gather data	______
d. Use evidence to communicate defensible explanations of cause and effect	______
e. Use scientific criteria to analyze alternative explanations and develop a preferred explanation	______

Comments:

2. Opportunities to develop understanding of scientific inquiry

Cite specific examples:	Page(s)
a. Discussion of both roles and limitations of skills such as organizing and interpreting data, constructing explanations	______
b. Discussion of how science advances through legitimate skepticism	______

WORKSHEET 2 (CONTINUED)

Page(s)

c. Discussion of how scientists evaluate proposed explanations of others by examining and comparing evidence, reasoning that goes beyond the evidence, suggesting alternative explanations for the same evidence _____

d. Opportunities for students to demonstrate these same understandings as part of their investigations _____

Comments:

Estimate of alignment with National Science Education Standards *Inquiry Standard*:

Excellent [ ] Good [ ] Some [ ] Little [ ] None [ ]

Rationale for alignment estimate:

WORKSHEET 3: ANALYSIS OF PEDAGOGY

	Yes	No
1. Do the materials identify specific learning goals and outcomes for students that focus on one or more of the fundamental abilities and understandings of inquiry?	___	___

Comments:

2. Do the materials engage and focus student thinking on interesting questions, problems, or relevant issues rather than opening with statements of fact and vocabulary?	___	___

Comments:

3. Do materials provide a sequence of learning activities connected in such a way as to help students build abilities of inquiry, understandings of inquiry, and/or fundamental science subject matter concepts?	___	___
Does the material provide specific means (e.g., connections among activities, linkage between text and activities, building from concrete to abstract, and embedded assessments) to help the teacher keep students focused on the purpose of the lesson?	___	___

Comments:

WORKSHEET 3 (CONTINUED)

	Yes	No
4. Are student subject matter learning goals reached through an inquiry that contains all five essential features of classroom inquiry learning (Table 2-5, p. 25)?	___	___

Comments:

5. Does the teacher's guide present common student difficulties in learning inquiry abilities and understandings?	___	___
Are suggestions provided to access prior abilities and understandings of students?	___	___

Comments:

Estimate of alignment with National Science Education Standards *Teaching Standard*:

Excellent [ ] Good [ ] Some [ ] Little [ ] None [ ]

Rationale for alignment estimate:

WORKSHEET 4:
ANALYSIS OF ASSESSMENT PROCESS

Cite example or evidence of:	Yes	No
1. Consistency between learning goals and assessment	___	___
2. Assessments stressing application of abilities and concepts to new or different situations	___	___
3. Fairness of assessment tasks for all students — for example, task does not rely heavily upon the student's ability to read complex items or write explanations, as opposed to demonstrating inquiry abilities of understanding fundamental science subject matter concepts	___	___
4. The inclusion of actual assessment instruments, scoring criteria or rubrics, and specific suggestions provided regarding their use	___	___

Comments:

Estimate of alignment with National Science Education Standards *Assessment Standard*:

Excellent [ ] Good [ ] Some [ ] Little [ ] None [ ]

Rationale for alignment estimate:

WORKSHOP 5: EVALUATING THE TEACHER'S GUIDE

	Yes	No
1. Is appropriate and sufficient background in science presented?	___	___
2. Are the suggested teaching strategies usable by most teachers?	___	___
3. Are suggestions provided for pre- and post-investigation discussions focusing on subject matter, concept development, inquiry abilities, and inquiry understandings?	___	___
4. Is additional professional development recommended?	___	___
5. Are the types of support teachers will need for the instructional materials indicated?	___	___

Comments:

Estimate of usefulness of guide in overall instructional materials management:

Excellent [ ] Good [ ] Fair [ ] Poor [ ]

Rationale for alignment estimate:

WORKSHEET 6: ANALYSIS OF MATERIALS USE AND MANAGEMENT

1. How many different types of materials must be managed and orchestrated during a typical chapter, unit, or teaching sequence (e.g., student text, teacher's guide, student materials, transparencies, handouts, videos, software)?

   Comments:

	Yes	No
2. Does the teacher's guide contain suggestions for effectively managing instructional materials?	___	___
Comments:		
3. Do instructional materials call for equipment, supplies, and technology that teachers using these materials might not have?	___	___
Comments:		
4. Is the cost for the materials and replacements reasonable?	___	___
Are there special requirements?	___	___
Comments:		

Estimate of use and management:

Easy [ ] Satisfactory [ ] Difficult [ ]

Rationale for overall estimate:

Appendix C
Resources for Teaching Science Through Inquiry

The following list represents a sampling of the many resources available to help teachers and others use inquiry as a basis for teaching and learning science. Whenever possible, we have listed Web sites or materials that themselves contain lists of resources. The reader is encouraged also to consult the References section in this publication for further information.

WEB SITES

These Web sites contain references to a wide variety of resources, including student curriculum materials, bibliographies, and professional development opportunities.

Eisenhower National Clearinghouse
The Ohio State University
http://www.enc.org/

Exploratorium Institute for Inquiry
http://www.exploratorium.edu/IFI/resources/websites.html

The Science Learning Network
http://www.sln.org/

Project 2061
American Association for the Advancement of Science
http://www.project2061.org/

Science Education Projects Funded by the National Science Foundation
http://watt.enc.org/nsf.html

Professional Development Summer Opportunities for Teachers
NSF-Funded Projects
http://www.ehr.nsf.gov/ehr/esie/teso/

BOOKS

Science for All Children: A Guide to Improving Elementary Education in Your School District
National Science Resources Center/ Smithsonian Institution
National Academy Press, Washington, DC: 1997.
http://www.nationalacademies.org/publications/

Inquiry: Thoughts, Views, and Strategies for the K-5 Classroom
Foundations, Volume 2
Division of Elementary, Secondary, and Informal Education
National Science Foundation, Arlington, VA: 1999.

Inquiry and Learning: Realizing Science Standards in the Classroom
John W. Layman, George Ochoa, and Henry Heikkinen
The National Center for Cross Disciplinary Teaching and Learning
College Entrance Examination Board, New York: 1996.

Physics by Inquiry, Volumes I and II
Lillian C. McDermott and the Physics Education Group, University of Washington
John Wiley & Sons, Inc., New York: 1996.

JOURNALS

The Science Teacher; Science and Children
National Science Teachers Association
http://www.nsta.org/pubs/tst/

Hands On!
TERC, Inc.
http://www.terc.edu/handson/handson.html

Journal of Research in Science Teaching
National Association for Research in Science Teaching
http://science.coe.uwf.edu/narst/jrstinfo.htm

ENC Focus, A Magazine for Classroom Innovators
Eisenhower National Clearinghouse for Mathematics and Science Education
http://www.enc.org/order/

Connect
Synergy Learning International, Inc.
http://www.synergylearning.org

RESOURCE GUIDES

Resources for Teaching Elementary School Science
National Science Resources Center/ Smithsonian Institution
National Academy Press, Washington, DC: 1996.
http://www.nap.edu

Resources for Teaching Middle School Science
National Science Resources Center/ Smithsonian Institution
National Academy Press, Washington, DC: 1998.
http://www.nap.edu

INSTRUCTIONAL MATERIALS

"Resource List: The ENC Collection"
ENC Focus: A Magazine for Classroom Innovators, vol. 6, no. 1, 1999, pp. 39-62.
Eisenhower National Clearinghouse for Mathematics and Science Education
http://www.enc.org/order/

VIDEO COLLECTIONS

Collections of videos (with guidebooks) portraying inquiry-based teaching and learning include:

Available from the Annenberg/ Corporation for Public Broadcasting (http://www.learner.org/):

Private Universe Teacher Workshops, developed by The Harvard-Smithsonian Center for Astrophysics.

Science Images, developed by the North Central Regional Educational Laboratory.

Science K-6: Investigating Classrooms, developed by WGBH Boston.
http://www.wgbh.org/wgbh/learn/scilib/aboutvid.html/

Teaching High School Science (available Fall 2000), developed by WGBH Boston.
http://www.wgbh.org/wgbh/learn/THSS.html/

Visualizing Growth: Changing the Way We Teach Science, developed by WNED, the Buffalo Museum of Science, and the Buffalo Public Schools.

Available from the New York State Education Department (518-474-5862):
Just Think: Problem Solving through Inquiry.

Available from Heinemann (800-541-2086):
Sense Making in Science Video Series, developed by TERC.

Available from the Mr. Wizard Institute (800-537-0008):
Teacher to Teacher with Mr. Wizard, developed by the Mr. Wizard Foundation.

Index

A

B

C

D

E

P

Q

R

S

T

V

W

Credits

Cover and page xix: Students at Glebe Elementary School, Arlington, VA, work on an activity from *Organisms*, a first-grade unit in the Science and Technology for Children (STC) curriculum program. Eric Long, photographer. Courtesy of the National Science Rsources Center (NSRC).

Page viii and page 6: Illustration by student at Edmund Burke School, Washington, DC.

Page viii and page 7: Students at Edmund Burke School, Washington, DC. Danyelle Miller-Coe, photographer.

Page viii and page x: Students at Edmund Burke School, Washington, DC. Danyelle Miller-Coe, photographer.

Page viii: Student at Edmund Burke School, Washington, DC. Danyelle Miller-Coe, photographer.

Page viii and page 67: Students conducting an investigation of marine life. Courtesy of the Eisenhower Consortium @ SERVE.

Page viii and page 68: Students conducting an investigation of marine life. Courtesy of the Eisenhower Consortium @ SERVE.

Page ix and page 123: Students at Bailey's Elementary School, Fairfax, VA, work on an activity from *Animal Studies*, a fourth-grade unit. Rick Vargas, photographer. Courtesy of the NSRC.

Page ix and page 116: Student at Edmund Burke School, Washington, DC. Danyelle Miller-Coe, photographer.

Page ix and page 133: Courtesy of the Biological Sciences Curriculum Study (BSCS).

Page ix and page 86: Courtesy of the Physics Education Group, University of Washington, Seattle.

Page ix and page 147: Courtesy of the Physics Education Group, University of Washington, Seattle.

Page ix and page 107: Teachers participating in an NSRC Leadership Institute. Rick Vargas, photographer. Courtesy of the NSRC.

Page xi: Students at Edmund Burke School, Washington, DC. Danyelle Miller-Coe, photographer.

Page xiv: Drawing by Van Nguyen, National Academy Press.

Page xx: Students at Edmund Burke School, Washington, DC. Danyelle Miller-Coe, photographer.

Page 2: Courtesy of Brian Atwater and Mary Lou Zoback, U.S. Geological Survey.

Page 4: Image of article reprinted by permission from *Nature* 378:371-372. Copyright 1995 Macmillan Magazines Ltd.

Page 9: Letter written by student, Janney Elementary School, Washington, DC.

Page 12: Student and teacher at Edmund Burke School, Washington, DC. Danyelle Miller-Coe, photographer.

Page 15: Probably Tuskegee Institute. From the Library of Congress Photo Collections.

Page 16: From the Library of Congress Photo Collections.

Page 17: From the Library of Congress Photo Collections.

Page 24: Courtesy of Lawrence Hall of Science, University of California, Berkeley.

Page 28: Students working on an activity from *Floating and Sinking*, a fifth-grade STC unit. Courtesy of the NSRC.

Page 30: Courtesy of the Lawrence Hall of Science, University of California, Berkeley.

Page 31: Student at Edmund Burke School, Washington, DC. Danyelle Miller-Coe, photographer.

Page 32: Students at Edmund Burke School, Washington, DC. Danyelle Miller-Coe, photographer.

Page 38: Students at Edmund Burke School, Washington, DC. Danyelle Miller-Coe, photographer.

Page 38: Student at Edmund Burke School, Washington, DC. Danyelle Miller-Coe, photographer.

Page 38: Students at Edmund Burke School, Washington, DC. Danyelle Miller-Coe, photographer.

Page 40: Courtesy of BSCS.

Page 42: Courtesy of BSCS.

Page 43: Student at Edmund Burke School, Washington, DC. Danyelle Miller-Coe, photographer.

Page 45: Students at Glebe Elementary School, Arlington, VA, work on an activity from *Organisms*, a first-grade STC unit. Courtesy of the NSRC.

Page 49: Illustration by National Academy Press.

Page 51: Courtesy of BSCS.

Page 52: Students at Chevy Chase Elementary School, Chevy Chase, MD. David Savage, photographer. Courtesy of the NSRC.

Page 53: Moon phase photos courtesy of BSCS.

Page 55: Student at Eastern Middle School, Silver Spring, MD. Robert Allen Strawn, photographer.

Page 56: Image of the Copernican model of the universe. Reproduced from the Collections of the Library of Congress.

Page 57: Page from Galileo's "Starry Messenger." Reproduced from the Collections of the Library of Congress.

Page 62: Sketch drawn by student at Woodrow Wilson Senior High School, Washington, DC.

Page 73: Students at Edmund Burke School, Washington, DC. Danyelle Miller-Coe, photographer.

Page 74: Worksheet from students at Edmund Burke School, Washington, DC.

Page 77: Students at Glebe Elementary School, Arlington, VA, working on an activity from *Organisms*, a first-grade STC unit. Courtesy of the NSRC.

Page 81: Courtesy of BSCS.

Page 88: BASEE workshop, summer 1999. Courtesy of Mary Lou Zoback, U.S. Geological Survey.

Page 89: Students observing a Rube Goldberg device. Courtesy of Argonne National Laboratory.

Page 92: Students and teacher at Piney Branch Elementary School, Takoma Park, MD. Robert Allen Strawn, photographer.

Page 94: Teachers participating in an NSRC Leadership Institute. Rick Vargas, photographer. Courtesy of the NSRC.

Page 97: Teachers at Bellevue School District, Bellevue, WA, participating in a *Physics by Inquiry* class conducted by the Physics Education Group. Courtesy of the Physics Education Group, University of Washington, Seattle.

Page 100: Courtesy of the Exploratorium, San Francisco, CA.

Page 102: Courtesy of the Exploratorium, San Francisco, CA.

Page 104: Courtesy of BSCS.

Page 110: Students and teacher at Edmund Burke School, Washington, DC. Danyelle Miller-Coe, photographer.

Page 111: BAESI field trip. Courtesy of Mary Lou Zoback, U.S. Geological Survey.

Page 113: Principal and teacher at East Silver Spring Elementary School, Silver Spring, MD. Robert Allen Strawn, photographer.

Page 114: Students at Eastern Middle School, Silver Spring, MD. Robert Allen Strawn, photographer.

Page 118: Students at Edmund Burke School, Washington, DC. Danyelle Miller-Coe, photographer.

Page 121: Student at Montgomery Blair High School, Silver Spring, MD. Robert Allen Strawn, photographer.

Page 125: Student at Amidon Elementary School, Washington, DC, working on an activity from *Floating and Sinking*, a fifth-grade STC unit. Courtesy of the NSRC.

Page 130: Student at Piney Branch Elementary School, Takoma Park, MD. Robert Allen Strawn, photographer.

Page 134: Students at Amidon Elementary School, Washington, DC, working on an activity from *Floating and Sinking*, a fifth-grade STC unit. Courtesy of the NSRC.

Page 136: Courtesy of Lawrence Hall of Science, University of California, Berkeley.

Page 138: Courtesy of the NSRC.

Page 142: Courtesy of the Physics Education Group, University of Washington, Seattle.

Page 148: High school science supply shelves. Lisa Vandemark, photographer.

Page 151: Photodisk image.

ЭER FORM
tomers in North America Only)

INQUIRY AND THE NATIONAL SCIENCE EDUCATION STANDARDS

:ASE SEND ME:

.	Code	Title	Price
_	INQSCB	Inquiry and the National Science Education Standards	
		single copy	$21.95
		2-9 copies	$18.50 each*
		10+ copies	$15.95 each*
_	SCISTB	National Science Education Standards	
		single copy	$19.95
		2-9 copies	$16.50 each*
		10+ copies	$13.95 each*

Qty.	Code	Title	Price
____	INSMAT	Selecting Instructional Materials	
		single copy	$18.95
		2-9 copies	$16.50 each*
		10+ copies	$13.95 each*
____	DESMAT	Designing Math & Science Curriculum	
		single copy	$12.95
		2-9 copies	$10.50 each*
		10+ copies	$ 8.95 each*

*No other discounts apply

s form to order copies of INQUIRY AND THE NATIONAL SCIENCE EDUCATION STANDARDS. All orders must be prepaid. Please add $4.50 for g and handling for the first copy ordered and $0.95 for each additional copy. If you live in CA, DC, FL, MD, MO, TX, or Canada, add applicable sales tax . Prices apply only in the United States, Canada, and Mexico and are subject to change without notice.

ɱ enclosing a U.S. check or money order for $___________

ase charge my VISA/MasterCard/American Express account.

r: ________________________

ion Date: ________________________

re: ________________________

Name : ________________________

Address: ________________________

City ____________ State ______ Zip Code: __________

6476

DER FORM
stomers in North America Only)

INQUIRY AND THE NATIONAL SCIENCE EDUCATION STANDARDS

EASE SEND ME:

/.	Code	Title	Price
_	INQSCB	Inquiry and the National Science Education Standards	
		single copy	$21.95
		2-9 copies	$18.50 each*
		10+ copies	$15.95 each*
_	SCISTB	National Science Education Standards	
		single copy	$19.95
		2-9 copies	$16.50 each*
		10+ copies	$13.95 each*

Qty.	Code	Title	Price
____	INSMAT	Selecting Instructional Materials	
		single copy	$18.95
		2-9 copies	$16.50 each*
		10+ copies	$13.95 each*
____	DESMAT	Designing Math & Science Curriculum	
		single copy	$12.95
		2-9 copies	$10.50 each*
		10+ copies	$ 8.95 each*

*No other discounts apply

is form to order copies of INQUIRY AND THE NATIONAL SCIENCE EDUCATION STANDARDS. All orders must be prepaid. Please add $4.50 for g and handling for the first copy ordered and $0.95 for each additional copy. If you live in CA, DC, FL, MD, MO, TX, or Canada, add applicable sales tax . Prices apply only in the United States, Canada, and Mexico and are subject to change without notice.

m enclosing a U.S. check or money order for $___________

ease charge my VISA/MasterCard/American Express account.

r: ________________________

tion Date: ________________________

ıre: ________________________

Name : ________________________

Address: ________________________

City ____________ State ______ Zip Code: __________

6476

INQUIRY AND THE NATIONAL SCIENCE EDUCATION STANDARDS

Inquiry and the National Science Education Standards is the book that educators have been waiting for--a practical guide to teaching inquiry and teaching through inquiry, as recommended by the National Science Education Standards. This will be an important resource for educators who must help school boards, parents, and teachers understand "why we can't teach the way we used to." We now recognize that inquisitiveness is a natural state of mind, especially in children; it follows that scientific inquiry is a form of human endeavor. As a learning process, "inquiry" refers to the diverse ways in which scientists study the natural world. It also speaks to the way in which students grasp science knowledge and the methods by which that knowledge is produced. **Inquiry and the National Science Education Standards** explains and illustrates how inquiry-based education helps students learn science content, master how to do science, and truly understand the very nature of science. Other books of interest are National Science Education Standards, Selecting Instructional Materials, and Designing Math & Science Curriculum.

ISBN 0-309-06476-7; 2000, 180 pages, 8.5 x 11, hardbound, index, $21.95

FOUR EASY WAYS TO ORDER:

By phone: Call toll-free 1-888-624-8422 or (202) 33 3313.

By fax: Copy the order card and fax to (202) 334-24

By electronic mail: Order via internet at http://www.nap.edu/bookstore.

By mail: Photocopy this form and send with your pa to National Academy Press, 2101 Constitution Aven NW, Lockbox 285, Washington, DC 20055.

All international customers please contact National Academy Pres export prices and ordering information.

Use the form on the reverse of this card to order your copies of Inquiry and the National Science Education Standards, plus the other books in the series.

INQUIRY AND THE NATIONAL SCIENCE EDUCATION STANDARDS

Inquiry and the National Science Education Standards is the book that educators have been waiting for--a practical guide to teaching inquiry and teaching through inquiry, as recommended by the National Science Education Standards. This will be an important resource for educators who must help school boards, parents, and teachers understand "why we can't teach the way we used to." We now recognize that inquisitiveness is a natural state of mind, especially in children; it follows that scientific inquiry is a form of human endeavor. As a learning process, "inquiry" refers to the diverse ways in which scientists study the natural world. It also speaks to the way in which students grasp science knowledge and the methods by which that knowledge is produced. **Inquiry and the National Science Education Standards** explains and illustrates how inquiry-based education helps students learn science content, master how to do science, and truly understand the very nature of science. Other books of interest are National Science Education Standards, Selecting Instructional Materials, and Designing Math & Science Curriculum.

ISBN 0-309-06476-7; 2000, 180 pages, 8.5 x 11, hardbound, index, $21.95

FOUR EASY WAYS TO ORDER:

By phone: Call toll-free 1-888-624-8422 or (202) 33 3313.

By fax: Copy the order card and fax to (202) 334-24

By electronic mail: Order via internet at http://www.nap.edu/bookstore.

By mail: Photocopy this form and send with your pa to National Academy Press, 2101 Constitution Aven NW, Lockbox 285, Washington, DC 20055.

All international customers please contact National Academy Pres export prices and ordering information.

Use the form on the reverse of this card to order your copies of Inquiry and the National Science Education Standards, plus the other books in the series.